ECONOMIC HISTORY OF MEDIEVAL INDIA

Encyclopaedic History of India Series

ECONOMIC HISTORY OF MEDIEVAL INDIA

Dr. Mahesh Vikram Singh
Professor, Deptt. of History
Mahatma Gandhi Kashi Vidyapeeth
Varanasi (UP)

Dr. Brij Bhushan Shrivastava
Head of Deptt., Ancient History, Archeology & Culture
SMMTPG College, Ballia (UP)

CENTRUM PRESS
NEW DELHI-110002 (INDIA)

CENTRUM PRESS
H.O.: 4360/4, Ansari Road, Daryaganj,
New Delhi-110002 (India)
Tel: 23278000, 23261597, 23255577, 23286875
B.O.: No. 1015, Ist Main Road, BSK IIIrd Stage,
IIIrd Phase, IIIrd Block, Bangalore-560085 (INDIA)
Tel: 080-41723429
Email: centrumpress@gmail.com
Visit us at: www.centrumpress.com

Economic History of Medieval India

First Edition, 2011

ISBN 978-93-80836-79-9

PRINTED IN INDIA

Printed at Mehra Offset Press, Delhi

प्रो. विपिन चंद्रा
अध्यक्ष
Prof. Bipan Chandra
Chairman

नेशनल बुक ट्रस्ट, इंडिया
नेहरू भवन
5 इंस्टीट्यूशनल एरिया, फेज़-II, वसंत कुंज, नई दिल्ली-110 070
फोन/ Phone: 011-26121880 फैक्स/ Fax: 011-26121883

NATIONAL BOOK TRUST, INDIA
Nehru Bhawan
5 Institutional Area, Phase II, Vasant Kunj, New Delhi-110 070
ई-मेल / E-mail: chairman@nbtindia.org.in
वेबसाइट / Website: www.nbtindia.org.in

FOREWORD

The term 'history' is derived from the Greek word 'historia' that means knowledge acquired through investigation. Obviously, this knowledge can be correct if the method of investigation is objective and not vitiated by any kind of bias. In other words, if the study of human past is comprehensive and obtained through scientific inquiry, it can provide perspective on the present day problems and help one plan for the future.

A true historian has to identify the sources that can be most useful in a given context. Documents, coins, archaeology, anthropology, geography, travel accounts, oral traditions, mythology and so on can be useful but they can be used only after their veracity is tested and they are critically examined. They should be checked and counter-checked.

Over the centuries, one finds the study and writing of history vitiated by biases. There are numerous instances in which historical data have been distorted to support or oppose certain preconceived ideas and purposes. Strictly speaking such history is just like fiction to accord with preconceived notions and serve some ulterior purposes.

The study of the past has never been static. Conclusions go on changing because of the discovery of new materials and tools of investigation. To give a concrete example, the carbon 14 or radiocarbon dating test has revolutionized the study of civilizations and settlements, especially of prehistoric times, for which written documents, coins, etc. are seldom available. This method has enabled historians to determine more accurately than before the time period of a particular civilization or settlement. This method was discovered only 70 years ago by American scientists.

In our country, excavations brought to light the Indus Valley Civilization and its various features, hitherto unknown. Similarly, no complete text of Kautilya's Arthashastra was available before it was discovered by Shamasastry, the chief of the Mysore Government Oriental Library in the first decade of the last century. Likewise, people's knowledge of the history of the Buddhist period got extended after excavations at Sarnath and the ruins of the Asokan period at Patna. In the future, if the Harappan inscriptions are deciphered, our knowledge of the Indus Valley Civilization will increase enormously. All these instances underline the fact that our knowledge of history is never static and its frontiers go on extending.

In the light of what has been said above the encyclopedic history is going to be of great help to students interested in Indian history. It is comprehensive and as far as possible free from biases. It includes the latest materials, and objective conclusions.

Prof . Bipan Chandra
Professor Emeritus, JNU
Chairman, National Book Trust, India

Contents

Preface

The people of India have had a continuous civilization since 2500 B.C., when the inhabitants of the Indus River valley developed an urban culture based on commerce and sustained by agricultural trade. This civilization declined around 1500 B.C., probably due to ecological changes. During the second millennium B.C., pastoral, Aryan-speaking tribes migrated from the northwest into the subcontinent. As they settled in the middle Ganges River valley, they adapted to antecedent cultures.

The political map of ancient and medieval India was made up of myriad kingdoms with fluctuating boundaries. In the 4th and 5th centuries A.D., northern India was unified under the Gupta Dynasty. During this period, known as India's Golden Age, Hindu culture and political administration reached new heights. Islam spread across the Indian subcontinent over a period of 500 years. In the 10th and 11th centuries, Turks and Afghans invaded India and established sultanates in Delhi. In the early 16th century, descendants of Genghis Khan swept across the Khyber Pass and established the Mughal (Mogul) Dynasty, which lasted for 200 years. From the 11th to the 15th centuries, southern India was dominated by Hindu Chola and Vijayanagar Dynasties. During this time, the two systems—the prevailing Hindu and Muslim—mingled, leaving lasting cultural influences on each other.

The first British outpost in South Asia was established in 1619 at Surat on the northwestern coast. Later in the century, the East India Company opened permanent trading stations at Madras, Bombay, and Calcutta, each under the protection of native rulers. The British expanded their influence from these footholds until, by the 1850s, they controlled most of present-day India, Pakistan, and Bangladesh. In 1857, a rebellion in north India led by mutinous Indian soldiers caused the British Parliament to transfer all political power from the East India Company to the Crown. Great Britain began administering most of India directly while controlling the rest through treaties with local rulers.

In the late 1800s, the first steps were taken toward self-government in British India with the appointment of Indian councillors to advise the British viceroy and the establishment of provincial councils with Indian members; the British subsequently widened participation in legislative councils. Beginning in 1920, Indian leader Mohandas K. Gandhi transformed the Indian National Congress political party into a mass movement to campaign against British colonial rule.

—*Authors*

1

Introduction

The known Economic history of India begins with the Indus Valley civilization. The Indus civilization's economy appears to have depended significantly on trade, which was facilitated by major advances in transport technology. These advances included bullock-driven carts that are identical to those seen throughout South Asia today, as well as boats. Most of these boats were probably small, flat-bottomed craft, perhaps driven by sail, similar to those one can see on the Indus River today; however, there is secondary evidence of sea-going craft. Archaeologists have discovered a massive, dredged canal and docking facility at the coastal city of Lothal.

Around 600 BC, the Mahajanapadas minted punch-marked silver coins. The period was marked by intensive trade activity and urban development. By 300 BC the Maurya Empire united most of the Indian subcontinent. Trade routes became more secure and the road system was expanded. The political unity and military security allowed for a common economic system and enhanced trade and commerce, with increased agricultural productivity. Farmers were freed of tax and crop collection burdens from regional kings, paying instead to a nationally-administered and strict-but-fair system of taxation as advised by the principles in the Arthashastra. Chandragupta Maurya established a single currency across India, and a network of regional governors and administrators and a civil service provided justice and security for merchants, farmers and traders.

For the next 1500 years, India produced its classical civilizations such as the Rashtrakutas, Hoysalas and Western Gangas. During this period India is estimated to have had the largest economy of the ancient and medieval world between the 1st and 15th centuries AD, controlling between one third and one fourth of the world's wealth up to the time of the Marathas, from whence it rapidly declined during European rule.

India has followed central planning for most of its independent history, which have included extensive public ownership, regulation, red tape, and trade barriers. India slipped behind many other Asian countries. After the 1991 economic crisis, the central government launched economic liberalization. India has turned towards a more capitalist system and has emerged as one of the fastest growing large economies of the world.

The Indus Valley civilization, the first known permanent and predominantly urban settlement that flourished between 2800 BC to 1800 BC boasted of an advanced and thriving economic system. Its citizens practiced agriculture, domesticated animals, made sharp tools and weapons from copper, bronze and tin and traded with other cities. Evidence of well laid streets, layouts, drainage system and water supply in the valley's major cities, Harappa, Lothal, Mohenjodaro and Rakhigarhi reveals their knowledge of urban planning. One of the theories about their end is that they eventually overused their resources, and slowly died out. There have been few weapons found in the Indus Valley, showing that they were peaceful people, and they did not get slaughtered by the Aryans.

Ancient and Medieval Characteristics

Though ancient India had a significant urban population, much of India's population resided in villages, whose economy was largely isolated and self-sustaining. Agriculture was the predominant occupation of the populace and satisfied a village's food requirements besides providing raw materials for hand based industries like textile, food processing and crafts. Besides farmers, other classes of people were barbers, carpenters, doctors (Ayurvedic practitioners), goldsmiths, weavers etc.

Religion

Religion, especially Hinduism, played an influential role in shaping economic activities. The Indian caste system castes and sub-castes functioned much like medieval European guilds, ensuring division of labour and provided for training of apprentices. The caste system restricted people from changing one's occupation and aspiring to an upper caste's lifestyle. Thus, a barber could not become a goldsmith and even a highly skilled carpenter could not aspire to the lifestyle or privileges enjoyed by a Kshatriya (person of a warrior class). This barrier to mobility on labour restricted economic prosperity to a few castes.

Pilgrimage towns like Allahabad, Benares, Nasik and Puri, mostly centred around rivers, developed into centres of trade and commerce. Religious functions, festivals and the practice of taking a pilgrimage resulted in a flourishing pilgrimage economy.

Family Business

In the joint family system, members of a family pooled their resources to maintain the family and invest in business ventures. The system ensured younger members were trained and employed in the family business and the older and disabled persons would be supported by the family. The system, by preventing the agricultural land from being split ensured higher yield because of the benefits of scale. The system curbed members from taking initiative because of the support system and family or work.

Organizational Entities

Along with the family-run business and individually owned business enterprises, ancient India possessed a number of other forms of engaging in business or collective activity, including the gana, pani, puga, Sangha, nigama and serine. Nigama, pani and serine refer most often to economic organizations of merchants, crafts people and artisans, and perhaps even para-military entities. In particular, the serine was a complex organizational entity that shares many similarities with modern corporations, which were being used in India from around the 8th century BC until around the 10th century AD. The use of such entities in ancient India was widespread including virtually every kind of business, political and municipal activity.

The serine was a separate legal entity which had the ability to hold property separately from its owners, construct its own rules for governing the behaviour of its members, and for it to contract, sue and be sued in its own name. Some ancient sources such as Laws of Manu VIII and Chanakya's Arthashastra have rules for lawsuits between two or more serine and some sources make reference to a government official (Bhandagarika) who worked as an arbitrator for disputes amongst serine from at least the 6th century BC onwards. There were between 18 to 150 serine at various times in ancient India covering both trading and craft activities. This level of specialization of occupations is indicative of a developed economy in which the serine played a critical role. Some serine could have over 1000 members as there were apparently no upper limits on the number of members.

The serine had a considerable degree of centralized management. The headman of the serine represented the interests of the serine in the king's court and in many official business matters. The headman could also bind the serine in contracts, set the conditions of work within the serine, often received a higher salary, and was the administrative authority within the serine. The headman was often selected via an election by the members of the serine, who could also be removed from power by the general assembly. The headman often ran the enterprise with two to five executive officers, who were also elected by the assembly.

Coinage

Punch marked silver ingots, in circulation around the fifth century BC and the first metallic coins were minted around sixth century BC by the Mahajanapadas of the Gangetic plains were the earliest traces of coinage in India. While India's many kingdoms and rulers issued coins, barter was still widely prevalent. Villages paid a portion of their agricultural produce as revenue while its craftsmen received a stipend out of the crops at harvest time for their services. Each village, as an economic unit, was mostly self-sufficient.

Exports

Surplus of Indian manufactures, like the muslin of Dacca, calicos of Bengal, shawls of Kashmir, steel and iron works, silk, and other textiles and handicrafts, agricultural products like pepper, cinnamon, opium and indigo were exported to Europe, the Middle East and South East Asia in return for gold and silver.

GDP Estimate

According to economic historian Angus Maddison in his book The World Economy: A Millennial Perspective, India had the world's largest economy from the first to eleventh century, and in the eighteenth century, with a (32.9%) share of world GDP in the first century to (28.9%) in 1000 AD, and in 1700 AD with (24.4%).

Maurya Empire

During the Maurya Empire (c. 321-185 BC), there were a number of important changes and developments to the Indian economy. It was the first time most of India was unified under one ruler. With an empire in place, the trade routes throughout India became more secure thereby reducing the risk associated with the transportation of goods. The empire spent considerable resources building roads and maintaining them throughout India. The improved infrastructure combined with increased security, greater uniformity in measurements, and increasing usage of coins as currency enhanced trade. During this time, the Arthasastra ("science of the state") was written by the Chanakya, an adviser to Chandragupta Maurya. The Arthasastra is one of the most important ancient texts on economics, politics and administration. It was a treatise on how to maintain and expand power, obtain material gain, and administer an empire. It covers both theory and implementation and contains many clear and detailed rules regarding the governing of an empire. The exhaustive account of the economic ideas embedded in the Arthashastra has been given by Ratan Lal Basu in his famous work "Ancient Indian Economic Thought, Relevance For Today". In course of an International Conference held in 1902 at Oriental Research Institute, Myore, India to celebrate the Centenary of discovery of the manuscript of the Arthashastra by R. Shamasastry, eminent Chanakya experts from all over the world had discussed various aspects of Chanakya's thought in the light of present day scenario. Most of the papers presented in the Conference have been compiled in an edited volume by Raj Kumar Sen and Ratan Lal Basu.

The economic situation in the Maurya Empire is comparable to the Roman Empire several centuries later, which both had extensive trade connections and both had organizations similar to corporations. While Rome had organizational entities which were largely used for public state-driven projects, Maurya India had numerous private commercial entities which existed purely for private commerce. This was due to the Mauryas having to contend with pre-existing serine hence they were more concerned about keeping the support of these pre-existing private commercial entities. The Romans did not have such pre-existing entities to contend with; hence, they were able to prevent such entities from developing.

Mughal Empire

1526

During this period, Mughal India was the second largest economy in the world. The gross domestic product of India in the 16th century was estimated at about 24.5% of the world economy, in comparison to Ming China's 25% share.

1600

An estimate of India's pre-colonial economy puts the annual revenue of Emperor Akbar's treasury in 1600 at £17.5 million, in contrast to the entire treasury of Great Britain in 1800, which totalled £16 million. The gross domestic product of Mughal India in 1600 was estimated at about 22.6% the world economy, in comparison to Ming China's 29.2% share.

1700

By this time, the Mughal Empire expanded to almost 1,000 million acres (4,000,000 km^2), or 90 percent of South Asia, and a uniform customs and tax administration system was enforced. Annual revenue reported by the Emperor Aurangzeb's exchequer exceeded £100 million in 1700 (twice that of Europe then). Thus, India emerged as the world's largest economy, followed by Manchu China and Western Europe.

Nawabs, Marathas and Nizams

1725-1750

During this period, Mughals were replaced by the Nawabs in north India, the Marathas in central India and the Nizams in south India. However, the Mughal tax administration system was left largely intact. China was the world's largest economy followed by India and France. The gross domestic product of India in 1750 was estimated at about 80 percent that of China.

1750-1775

During this period, about two-thirds of the civil service in India was still dominated by Muslim officers though the Maratha empire expanded to almost 250 million acres (1,000,000 km^2), or 34 percent of Indian landscape, while the Nizam's dominion expanded to almost 125 million acres (510,000 km^2), or 17 percent of Indian landscape. China was the world's largest economy followed by India and France. The gross domestic product of India in 1775 was estimated at about 70 percent that of China. Nevertheless, a devastating famine broke out in the eastern coast in early 1770s killing 5 percent of the national population.

British Rule

The British colonial rule created an institutional environment that did stabilize the law and order situation to a large extent. The British foreign policies however stifled the trade with rest of the world. They created a well developed system of railways, telegraphs and a modern legal system. The infrastructure the British created was mainly geared towards the exploitation of resources of India. By the end of the colonial rule India inherited an economy that was one of the poorest in the world and totally stagnant, with industrial development stalled, agriculture unable to feed a rapidly accelerating population. They were subject to frequent famines, had one of the world's lowest life expectancies, suffered from pervasive malnutrition and were largely illiterate.

GDP Estimates

An estimate by Angus Maddison, formerly of Groningen University, reveals that India's share of the world income went from 24.4% in 1700, comparable to Europe's share of 23.3%, to a low of 3.8% in 1952. While Indian leaders during the Independence struggle and left-nationalist economic historians have blamed the colonial rule for the dismal state of India's economy, a broader macroeconomic view of India during this period reveals that there were segments of both growth and decline, resulting from changes brought about by colonialism and a world that was moving towards industrialization and economic integration.

2

Islam and the Expansion of Trade and Economy

It was in the expansion of trade where Islam's impact was the greatest. One of the most significant aspects of the Islamic period in world history was the emergence of Islamic courts capable of imposing a common commercial and legal system that extended from Morocco in the West to Mongolia in the North East and Indonesia in the South East. Although this was not of significant benefit to countries such as India that enjoyed a substantial trade surplus, it was probably of great significance to the people of the Arabian or Central Asian deserts whose oasis depended heavily on trade.

As the Hindu and Buddhist kingdoms of Asia were subjugated by Islam, and as Islam spread through Africa-it became a highly centralising force that facilitated in the creation of a common legal system that allowed letters of credit issued in say Egypt or Tunisia to be honoured in India or Indonesia. To create and sustain such an internationally consistent legal system, Islamic rulers had to undercut the local and traditional systems of governance that prevailed. This also meant that they often preferred to deal with foreigners who had no interest in preserving the older systems. It is also possible that the terms of trade were structured in ways that disadvantaged local artisans and peasants, but favoured the rich traders and ruling elites in the newly established and aggressively expanding Islamic kingdoms.

As the old contractual obligations in society were weakened, Islam became the new binding force of these newly conquered societies. And in order to cement their rule, Islamic rulers initially promoted a system in which there was a revolving door between the clergy, the administrative nobility and the mercantile classes. Ibn Batuta is a classic example of this phenomenon. He served as an Imam in Delhi, as a judicial official in the Maldives, and as an envoy and trader in the Malabar. There was never a contradiction in any of his positions because each of these roles complemented the other. Islam created a compact under which political power, law and religion became fused in a manner so as to safeguard the interests of the mercantile class. This led world trade to expand to the maximum extent possible in the medieval world.

Agriculturally developed societies played a crucial role in this transformation. The interests of the mercantile community were such that they wished agricultural taxes to be high but trade duties to be low. By and large, Islamic rulers implemented exactly such a regime. This enabled the founding of new trading and manufacturing centres that emerged wherever Islam took hold. For the desert areas of the world, Islam came as a big boon-providing wealth from trade that would have been unimaginable considering the poverty of the natural landscape. For the world's largely self-sufficient and more advanced agricultural civilisations like India (or Egypt or Indonesia)-this growth in trade was probably of lesser significance and more of a mixed bag.

Islam and the Spread of Technology

With the growth of international trade also came the spread of manufacturing technology and a more advanced urban culture. Local inventions and regional technologies became more easily globalised. This was of profound importance to those parts of the world that had lagged in terms of technological development. On the other hand, for a nation like India which had a rich intellectual tradition of its own, and was already a relatively advanced civilisation, this may have been of lesser import. Nevertheless, no country has a lock on technology, and to the extent that the arrival of Islam was concomitant with the adoption of new technologies it helped India too. Although there is considerable debate amongst historians as to how much technology was actually brought into India by Islamic invaders, there is one (albeit controversial) school of thought that argues that inventions like the water-wheel for irrigation were imported during the Islamic period. In some other cases, the evidence is much clearer. The use of ceramic tiles in construction was inspired by architectural traditions prevalent in Iraq, Iran, and in Central Asia. Rajasthan's blue pottery was an adaptation of Chinese pottery which was imported in large quantities by the Mughal rulers. There is also the example of Sultan Abidin (1420-70) sending Kashmiri artisans to Samarqand to learn book-binding and paper making.

But regardless of whether the Islamic rulers introduced new technology or not, there is considerable evidence that many Islamic rulers developed Karkhanas, *i.e.* small factories during their reign. Of even greater significance is how new towns that specialised in a particular category of manufactured goods emerged throughout the country. Khurja and Siwan became renowned for pottery, Moradabad for brass ware, Mirzapur for carpets, Firozabad for glass wares, Farrukhabad for printing, Sahranpur and Nagina for wood-carving, Bidar and Lucknow for bidriware, Srinagar for papier-mache, Benaras for jewellery and textiles, and so on.

Impact on the Peasantry

The impact on the peasantry varied from region to region, and from ruler to ruler. Even as urbanisation created opportunities for some, it also created new problems for the countryside. The growth of the urban centres and the manufacture of luxury goods that were popular in the lavish courts of some of the Islamic rulers often came at a heavy cost on large sections of the peasantry. While trading communities and certain categories of skilled artisans may have been able to take advantage of new avenues for social mobility, other sections suffered a setback.

The invading rulers, particularly during the Delhi Sultanate (or even the Mughal) period had a fairly narrow local support base-(especially if they were not born and raised in India, and were driven to enforcing their particular idea of Islamic law on a resistant population). This meant that they had to rely on greater violence to sustain their rule. It appears that military campaigns became more frequent and more brutal. Punishments became more severe and torture and the death penalty were used with less restraint.

During the early period of Islamic conquest, many Islamic rulers resorted to the hated jaziya, or poll tax levied on non-believers-*i.e.* non-Muslims. In some instances, this pushed the poorest sections of the peasantry into slavery. In other instances this may have coerced some of the peasantry into converting, or else led to local uprisings and tax rebellions. But the consequences of failed rebellions were just as disastrous.

Growth of Slavery

During the period of the Delhi Sultanate, the practice of slavery grew to levels previously unseen in Indian history. S.A.A. Rizvi reports that Delhi's 14th C. ruler Firuz Shah Tughlaq kept 180,000 slaves.

Impoverished peasants were often forced into selling their children, both boys and girls into slavery. According to Ibn Batuta, captive girls were very cheap, and even skilled girls were relatively inexpensive.

Slaves acquired through wars and armed raids against Hindu chiefs were sold in local markets. Noblemen kept an enormous number of slaves and feudal lords maintained entire armies of slaves. A significant number were captured and sent to the slave markets of Central Asia. However, slaves utilised in the military often fought their way to the top and took their revenge on the ruling clans.

This occurred not only in Delhi but also in Aurangabad and Ahmednagar in the Deccan, and in Bengal.

As a result, the Sultanate period was a period of great instability with rulers being deposed in quick succession. It is quite likely that the Rajput practice of Jauhar emerged as a means of fending off such degradation in the face of impending military defeat.

During famines, both Hindus and Muslims sold their children into slavery thus forcing the clergy to speak out against the practice. In 1562, Akbar abolished the practice of taking the wives and children of defeated rebels as captives and from then on, it appears that the practice of slavery may have gone into decline but was not entirely discontinued.

The special tax 'Jazia' on non-Muslims, was also abolished. Nevertheless, taxes on the peasantry went up from a sixth or a fourth of the produce to a third under the Mughals. While some of these increased taxes may have been made possible through improved irrigation methods-at some point these taxes far exceeded any gains in productivity and came to be viewed as unbearable, and eventually led to the Sikh and Maratha revolts that permanently fractured Mughal rule.

But not all Islamic rulers bled the peasantry. Shah Mir who became king of Kashmir in 1339 fixed the land tax at 17%. Later rulers like Tipu Sultan of Mysore were also not viewed as unreasonable taxers and became especially popular. Even more profligate rulers like the Awadh Nawabs managed to juggle the interests of the peasantry with the interests of urban-dwellers thus maintaining a certain amount of popular support. It is thus no surprise that only such popular rulers (like Tipu and the Awadh Nawabs) were able to offer any significant resistance to British rule.

Trade Under the Sultanate and Mughals

The trade advantages enjoyed by the Chola, Gujarati, and Bengali cotton manufacturers dramatically ended after 1200 when Muslim Turkish invaders from Afghanistan swept into northern India and established the sultanate of Delhi. In the following two centuries the new Turkish dynasties took over the Gujarati and Bengali trade and controlled much of the textile manufacturing as well.

However, in 1401 Gujarat declared independence from the sultanate and expanded its trade with the West. By the mid-fifteenth century, Ahmedabad, its capital city, was widely known as the "Venice of India."

The Gujarati trading castes called banias, riding the winds of Indian ocean trade, amassed such great riches that they were envied by both Indians and foreigners.

From 1400 to 1750 Indian coastal cities, strung like a necklace from Gujarat in the northwest around the southern tip of India all the way to Bengal in the northeast, played a central role in the Eurasian trading system.

By 1750 India's population stood at 200 million and produced about a fourth of the world's manufactures. Besides dominating the shipping lanes, Indian traders travelled by land along the Silk Roads as well as across the sub-continent. Caravans of up to 40,000 pack animals linked the port cities and brought manufactured goods from the hinterlands. World historians Andre Gunder Frank and Kenneth Pomeranz have established that until 1800 India maintained a massively favourable balance of trade with most of the world, especially with Europe. Indian products were traded to the north, west, and east: cotton textiles, indigo, silk cloth, iron and steel products, housewares, glass, rice, wheat, spices, incense, shawls, blankets, paper, and saltpeter.

Europe and West Asia paid for this vast trade imbalance with gold but mostly silver, much of it dug by slaves from Spanish mines in Peru and Mexico.

Colonialism and Imperialism

During the height of Mughal rule (1526–1707 C.E.) artisans and entrepreneurs made India what one economic historian has called the "industrial workshop of the world":

Indian economic and financial organisation and techniques of production were far more advanced than in Europe. Only in the seventeenth century did European traders attempt to take over some cotton mills and begin to retail cloth in European cities.

By the end of the century Indian luxury cloth was so prized by Europeans that France prohibited the import of chintz to protect its own textile industry.

In spite of this ban, French consumers continued to buy Indian cloth. Few European producers could master the Indian art of mordant dyeing which created cloth of intense colours. The enormous manufacturing and trade balance advantages that India had enjoyed for some 2,500 years were slowly wiped out as a result of British colonial control of the sub-continent.

In 1750, with the start of significant British presence in the north, India at the end of Mughal power was still producing about one-fourth of the world's manufactured goods. It was not until the nineteenth century that British manufacturers could cheaply produce cotton cloth that equalled Indian quality.

By using Indian-grown cotton to make cloth by machine at home, they finally ended India's superiority. With increasing political control, the British were even able to force Indian consumers to buy inferior British fabrics.

By 1850, with the establishment of British control over political and economic life, India's share of world manufacturing had sunk to a mere 8.6 percent of world production. At the time of India's independence from England, India was producing only 1.5 percent of world manufactures. Clearly colonialism had "underdeveloped" India as an economic giant.

The Land Revenue System of Akbar

When Akbar became ruler of the Mughal Empire he inherited a land revenue system that did not have great influence upon the local economy. He understood the usefulness of the land revenue system which prior Indo-Muslim regimes, such as the ruler Sher Shah Suri, had begun, so rather than try to create a new revenue system, Akbar employed the help of his advisers to reform preexisting systems.

Akbar's fiscal reforms were for the administrative purpose of stabilising the village-level peasant population while consolidating regional rule directly under his command. It was imperative that Akbar create a land revenue system and administration that gave the appearance of a cohesive central government to all of his subjects, so they would unquestionably view Akbar and the Mughals as legitimate rulers. Here we see how important Akbar considered support from all classes of the population and not just from the ruling class in order to legitimize his rule to all within the empire, and includes reorganising all of the Mughals' land and correcting the inherent corruption of the system.

He began by reclassifying all land holdings into five categories based on the fertility of the soil. Under the new regulation land tax system, imperial revenue officials, theoretically, gathered reports on the status of the cultivation of each peasant in each village.

From the reports they assessed taxes based on the recorded prices and yields specific to each locality. In 1580, Akbar and his advisers succeeded in the reorganisation of the empire on the provincial level of the tax revenue system with the establishment of twelve provinces. Each province, by imperial decree, was to have its own administration consisting of seven posts that were functionaries of the province and who reported to the central administration as well. The governors had military control over the region, but not administrative free reign. The importance of this division between civil and military authority is that Akbar had begun to restrict the autonomy of the provincial governors. Another reform, which shocked the upper rung of the Muslim hierarchy, was the re-examination of all religious land grants. Akbar analysed each grant and reassessed them personally. This entailed the arrangement of private interviews with the sheikhs and ulemas (leaders of Sufi brotherhoods and scholars) to decide whether each land grant was valid.

He upheld the validity of many land grants if he was satisfied, but those religious leaders who had disciples, held spiritual soirees, or claimed to have accomplished miracles were punished by a withdrawal of their grants. The reassessment of all land grants shows that Akbar wanted to establish from the beginning of his rule the idea that he kept close watch over the religious Muslim authorities, the sheikhs and ulemas. This demonstrates the sultan's commitment to establishing Mughal legitimacy in Hindustan and to separating himself from the corrupt, dysfunctional elements of a Muslim-run empire. The greatest improvement to the administration and land revenue system was the development of the mansabdari system which created a hierarchy of officials all of which were exclusively loyal to the sultan.

This new system for administration was a meritocratic and was not based on a religious aristocracy. Previously, the Muslims in India formed the governing class from which all high officials were drawn. However, Akbar ended Muslim superiority in his empire by choosing men on merit, rather than on the basis of kinship, religion, or nepotism, including many very able non-Muslims.

The inclusion of Hindus into high posts of the administration was a form of tokenism. Their elevated stature would allow other Hindus who came to court to recognise the superiority of Akbar because Hindus would already be standing near him. It also expressed to every person that the Mughal Empire was not subject to a harsh, fundamentalist Muslim rule, but was subject to the goal of the equality of all of its subjects. The hierarchial system of imperial rank existed in his Mughal lineage but Akbar viewed it as inefficient for his ideal administration. Babur was the first to bring this Mongol system to the Indian sub-continent and with the exception of the numerical rank, his system had a division between high officials, labelled "great Begs", and lower officials, "Begs." All of Babur's officials were members of a regular service which had formal appointments and promotions as well. The formality of the regular service system reflects the mansabdari system under Akbar because he also sought to distinguish levels between rank holders. Akbar differed from Babur's system because he was the first of his Mughal lineage to create the dual status of a separate civil and military rank for each rank holder.

Akbar introduced giving each mansab two rank numbers which expanded the officials' responsibility to the empire into civilian duty. The first rank was the zat and was the personal numerical rank which was given to middle and high officials and determined their salary.

The addition of the zat rank denoted numerically how that official stood in relation to the sultan. The higher the rank, the more important that official's relationship was to Akbar. The second number, the suwar, was the numerical rank given to officials denoting the number of soldiers and cavalry the mansab was responsible for when called upon. Suwar was a "trooper rank" and was first introduced in his eleventh regnal year. This separation between civil and military ranks for each official, which could be changed at Akbar's will, allowed him to maintain a civil hierarchy which depended exclusively on his will while concurrently maintaining the strength of the imperial army.

Akbar limited the power of his mansabdars by personally appointing each mansabdar and imposing his will over them through legislative procedure. Syed Giasuddin Ahmed states: "officials (in the mansabdari system) were bound to the ruler not through serfdom, but through a free and mutual contract." All officials were subject to dismissal or transfer to another region because Akbar never wanted any official to gain too much loyalty or power in a region. This transfer was not without warrant, because in the provinces, the provincial governor was viewed as the incarnation of the sultan himself, and would gain allegiances in his region as such. Also, every mansabdar, theoretically, was chosen personally by Akbar entailing an elaborate process by which each mansab had to be appointed twice.

The reason behind Akbar's use of personal appointment was that the imperial eye was sharp enough to discern the merits of every man. Abul Fazl states: "His majesty sees through some men at the first glance, and confers upon them high rank." The sultan did not allow for many officials to be trained in important administrative practices, such as fiscal matters, which meant that Akbar only allowed for a select few to have the knowledge of how the empire was run. The limited amount of specialisation was so officials could not learn how to manipulate the system by knowing its intricacies. It was, in effect, one more method of checking the power of his officials. Closest to Akbar in the administration were only four primary ministers.

The Divan-i-Kul was the head financial minister in charge of revenue and expenditure; the Mir Bakhshi was primarily responsible for military and the mansabdari; the Khan-i-Zaman was in charge of factories and stores and the imperial household; and the Sadr-us-Sudar was the chief justice who was the head of ecclesiastic and judiciary matters. The post of the Vakil (prime minister) remained unfilled through much of Akbar's reign; when it was filled, it had very limited power. Akbar allowed for the officers to act autonomously and check each other while in office, but he still retained the right to impose his will.

The overlap of these high posts inherently regulated each office because none of the imperial officials could act without the aid of another office; nor could they act without the final approval of Akbar. For example, the Sadr-us-Sudar was the chief theologian in the state, and when in office had the autonomous power of declaring legal fatawi (legal pronouncements). But Akbar appointed the Sadr and could dismiss him at any time. Thus, the incumbent was kept in the predicament of being autonomous while having to make judgments according to the sultan's will.

Some officials received their salaries directly from the imperial treasury, but the majority received their salary by way of a decree (jagir). The jagir system of salary assignment was important because it was a convenient way for the central government to maintain the bureaucracy: "it rid the central government of a fair measure of responsibility with regard to collection and disbursement without any corresponding reduction in authority or increases in the revenue burden." Under this system, local officials were paid through jagirs, the order to collect revenue from certain areas in lieu of a salary. Any official, regardless how high or low their rank, could receive a salary in this way, and those who were assigned a jagir were labelled jagirdars.

To classify the central government's relationship to these regional officials in Marxist terms: "the jagirdar represented the despotic government suspended over the small community." The region they were to collect from may or may not have been near their region of rule. In practice, however, jagirdars tended to obtain salary assignments within the provinces they were currently serving. In Akbar's quest to establish Mughal legitimacy and his own legacy on the sub-continent, he had effectively created an imperial administration which inherently checked itself. Whether the ruler and his judgment were present or not, the Mughal administration would continue to run without major problems.

Although the Mughal Empire begun its decline with Akbar's successor and son, Jahangir, the mansabdari system lasted through British rule and into the mid-1800s. The thousands of zamindars in the empire had a very important relationship with Akbar. The term zamindar was coined by the Mughals and referred to the "various holders of hereditary interests, ranging from powerful, independent, and autonomous chieftains to petty intermediaries at the village level." Zamindars exercised tremendous power over the economic life of the country, including agricultural production, handicrafts, and trade. They maintained the economy of the empire on the village level and collected revenue for either a jagirdar or in certain cases, the imperial treasury.

Douglas Streusand has referred to Akbar's relationship to the village level of his empire as the "Akbari Compromise." Streusand's interpretation builds on the idea that Akbar wanted to run the empire with a focus on individual households, through central officials reporting directly to him on the status of the people. But, he quickly discovered the central administration could not penetrate into the village level because of the long existing regional system of rule which was backed by a loyal armed peasantry.

Therefore, Akbar abandoned his dream of a fully centralised administration and entered into a compromise of keeping the regional rulers in similar positions as they were prior to his rule. Streusand claims that the compromise consisted of regional rulers who need not fear losing their position as long as they maintained the sultan's trust and did not abuse their authority by being disloyal to him. Akbar inherited a hierarchial system of land revenue that had been developing since the establishment of the Sultanate in the twelfth century. In the land revenue system, the sultan's relationship to the chieftains depended on constant military coercion for tax revenue. This meant that there existed a never ending power struggle between the state's efforts for a consolidation of power and the chieftains' desire for territorial autonomy.

Akbar saw the inefficiency of the existing tax revenue system and sought to reform it in a way that would legitimise the state in order to end the need for military coercion while continuing to demand the same from chieftains as did his predecessors: recognition of the central government's superiority, the obedient remit of tax revenue, and the rendering of military assistance. Akbar made the system of regional control more effective because he developed a lucrative policy of incorporation for his opponents into the Mughal hierarchial administration. He was the first ruler to realise the importance of forging links between the position of the sultan and the chieftains by incorporating them into the imperial hierarchy of administration.

Akbar understood that military coercion was not the right method for consolidation. He received the empire's revenue through aggressive diplomacy which was designed to achieve his main objective of reducing the chieftains' status to intermediaries for the empire, for which they would receive just compensation. The first step in the reductive process was the introduction of using the same generic term (zamindar) to refer to all of the holders of widely varying types of landed interests. In doing this, Akbar destroyed the preexisting hierarchy on the local level because all persons that were previously in that hierarchy were now all equal in the community. From autonomous chieftains to village heads, all possessed the same rank in the view of the Mughal Empire.

Akbar did not hesitate to use force to establish his supremacy over some staunch opponents, although diplomacy was preferred. During the beginning of his rule, he would conquer his opponents by whatever means necessary, which included personally leading his army on campaigns of bloody battles and sometimes enduring long devastating sieges. The power of Akbar and his empire came from one important fact: he always won. Later in his rule many opposing chieftains began to understand the extent of his power and realised the positive benefits of his policy of incorporation by conceding to his superiority without much bloodshed. In Akbar's policy of incorporation, a chieftain's submission brought the possibility for advancement within the imperial bureaucracy. The usual appointment of chieftains was to mansabdars who were allowed to rule their territory much in the same way as before. The new treatment of the chieftains made them depend on the goodwill of Akbar for their positions and not on their prior hereditary rights.

This dependency for their livelihood, combined with the Mughal-reserved right of the transfer of officials meant that the sultan effectively had full control over the former chieftain's territory. Akbar was the first foreign ruler of Hindustan to make a direct relationship with the vassals. Prior Indo-Muslim rulers only tried to control the various levels of chieftains, and did not attempt to penetrate deeper into the multi-layered agrarian system. Akbar forged new relationships on the local level in an attempt to undermine the power of formerly autonomous chieftains and form new allies who would act as imperial spies for the welfare of the state.

Akbar's treatment of the village level demonstrates his concern for legitimising the Mughal Empire to all of his subjects and not just to the bureaucracy. He created a system which ventured deep into the local sphere in order to discover how his policies were being implemented. His generous policy of incorporation left prior autonomous rulers with a comfortable position in the Mughal administration and allowed them to rule over their regions with almost the same power, but with a new allegiance. As long as they identified themselves as part of the Mughal Empire, they were allowed to prosper along with it.

Conclusion

Prior to Akbar's ascension to the throne of Hindustan, Muslim sultans had been trying to establish their hold over the majority Hindu population for three-hundred years. Prior Muslim rulers had been unsuccessful because they did not understand the importance of appealing to the Hindu majority rather than trying to win the fierce Hindu warriors over by might. Akbar also had the advantage of being raised in exile and witnessing his father's political failures which had a great influence on his quest to establish a lasting Mughal Empire.

For Akbar's new vision for the ruler of Hindustan to be finalised, he first had to legitimise the Mughal state to the Hindus as well as the competing Muslim factions for the throne of Hindustan. Akbar's re-imagining of legislative policies and administrative reforms in the sub-continent should be viewed as tools to aid in the fulfilment the larger objective of the legitimisation of his rule and more importantly, the Mughal Empire. Akbar reformed the legislative policy, administration, and the land revenue system in order to centralise and legitimise rule in Hindustan under himself.

In the legal sphere, Akbar moved away from the Muslim custom of appealing to orthodox mullah judgment and towards his own amicable policy of sulh-i-kull. Under sulh-i-kull, both Muslim and Hindu were equal in the eyes of the law which included the abolition of many customary Muslim policies such as the jizya and the pilgrim tax. Subjects of the new Mughal Empire were also free to convert to or from religions as long as it was not a forced conversion. The culmination of Akbar's legal reform policy came with the 1579 mahzar, or "Infallibility Decree," which effectively established Akbar's freedom from orthodox mullah opinion as well as the creation of the legitimate Mughal Empire to the rest of the Islamic World.

For his imperial administration, Akbar created the efficient mansabdari system. Most every imperial official from all levels of administration was included in this system, and the higher their rank determined the closer they were to Akbar, as well as the higher they were in society. The hierarchial mansabdari system was indiscriminate of religious affiliation and served the larger purpose of having all in the administration identify directly with the Mughal sultan for their status in the empire and not with a religious hierarchy. Most mansabdars were paid by the jagir system of salary assignment in which mansabdars collected their own salary from specified regions. This self-generating tax revenue system was efficient for Akbar because he could focus more energy on expanding the empire rather than on running the land that was already incorporated. Life indoctrinating ritual interaction was the glue which held Akbar's administration together. In this system, higher prostration to the sultan became synonymous with higher status within the empire. Some rituals were incorporated from the Hindu style of kingship which allowed for Hindus to easily recognize the sovereign. By drawing on Hindu methods, ritual served as an effective tool for overcoming preexisting loyalties. Through the ritual interaction, Akbar's subordinates became a visible representative and reminder of the effulgence of the sultan throughout the empire. Akbar's administration outlived his horribly inefficient successors, Jahangir, Shah Jahan, and Aurangazeb, who seemingly tried to destroy the system their brilliant forefather created. Jahangir and Shah Jahan allowed personal greed to overwhelm their rule and by the end of the latter's reign the imperial coffers were almost empty.

Aurangazeb was the worst ruler towards the system created by Akbar because he attempted to return the rule of Hindustan back to that of a fundamentalist Muslim vision, where the empire was run by the mullahs' judgment. His vehement, yet futile, attempts to secure the status of Hindus as inferior people were no match for the legitimacy Akbar had created one hundred years earlier. Akbar was so successful at creating an efficient method for rule in Hindustan that even after the Mughal Empire's collapse, Mughal rule was still legitimate in the eyes of the peasants. During the War of 1857, after which the British government formally took control over the Indian sub-continent, a British officer killed off the sons of the last Mughal and that ruler was exiled to Burma, despite the fact that these Mughals possessed little to no actual power. This effort by the British to emasculate the Mughal line demonstrates the effectiveness of the Mughal Empire created by Akbar. The vile treatment given to the last of his lineal descendants even though they were reduced to less than a shadow of their former power, mere figureheads, was necessary in part because the Great Mughal still retained enough of the aura of legitimate grandeur that Hindustan had once experienced under Muslim rule that the British felt compelled to humiliate them in order to establish their own right to rule. By the late nineteenth century, the British began to realise the magnitude of Akbar's achievement insofar as his rule appealed to both Hindu and Muslim, but by then it was too late. They had gone too far down the road of rule by force and fear, leaving the rule by divide to become the order of that day. As a result, the British found that their rule never acquired what Akbar had made central to Mughal society and without which no empire can long survive: legitimacy.

3

The Origins of Muslim Slave System

From the day India became a target of Muslim invaders its people began to be enslaved in droves to be sold in foreign lands or employed in various capacities on menial and not-so-menial jobs within the country. To understand this phenomenon it is necessary to go into the origins and development of the Islamic system of slavery.

For, wherever the Muslims went, mostly as conquerors but also as traders, there developed a system of slavery peculiar to the climate, terrain and populace of the place. For example, simultaneously with Mohammad bin Qasim's invasion of Sindh in early 8th century, the expansion of Arab Islam had gone apace as far as Egypt, North Africa and the Iberian Peninsula in the West, as well as in Syria, Asia Minor, Palestine, Iraq, Iran, Khurasan, Sistan and Transoxiana. In all these countries Muslim slave system grew and developed in its own way. There was constant contact between India and most of these countries in the medieval times.

For example, as early as during the reigns of the slave sultans Iltutmish and Balban (1210-86), there arrived at their courts in Delhi a large number of princes with their followers from Iraq, Khurasan and Mawar-un-Nahr because of the Mongol upheaval. Many localities in Delhi and its environs were settled by these elites and their slaves, soldiers and scholars. In Balban's royal procession 500 Sistani, Ghauri and Samarqandi slave-troops with drawn swords used to march by his side pointing to the fact that a large number of foreign slaves from these lands had come to India in 13th-14th centuries. When the Mughals launched their conquest of India, there was the establishment of the Ottoman Empire in Turkey which at its height included present-day Albania, Greece, Bulgaria, Serbia, Romania and several other contiguous countries. Then there was the Safavid empire in Iran. The Ottoman Empire traded with Europe and imported 'there indispensable stock of slaves. (Slav, as the word indicates), supplied by merchants, sometimes Jewish, from Verdun, Venice or elsewhere in Italy. Other slaves were brought from black Africa, eastern Europe and Turkish Central Asia.' The Mughals of India had very close contacts with the Turkish Ottoman and Iranian Safavid empires. This contact certainly included exchange of slaves and ideas on slavery. But any attempt in this area of study, which is so vast and labyrinthine, is bound to deflect us from our main theme which is restricted to India. We shall therefore confine ourselves to the barest particulars of the beginnings of the institution outside India which will suffice for understanding the Muslim slave system in India in the medieval period.

Prophet Mohammad found slavery existing in Arabia, and recognised it in the Quran. The origins of Muslim slave system can thus be traced to Arabia, the original Muslim homeland, and the regions into which Islam spread. Quranic injunctions, Islamic conquests and Muslim administrative institutions gave it a continuity and legitimacy. According to T.P. Hughes, 'Slavery is in complete harmony with the spirit of Islam' That Mohammad ameliorated the condition of the slave, as it existed under the heathen law of Arabia, we cannot doubt; but it is equally certain that the Arabian legislator intended it to be a permanent institution.' D.S. Margoliouth elaborates on the theme adding that 'On the whole' the Prophet did something to alleviate the existence of the captives' manumission was declared by him to be an act of piety' and murder or maiming of slaves was to be punished by retaliation.' In one of his last sermons, Mohammad exhorted his followers thus: 'And your Slaves! See that ye feed them with such food as ye eat yourselves; and clothe them with the stuff ye wear. And if they commit a fault which ye are not inclined to forgive, then sell them, for they are the servants of the Lord, and are not to be tormented.' His first orthodox biographer, Ibn Ishaq, however mentions a transaction which set a precedent for Islamic slave trade at a later, stage: 'Then the apostle sent Saad b. Zayd Al-Ansari' with some of the captive women of B Qurayza to Najd and he sold them for horses and weapons.' The women had been made captive after their menfolk had been slaughtered enmasse in the market place at Medina.

Status of Slaves in Islam

The appeal of Mohammad contained some fundamental perceptions about the status of slaves in Islam. It recognised the slave as the property of the master. A slave could be sold but, being a Muslim or servant of the Lord, was not to be treated harshly. Here it needs to be observed that in the early days of Islam it was the scum of the society that flocked to the standard of Mohammad and became his fighting force. 'Koran acknowledges so distinctly that the followers of the Prophet were the lowest of the people.' Arabian aristocracy 'requested him to send away this scum before they would argue with him', (as did the Turkish ruling classes treat the early Muslim converts in India). But the mission of Mohammad was to spread his creed and any non-humane regulations would have presented a very unfavourable picture of Islam to the captives. This would have discouraged proselytization. On conversion also Muslim slaves could not be treated badly for that again would have been damaging to the reputation of the new creed and galling to the lives of the new converts. How these injunctions were later on followed or flouted by Muslim invaders and rulers in other countries is a different matter. In the original land of Islam, in Arabia, it was enjoined not to treat the slaves harshly; instead the masters were encouraged to utilize to the best services of men slaves and enjoy the intimate company of women slaves.

This tolerant treatment was not without conditions. A slave was the property of his master. His tenor of life was determined by the latter. For example, he could not marry without the master's permission. Although he was free to move from place to place, he could not hold pleasure parties nor pay visits to friends. A slave could not bestow aims or grant a loan or make a pilgrimage. If he managed to accumulate any property, it was inherited not by his sons but by the master. In theory a slave could purchase his freedom, but bond of freedom was granted to a slave in return for money paid, and until full money was paid there was no total redemption. A slave should not seek his emancipation by running away, 'The slave who fled from his master committed an act of infidelity', says Mohammad. The emancipation of slaves was not unknown in pre-Islamic Arabia. It was an old custom among the Arabs of more pious disposition to will that their slaves would be freed at their death. To Mohammad, the freeing of a slave was an act of charity on the part of the master, not a matter of justice, and only a believing slave deserved freedom.

In short, slavery in Islam is a permanent and perennial institution. As Margoliouth points out, 'the abolition of slavery was not a notion that ever entered the Prophet's mind.' 'The fact remains,' writes Ram Swarup 'that Mohammad, by introducing the concept of religious war and by denying human rights to non-Muslims, sanctioned slavery on an unprecedented scale' (and on) such massive proportions. Zubair, a close companion of the Prophet, owned one thousand slaves when he died. The Prophet himself possessed at least fifty-nine slaves at one stage or another, besides thirty-eight servants, both male and female. Mirkhond, the Prophet's fifteenth century biographer, names them all in his *Rauzat-us-Safa*. The fact is that slavery, tribute, and booty became the main props of the new Arab aristocracy'..?

The Slavery of Islam is interwoven with the Law of marriage, the Law of sale, and the Law of inheritance, of the system, and its abolition would strike at the very foundations of the code of Muhammadanism.'

Extension of Islamic Slavery

Islamic slave system spread and developed wherever Muslim rule was established. *Ghulam or quallar* (slave) was the creation of the Safavid state. Mamluks were found in Egypt. In the Ottoman empire they were called kapi-kulus. 'Kapi-kulu were recruited originally from the Sultan's share of prisoners of war, and subsequently from a periodical levy (*depshrime*) of Christian boys. Most of the youths entered the Janissary corps.' Christian slaves were drawn from the ranks of the Georgian, Armenian and Circassian prisoners or their descendants.' Black slaves, natives of East Africa, were called Zanj. Majority of slaves who penetrated and flourished in India were Turks.

Immediately after its birth, Muhammadanism entered upon a career of aggressive and expansionist conquest. Its Caliphs conquered extensively and set up autocratic governments based on the tenets of Islam rather than democratic governments based on the will of the people. Conquests required large armies; despotic governments could not be run without a train of bureaucrats. From the ninth to the thirteenth century in particular it was a period of feverish activity in Muslim Asia; empires were established and pulled down; cities were founded and destroyed. In other words, the whole of Central Asia, Transoxiana and Turkistan was a very disturbed region in the medieval period. Armies and bureaucrats were needed in large numbers to administer the ever expanding dominions of Islam. The Turks came handy for such services.

Turkish Slaves

The Abbasids had built up a very large empire with capital at Baghdad, and its provinces were administered by their Turkish slave officers and Turk mercenary troops. Caliph al-Mutasim (833-842 C.E.) introduced the Turkish element into the army, and he was the first Caliph to have Turkish slaves under his employment. For it was soon discovered that the young slaves acquired from Turkistan and Mawar-un-Nahr formed an excellent material for such a corps.

Turks is a generic term comprehending peoples of sundry denominations and tribes. The Turkistan of the medieval historians was an extensive country. It was bounded on the east by China, on the west by Rum or Turkey, on the north by the walls of Yajuj and Majuj (Gog and Magog) and on the south by the mountains of Hindustan. The Turks as a people were both civilised town-dwellers and the migratory tribes trekking across the desert or wilderness. With the extension of the Muslim frontier to the north and west of Persia one tribe after another, like Turks, Tartars, Turkomen and even Mongols and Afghans came under subjection. They attracted the attention of their conquerors by their bravery and spirit of adventure. They were acquired in groups and droves as slaves. The Caliphs of Islam also purchased Turkish slaves to manage their far-flung empire. The Turkish slaves helped the cause of Islam through their fighting spirit.

But as their numbers grew, they became unmanageable. For example, Caliph al-Mutasim's own guard was of 4000 Turks; the number later rose to 70,000 slave mercenaries. With time the tyranny, lawlessness and power of the Turks went on increasing.

The unscrupulous policy of religious persecution followed by the Caliph Mutawakkil was responsible for the alienation of the subject races. His own son entered into a conspiracy with the Turks, which ended in the Caliph's murder in 861. The Caliph Mutadid (892-902) was unable to suppress the power of the Turks. The final decline of the Caliphate set in just after the murder of Muqtadir in 932 C.E. 'The Turkish soldiers made and murdered Caliphs at their pleasure.' As the Caliphal empire disintegrated, in the third century of Islam, its provincial governors became independent.

But technically these Turkish governors were only slaves and their tenure of power rested on military force and chance-victory and not on any moral foundations. On the other hand, the Caliphs were objects of respect. The first four Caliphs were directly related to Mohammad. Muawiyah, the founder of the Ummayad Caliphate, was a cousin of Abbas, an uncle of the Prophet. Abbas himself was founder of the Abbasid Caliphate. The Turkish slaves, therefore, considered it politic to keep a sort of special relationship with the Caliph: they went on paying him tribute and seeking from him recognition of their 'sovereignty'. That is how, in course of time, their political power was firmly established.

Slave-taking during Muslim Rule

Slavery forms an integral part of the history of Islam. The Turks practised it on a large scale before they entered India as invaders. Slaves were abducted or captured by marauders (Subuktigin, Balban), they were sold by jealous or needy relatives (Iltutmish), and they were purchased by slave-traders to be sold for profit (Aibak). These methods were known to Muslim rulers in India. All these and many other methods were employed by them and their nobles in making slaves in India. The phenomenon and its application was shocking to the Hindu mind; the Muslims, however, thought otherwise. According to Ibn Khaldun, the captives were 'brought from the House of War to the House of Islam under the rule of slavery, which hides in itself a divine providence; cured by slavery, they enter the Muslim religion with the firm resolve of true believers'? Muslims took pride in enslaving people; the feelings of Hindu victims were just the opposite.

Qutbuddin Aibak entered upon a series of conquests. He dispatched Ikhtiyaruddin Bakhtiyar Khalji to the East and himself concentrated in Hindustan proper. He captured Kol (modern

Aligarh) in 1194. There 'those of the garrison who were wise and cute were converted to Islam, but those who stood by their ancient faith were slain with the sword.' Surely, those who embraced Islam during or immediately after the battle were 'cute' and wise, because by this initiative on their part they were counted as free-born Muslims as against those who fought, were captured in battle, and then enslaved. T.P. Hughes gives the legal position: 'If a captive embraced Islam on the field of battle he was a free man; but if he were made captive, and afterwards embraced Islam, the change of creed did not emancipate him.' Women captives were invariably taken prisoner. 'Atiyat-ul-Qurazi relates that, after the battle with the Banu Quraizah, the Prophet ordered all those who were able to fight to be killed, and the women and children to be enslaved.'

Both these traditions were followed in India. In 1195 when Raja Bhim was attacked by Aibak 20,000 slaves were captured, and 50,000 at Kalinjar in 1202. 'The temples were converted into mosques,' writes Hasan Nizami, 'and the voices of the summoners to prayer ascended to the highest heavens, and the very name of idolatry was annihilated.' Call to prayer five times a day with a loud voice carried an invitation and a message-join us, or else. People 'could refuse this invitation or call at their own peril, spiritual and physical. As His followers became more powerful, the peril became increasingly more physical.' This process helped in the conversion of captives. Murry Titus pertinently remarks that 'we may be sure that all those who were made slaves were compelled to embrace the religion of the masters to whom they were allotted.' Farishtah specifically mentions that during the capture of Kalinjar 'fifty thousand *kaniz va ghulam*, having suffered slavery, were rewarded with the honour of Islam.' Thus enslavement resulted in conversion and conversion in accelerated growth of Muslim population.

Minhaj Siraj assigns twenty (lunar) years to Qutbuddin's career in Hindustan from 'the first taking of Delhi' up to his death, both as a commander of Sultan Muizzuddin and as an independent ruler. During this period Aibak captured Hansi, Meerut, Delhi, Ranthambhor and Kol. When Sultan Muizzuddin personally mounted another campaign against Hindustan, Aibak proceeded as far as Peshawar to meet him, and the two together attacked the Khokhar stronghold in the Koh-i-Jud or the Salt Range. The Hindus

(Khokhars) fled to the highest in the mountains. They were pursued. Those that escaped the sword fled to the dense depth of the jungle; others were massacred or taken captive. Great plunder was obtained and many slaves. According to Farishtah three to four hundred thousand Khokhars were converted to Islam by Muizzuddin; but this figure is inflated. More than a hundred years later, Amir Khusrau refers to Khokhars as a non-Muslim tribe, and the way they were constantly attacked and killed by Sultans Iltutmish and Balban confirms Khusrau's contention. Minhaj also says that 'the Khokhars were not annihilated in this affair (Muizzuddin-Aibak attack) by any means, and gave great trouble in after years.'

Under Aibak most of Hindustan from Delhi to Gujarat, and Lakhnauti to Lahore, was brought under the sway of the Turks. In his time a large number of places were attacked and many more prisoners were captured than for which actual figures are available. Figures of slaves made during campaigns of Kannauj, Banaras (where the Muslims occupied 'a thousand' temples), Ajmer (attacked thrice), Gujarat, Bayana and Gwalior are not available. Similar is the case with regard to Bihar and Bengal. About the end of the twelfth or the beginning of the thirteenth century, Ikhtiyaruddin Bakhtiyar Khalji marched into Bihar and attacked the University centres at Nalanda, Vikramshila and Uddandpur.

The Buddhist monks and Brahmans mistaken for monks were massacred and the common people, deprived of their priests and teachers, became an easy prey to capture and enslavement. But no figures of such captives are known. Ibn Asir only says that Qutbuddin Aibak made 'war against the provinces of Hind'. He killed many, and returned with prisoners and booty.'

In Banaras, according to the same author, 'the slaughter of the Hindus was immense, none was spared except women and children,' who would have been enslaved as per practice. Habibullah writes that Muslim sway extended from Banaras through the strip of Shahabad, Patna, Monghyr and Bhagalpur districts, and repeated references to the presence of Muslims in this tract from the early times indicates that taking of slaves and conversion was common in the region. Fakhr-i-Mudabbir informs us that as a result of the Turkish achievements under Muizzuddin and Aibak, Eleven poor (Muslim) householder became owner of numerous slaves.'

The narratives of contemporary and later chroniclers should not lead us to the conclusion that taking of Hindus as slaves was a child's play. There was stiff resistance to Muslim conquest and Muslim rule. Besides, the Sultans of Delhi had always to deal with a number of problems simultaneously. Most of the time of Sultan Iltutmish (1210-1236) was spent in suppressing his Turkish opponents, Qutbi and Muizzi Amirs in Delhi and rivals Yaldoz and Qubacha in Punjab and Sindh. He also faced the threat of invasion from the Mongol conqueror Chingiz Khan and the Khwarizmi Prince Jalaluddin Mangbarni fleeing before Chingiz. Therefore it was only sixteen years after his accession that he could march against Ranthambhor in 1226. During this period many Hindu kingdoms subdued by Aibak were becoming independent. Mandor near Jodhpur was attacked a little later. Here 'much booty fell into the hands' of the victors, which obviously included slaves also. The year 1231 witnessed his invasion of Gwalior where he 'captured a large number of slaves'. In 1234-35 he attacked Ujjain, broke its temple of Mahakal, and as usual made captives 'women and children of the recalcitrants.' But most of his compatriot Muslims were not satisfied with the Sultan's achievements in the sphere of slave-taking and converting the land into Dar-ul-Islam all at once.

It is true that foreign Muslims-freemen and slaves were flocking into Hindustan and this development was of great significance for the Sultanate. Adventurers and job seekers were flocking into Hindustan, the new heaven of Islam. More importantly, because of the Mongol upheaval, as many as twenty-five Muslim refugee princes with their retinues arrived at the court of Iltutmish from Khurasan and Mawaraun Nahr. During the reign of Balban fifteen more refugee rulers and their nobles and slaves arrived from Turkistan, Khurasan, Iraq, Azarbaijan, Persia, Rum (Turkey) and Sham (Syria). Their followers comprised masters of pen and of sword, scholars and Mashaikh, historians and poets. The pressure of these groups on the Sultan for Islamization of Hindustan would have been great. In 1228 C.E. Iltutmish received a patent of investiture from Al-Mustansir Billah, the Khalifa of Baghdad, in recognition of his enormously augmenting the prestige of the Muhammadan government in India. This was a booster as well as a further pressure. No wonder, the capital city of Delhi looked like Dar-ul-Islam and its ruler the leader of the eastern world of Islam.

But since the whole country was not conquered and converted, it did not amuse the Ulama and the Mashaikh.

Slave-taking a Matter of Policy

Some Ulama therefore approached the 'pious' Sultan Iltutmish to rule according to the Shariat and confront the Hindus with choice between Islam and death. Muslims had set up their rule and so the country had become Dar-ul-Islam. Any opposition to it was an act of rebellion. The Hindus who naturally resisted Muslim occupation were considered to be rebels. Besides they were idolaters (*mushrik*) and could not be accorded the status of Kafirs, of the People of the Book-Christians and Jews. For them the law provided only Islam or death. Islamic jurisprudence had crystallized over the last five centuries. Besides the evolvement of the four schools of Islamic jurisprudence, Sheikh Burhauddin Ali's *Hidayah* (530-596 H./1135-1199 C.E.), the Compendium of Sunni Law, based on the Quran and the Hadis, was also readily available in the time of Iltutmish. Muslim scriptures and treatises advocated jihad against idolaters for whom the law advocated only Islam or death.

In such a situation the answer of the Sultan to the Ulama was: 'But at the moment in India' the Muslims are so few that they are like salt (in a large dish)' However, after a few years when in the capital and the regions and all the small towns, when the Muslims are well established and the troops are larger' it would be possible to give Hindus, the choice of death or Islam.' Such an apologetic plea was not necessary to put forward. The fact was that the Muslim regime was giving a choice between Islam and death only. Those who were killed in battle were dead and gone; but their dependents were made slaves. They ceased to be Hindus; they were made Musalmans in course of time if not immediately after captivity.

There was thus no let up in the policy of slave-taking. Minhaj Siraj writes that Ulugh Khan Balban's 'taking of captives, and his capture of the dependents of the great Ranas cannot be recounted'. Talking of his war in Awadh against Trailokyavarman of the Chandela dynasty (Dalaki va Malaki of Minhaj), the chronicler says that 'All the infidels' wives, sons and dependents' and children' fell into the hands of the victors.' In 1253, in his campaign against Ranthambhor also, Balban enslaved many people. In 1259, in an attack on Haryana, many women and children were enslaved. Twice Balban led expeditions against Kampil, Patiali, and Bhojpur, and in the process enslaved a large number of women and children. In Katehar he ordered a general massacre of the male population of over eight years of age and carried away women and children. In 658 H. (1260 C.E.) Ulugh Khan Balban marched with a large force on a campaign in the region of Ranthambhor, Mewat and Siwalik. He made a proclamation that a soldier who brought a live captive would be rewarded with two silver *tankahs* and one who brought the head of a dead would get one silver *tankah*. Soon three to four hundred living and dead were brought to his presence. Like Balban other slave commanders of Iltutmish, or the 'Shamsia Maliks of Hind' were marching up and down the Hindustan, raiding towns and villages and enslaving people. This was the situation prevailing from Lakhnauti to Lahore and from Ajmer to Ujjain. The Hindus used to reclaim their lands after the Muslim invaders had passed through them with fire and sword, and Turkish armies used to repeat their attacks to regain control of the cities so lost. But the captives once taken became slaves and then Musalmans for ever. The exact figures of such slaves have not been mentioned and therefore cannot be computed. All that is known is that they were captured in droves. Only one instance should suffice to convey an idea of their numbers. Even in the reign of a weak Sultan like Nasiruddin, son of Iltutmish, the ingress of captives was so large that once he presented *forty beads of staves* to our chronicler Minhaj Siraj to send to his 'dear sister' in Khurasan.

Enslavement Under the Khaljis

The process of enslavement during war gained momentum under the Khaljis and the Tughlaqs. In two or three generations after Iltutmish the Muslims were digging their heels firmly into the country. Their territories were expanding and their armies were becoming larger. All the time, the desire to convert or liquidate the idolaters remained ever restless. Achievements in this regard of course depended on the strength, resources and determination of individual Muslim rulers. For example, although Jalaluddin Khalji was an old and vacillating king, even he did not just remain content with expressing rage at the fact of not being able to deal with the Hindus according to the law. During six years of his reign (June 1290-July 1296), he mounted expeditions and captured prisoners. While suppressing the revolt of Malik Chhajju, a scion of the dynasty he had ousted, he marched towards Bhojpur in Farrukhabad district and ruthlessly attacked Hindus in the region of Katehar (later Rohilkhand). During his campaign in Ranthambhor he broke temples, sacked the neighbouring Jhain and took booty and captives, making 'a hell of paradise'. Later on Malwa was attacked and large quantity of loot, naturally including slaves, was brought to Delhi. His last expedition was directed against Gwalior.

Jalaluddin's nephew and successor Alauddin Khalji (1296-1316) turned out to be a very strong king. He marched against Devagiri in 1296. On his way through Gondwana and Khandesh he took prisoners a large number of Mahajans and cultivators, and ransomed them for wealth. At Devagiri he enslaved a number of the Raja's relatives, and Brahmans and Mahajans. He put them in shackles and chains and paraded them in front of the fort to pressure the besieged king. After victory, he released many of the captives because of compulsions of the situation. He was only a prince who had marched to the Deccan without the Sultan's permission. But his taking of slaves in large numbers was in consonance with the policy of Muslim sultans and gave a foretaste of what was to follow during the course of his reign.

After ascending the throne, Alauddin Khalji embarked upon a series of conquests. He turned out to be the greatest king of the Sultanate period (cir. 1200-1500), and his success as regards capture of slaves was stupendous. He started by seizing the families and slaves of his brothers and brother-in-law. In 1299 he despatched a large army for the invasion of Gujarat. There all the major towns and cities like Naharwala, Asaval, Vanmanthali, Surat, Cambay, Somnath etc. were sacked. There the temples were broken, wealth looted and large numbers of captives of both sexes captured, including the famous Malik Kafur and the Vaghela king's consort Kamala Devi. In the words of Wassaf, the Muslim army in the sack of Somnath 'took captive a great number of handsome and elegant maidens, amounting to 20,000, and children of both sexes' the Muhammadan army brought the country to utter ruin, and destroyed the lives of inhabitants, and plundered the cities and captured their offspring'' In 1301 Ranthambhor was attacked and in 1303 Chittor. In the invasion of Chittor, 30,000 people were massacred in cold blood and obviously females and minors of their families were captured. Slaves were also taken in large numbers in the expeditions to Malwa, Sevana and Jalor (1305-1311); these will be referred to again in the course of this study. Maybe the number of captives obtained from Rajasthan was not that large knowing the bravery and chivalry of the Rajputs and their prevailing customs of Jauhar and Sati. But the highly successful Deccan campaigns of Malik Kafur must have supplied a large corps of captives. Besides, Alauddin did not confine to obtaining Hindu slaves. During the invasion of the Mongol Saldi (1299), the commanders of the Sultan captured 1,700 of his officers, men and women and sent them as slaves to Delhi. During the raid of Ali Beg, Tartaq and Targhi (1305), 8,000 Mongol prisoners were executed and their heads displayed in the towers of the Siri Fort which were then under constructions. The women and children accompanying the Mongol raiders Kubak and Iqbalmand were sold in Delhi and the rest of Hindustan. 'The Mongol invaders were certainly infidels,' says Mahdi Husain. This enslavement was as beneficial to Islam as that of the Hindus. Muslims were not enslaved because they were already Muslim.

Sultan Alauddin's collection of slaves was a matter of successful routine. Under him the Sultanate had grown so strong that, according to Shams Siraj Afif, in his days 'no one dared to make an outcry.' Similar is the testimony of the Alim and Sufi Amir Khusrau. In *Nuh Sipehr* he writes that 'the Turks, whenever they please, can seize, buy or sell any Hindu.' No wonder, under him the process of enslavement went on with great vigour. As an example, he had 50,000 slave boys in his personal service and 70,000 slaves worked continuously on his buildings. We must feel obliged to Muslim chroniclers for providing such bits of information on the basis of which we can safely generalize. For instance, it is Barani alone who writes about the number of slaves working on buildings and Afif alone who speaks about the personal 'boys' of Sultan Alauddin who looked after his pigeons. Ziyauddin Barani's detailed description of the Slave Markets in Delhi and elsewhere during the reign of Alauddin Khalji, shows that fresh batches of captives were constantly arriving there.

Enslavement Under the Tughlaqs

All sultans were keen on making slaves, but Mohammad Tughlaq became notorious for enslaving people. He appears to have outstripped even Alauddin Khalji and his reputation in this regard spread far and wide. Shihabuddin Ahmad Abbas writes about him thus: 'The Sultan never ceases to show the greatest zeal in making war upon infidels'. Everyday thousands of slaves are sold at a very low price, so great is the number of prisoners'. Mohammad Tughlaq did not only enslave people during campaigns, he was also very fond of purchasing and collecting foreign and Indian slaves. According to Ibn Battutah one of the reasons of estrangement between Mohammad Tughlaq and his father Ghiyasuddin Tughlaq, when Mohammad was still a prince, was his extravagance in purchasing slaves. Even as Sultan, he made extensive conquests. He subjugated the country as far as Dwarsamudra, Malabar, Kampil, Warangal, Lakhnauti, Satgaon, Sonargaon, Nagarkot and Sambhal to give only few prominent place-names. There were sixteen major rebellions in his reign which were ruthlessly suppressed. In all these conquests and rebellions, slaves were taken with great gusto. For example, in the year 1342 Halajun rose in rebellion in Lahore. He was aided by the Khokhar chief Kulchand. They were defeated. 'About three hundred women of the rebels were taken captive, and sent to the fort of Gwalior where they were seen by Ibn Battutah.' Such was their influx that Ibn Battutah writes: 'At (one) time there arrived in Delhi some female infidel captives, ten of whom the Vazir sent to me. I gave one of them to the man who had brought them to me, but he was not satisfied. My companion took three young girls, and I do not know what happened to the rest.' Iltutmish, Mohammad Tughlaq and Firoz Tughlaq sent gifts of slaves to Khalifas outside India. To the Chinese emperor Mohammad Tughlaq sent, besides other presents, '100 Hindu slaves, 100 slave girls, accomplished in song and dance' and another 15 young slaves.'

Ibn Battutah's earwitness account of the Sultan's gifting captured slave girls to nobles or arranging their marriages with Muslims on a large scale on the occasion of the two Ids, corroborates the statement of Abbas. Ibn Batuta writes that during the celebrations in connection with the two Ids in the court of Mohammad bin Tughlaq, daughters of Hindu Rajas and those of commoners, captured during the course of the year were distributed among nobles, officers and important foreign slaves. 'On the fourth day men slaves are married and on the fifth slave-girls. On the sixth day men and women slaves are married off.' This was all in accordance with the Islamic law. According to it, slaves cannot marry on their own without the consent of their proprietors. The marriage of an infidel couple is not dissolved by their jointly embracing the faith. In the present case the slaves were probably already converted and their marriages performed with the initiative and permission the Sultan himself were valid. Thousands of non-Muslim women were captured by the Muslims in the yearly campaigns of Firoz Tughlaq, and under him the id celebrations were held on lines similar to those of his predecessor. In short, under the Tughlaqs the inflow of women captives never ceased.

Similar was the case with males, especially of tender and young age. Firoz Tughlaq acquired them by all kinds of methods and means, so that he collected 180,000 of them. Shams Siraj Afif, the contemporary historian, writes that under Firoz, 'slaves became too numerous' and adds that 'the institution took root in every centre of the land'. So that even after the Sultanate broke up into a number of kingdoms, slave-hunting continued in every '(Muslim) centre of the land.'

Sufferings of the Enslaved

This is the version of the slave-capturing victors. The humiliation and suffering of the victims finds no mention in Muslim chronicles. Sustained experience of grief and pain and loss of dignity and self-respect used to turn them into dumb driven animals. The practice and pattern of breaking the spirit of the captives under Aibak, Iltutmish and Balban, indeed throughout the medieval period, was the same as during the days of the Khaljis and the Tughlaqs. Only one case may be cited as an instance.

Balban, when he was Ulugh Khan Khan-i-Azam, once brought to Delhi (in about 1260) two hundred fifty 'Hindu leading men and men of position' from Mewar and Siwalik, bound and shackled and chained. During the expedition he had proclaimed that a royal soldier would be rewarded with two silver *tankahs* if he captured a person alive and one *tankah* if he brought the head of a dead one. They brought to his presence 300 to 400 living and dead everyday.

The reigning Sultan Nasiruddin ordered the death of the leading men. The others accompanying them were shaken to the bones and completely tamed. Depiction of their suffering is found in an Indian work-*Kanhadade Prabandha*. Written in 'old Rajasthani or old Gujarati', it was composed in mid-fifteenth century and records the exploits of King Kanhardeva of Jalor against Alauddin's General Ulugh Khan who had attacked Gujarat in 1299 and taken a number of prisoners. In the Sorath (Saurashtra) region 'they made people captive-Brahmanas and children, and women, in fact, people of all (description)' huddled them and tied them by straps of raw hide.

The number of prisoners made by them was beyond counting. The prisoners' quarters (*bandikhana*) were entrusted to the care of the Turks.' The prisoners suffered greatly and wept aloud. 'During the day they bore the heat of the scorching sun, without shade or shelter as they were [in the sandy desert region of Rajasthan], and the shivering cold during the night under the open sky. Children, tom away from their mother's breasts and homes, were crying.

Each one of the captives seemed as miserable as the other. Already writhing in agony due to thirst, the pangs of hunger' added to their distress. Some of the captives were sick, some unable to sit up. Some had no shoes to put on and no clothes to wear. 'Some had iron shackles on their feet. Separated from each other, they were huddled together and tied with straps of hide. Children were separated from their parents, the wives from their husbands, thrown apart by this cruel raid. Young and old were seen writhing in agony, as loud wailings arose from that part of the camp where they were all huddled up'. Weeping and wailing, they were hoping that some miracle might save them even now.' The miracle did happen and Kanhardeva was successful in rescuing them after a tough fight.

But the description provides the scenario in which the brave and the strong, the elite and the plebeian, were made captives and their spirit broken. That is how Timur was enabled to massacre in one day about 100,000 of captives he had taken prisoner on his march to Delhi. They had been distributed among his officers and kept tied and shackled. That is how Maulana Nasiruddin Umar, a man of learning in Timur's camp, 'slew with his own sword fifteen idolatrous Hindus, who were his captives'. If the prisoners could 'break their bonds', such a carnage could not have been possible. Prisoners were often brought to Timur's presence with hands bound to their necks. Jahangir (1605-27) also writes that 'prisoners were conducted to my presence yoked together.' Most of them were kept yoked together even when they were sent out to be sold in foreign lands or markets in India.

The captives, on their part, clung together and did not separate from one another even in their darkest hour. Nor were they permitted an opportunity to do so under Islamic law which the victors always observed with typical Muslim zeal. The *Hidayah* lays down that 'if the Mussulmans subdue an infidel territory before any capitation tax be established, the inhabitants, together with their wives and children, are all plunder, and the property of the state, as it is lawful to reduce to slavery all *infidels*, whether they be *Kitabees, Majoosees* or *idotters*.' The *Hidayah* also lays down that 'whoever slays an infidel is entitled to his private property,' which invariably included his women and children. That is how a large number of people were involved, whether it was a matter of taking captives, making converts, or ordering massacres. About women and children of a single family of a slain infidel, or of droves of slaves captured in an attack on a region or territory Fakhre Mudabbir furnishes information on, both counts during the campaigns of Mohammad Ghauri and Qutbuddin Aibak. He informs us that during their expeditions *ghulams* of all descriptions (*har jins*) were captured in groups and droves (*jauq jauq*) so that even a poor householder (or soldier) who did not possess a single slave (earlier) became the owner of numerous slaves?

In short, the captives swam or sank together so that if they were captured they were taken in large numbers. A manifest example of this phenomenon is that during a rebellion-suppressing expedition of Mohammad bin Tughlaq in the Deccan (1327), all the eleven sons of the Raja of Kampil (situated on the River Tungbhadra, Bellary District), were captured together, and made Muslims. Generally, able bodied men and soldiers were massacred, and their helpless women and children were made prisoners in large numbers or groups. Even in peace times people of one or more villages or groups acted in unison. When Firoz Shah Tughlaq proclaimed that those who accepted Islam would be exempted from payment of Jizyah, 'great number of Hindus presented themselves' Thus they came forward day by day from every quarter'? Similarly, from the time of entering Hindustan, up to the time of reaching the environs of Delhi, Amir Timur had 'taken more than 100,000 infidels and Hindu prisoners'? Timur massacred them all, but the fact that people could be made slaves in such unbelievably large numbers was due to their keeping together through thick and thin, howsoever desperate the situation. Nobody knew the reality better than Ibn Battutah who travelled in India extensively. During his sojourn he found villages after villages deserted. Nature's ravages or man's atrocities might have made them flee, or more probably they would have been enslaved and converted, or just carried away. But the fact of habitations being completely deserted shows that large groups suffered together and did not forsake one another in times of trial and tribulation. This factor swelled the number of slaves.

Special Slaves of Firoz Shah Tughlaq

By the time of Firoz Shah Tughlaq, the institution of slavery had taken root in every region of Muslim domination. The Sultanate of Delhi was now two hundred years old and well entrenched. The need of slaves for all kinds of errands was great. So that slaves were ever needed in hundreds, and slave-taking did not remain confined to their capture during wars. Firoz Tughlaq resorted to some other methods of acquiring slaves. One of these was akin to the famous Dewshrime widely practised in the Ottoman Empire.

The practice of Dewshrime (Greek for 'collecting boys'), 'is the name applied to the forcible pressing of Christian children to recruit the janissary regiments' of the Turkish Empire' mainly in the European parts with a Christian population (Greece, Macedonia, Albania, Serbia, Bosnia and Herzegovina, and Bulgaria).' These Christians, Jews and Gypsies turned Muslims were trained to fight against their own erstwhile brethren. 'Instituted by Urkhan in 1330, it formed for centuries the mainstay of the despotic power of the Turkish sultans, and was kept alive by a regular contribution exacted every four years (or so), when the officers of the Sultan visited the districts over and made a selection from among the children about the age of seven. The Muhammadan legists attempted to apologise for this inhuman tribute by representing these children as the fifth of the spoil which the Quran assigns to the sovereign.'

Sultan Firoz commanded his great fief-holders and officers to capture slaves whenever they were at war, and to pick out and send the best for the service of the court. The fifth part of slaves captured in war in India were always despatched to the ruler (or Caliph) ever since the days of Mohammad bin Qasim. Firoz Tughlaq desired slaves to be collected in the Dewshrime fashion. Great numbers of slaves were thus collected, and when they were found to be in excess, the Sultan sent them to Multan, Dipalpur, Hissar Firozah, Samana, Gujarat, and all the other feudal dependencies.'

The policy of Delhi Sultanate of leaving the bare minimum to the peasant helped in Firoz's 'Dewshrime'. Under Muslim rule, a substantial portion of the agricultural produce was taken away by the government as taxes and the people were left with the bare minimum for subsistence in order to impoverish them because it was thought that 'wealth' was the source of "rebellion and disaffection.' This policy was in practice throughout the medieval period, both under the Sultans and the Mughals. Conditions became intolerable by the time of Shahjahan as attested to by Manucci and Manrique. Peasants were compelled to sell their women and children to meet the revenue demand. Manrique writes that 'the peasants were carried off' to various markets and fairs (to be sold), with their poor unhappy wives behind them carrying their small children all crying and lamenting, to meet the revenue demand.'

Bernier too affirms that 'the unfortunate peasants who were incapable of discharging the demand of their rapacious lords, were bereft of their children Who were carried away as slaves.' As in the Ottoman Empire, Christians and Jews turned Muslim were trained to fight their erstwhile brethren, so also in India in the medieval period Hindus captured and converted were made to fight their erstwhile brethren in Muslim wars of conquest. Trained or accustomed to fighting their own people, these converts to Islam are posing various kinds of problems in the present-day India and Eastern Europe.

Employment of Slaves

Muslim regime in medieval times drafted slaves in every sphere of activity. Slaves were needed in thousands for any large enterprise which, in modern technological age, would be accomplished by a few machines or even gadgets. There was no dearth of slaves either. Muslim victories in India had provided kings and nobles with innumerable slaves. From government affairs to domestic errands slaves were employed on every work.

On Building Construction

The first thing the Muslim Sultanate of Delhi started on was construction of impressive buildings. It aimed at overawing the people of the land with the greatness and might of the new Islamic regime. This could be achieved by constructing huge Muslim edifices with the wealth obtained from war and materials from Hindu buildings after destroying them. Architecture was considered as the visual symbol of Muslim political power with which the Turks wished to impress and overawe the conquered people. It denoted victory with authority. Wherever the Muslim conquerors marched or ruled in Central Asia or India, they constructed edifices both gigantic and delicate. The important fact to note in this connection is that slaves were drafted to construct the buildings.

And so thousands of slaves were drafted to construct the edifices (many even now extant as monuments), so as to complete the work in the shortest possible time. Surely, the task could be accomplished only by pressing into service thousands and thousand of slaves captured in early victories who were made to do the job. The congregational mosque at Delhi named, purposefully, as the Masjid Quwwatul Islam (Might of Islam), was commenced by Aibak in 592/1195 within two years of its conquest. It was built with materials and gold obtained by destroying 27 Hindu and Jain temples in Delhi and its neighbourhood. A Persian inscription in the mosque testifies to this. The mosque at Ajmer erected by Qutbuddin Aibak soon after its occupation and known as the *Arhai din ka Jhonpra,* was also built from materials obtained from demolished temples. The Qutb Minar, planned and commenced by Aibak sometime in or before 1199 and completed by Iltutmish, was also constructed with similar materials, 'the sculptured figures on the stones being either defaced or concealed by turning them upside down.' *'In this improvisation,'* rightly observes Habibullah, *'was symbolised the whole Mamluk history'* (emphasis added).

How many slaves were needed to accomplish the task on these three and the other buildings of Qutbuddin Aibak and Iltutmish such as mosques, *madrasas,* mausoleums, *qasrs* and tanks (*e.g.* Hauz-i-Shamsi) in and outside Delhi' It is difficult to determine but easy to conjecture their numbers, for these two sultans had embarked on constructional activity on a very large scale. It is known that Alauddin Khalji, another great builder, had 70,000 slaves working on his buildings, as attested to by the contemporary chronicler Ziyauddin Barani. Alauddin built 'masjids, minars, citadels and tanks'. But his Qutb Minar alone was an edifice more than equal to all his undertakings. Thus the men working on the buildings of the first two sultans were probably not less than those of Alauddin Khalji; they may have been probably more.

These slaves were to dismantle standing temples, very carefully, stone by stone, carry the carved columns, shafts and pillars to the new sites of construction, and raise the new structures. Although Hasan Nizami says that temples were demolished with the help of elephants and one elephant could haul stones for which 500 men were needed, yet it has to be recognised that not many mechanical devices were available. Most of the work was done by human hands and muscles. The task was delicate and the slaves were freely flogged for any damage to stone slabs thus carried. The *korrah* (whip) of Bernier was not an invention of Shahjahan's time; it had been there all along during Muslim conquest and rule.

Hindu masons and architects were expert builders, they created wonderful specimens of architecture. About the temples of India, Alberuni says that his own people 'are unable to describe them, much less to construct anything like them'. Indian builders would never have liked to destroy their own splendid creations and dismantle their own sacred temples, to build in their instead mosques and minars for foreign invaders and rulers. But they had no choice. All Turkish slaves from abroad had become masters in India as kings, nobles, army officers and even soldiers, lording over the native workers who had been reduced to the position of slaves. Furthermore, Hindu masons and labourers turned slaves under the new dispensation had to do the work in record time. Barani in his enthusiasm hyperbolically says that during Alauddin's reign a palace could be built in 2-3 days and a citadel in two weeks.

It was considered a matter of pride for a newly crowned king to build a city of his own to give name and fame to himself and his dynasty. The old city of Iltutmish was abandoned by Balban who built the Qasr-i-Lal or the Red Palace, and Kaiqubad built the city of Kilughari. 'It is their custom,' writes Ibn Battutah, 'that the king's palace is deserted on his death' and his successor builds a new palace for himself.'

The slaves had often to do double the work, destroy Hindu buildings and construct new ones from the materials of earlier ones. In those times people lived in congested localities for reasons of security. A city used to get dirty and uninhabitable after a few years because of lack of means of disposing off garbage and filth. Ibn Battutah and Babur affirm that all was destroyed because of moisture. It is because of this reason also that it was thought better to found and shift to a new town where everything was clean and tidy. Hindu slaves toiled as scavengers and cleaners in old cities. They toiled with blood and sweat to create new ones.

Mohammad Tughlaq and Firoz Tughlaq were as keen as Aibak, Iltutmish and Alauddin about founding new cities, raising new buildings and repairing old edifices of earlier Muslim rulers. Shams Siraj Afif counts Firoz's builders among the 180,000 (or about 2 lakh) slaves of Firoz Tughlaq, but the break up for various duties would point to there being separate contingent of masons and builders with 12,000 slaves as stone-cutters alone. Even the shifting of the two Ashokan pillars to Delhi required the services of a few thousand men (*chandin hazar admi*). No wonder the invader Timur (1399 C.E.) found in India exquisite Muslim buildings, and enslaved thousands of craftsmen and builders many of whom he took with him to Samarqand to construct edifices similar to the Jama Masjid built by Firoz Shah and the Qutb Minar built by Aibak. But after his departure from India new slaves soon replaced those taken away by Timur, and every sultan and noble embarked on building enterprises as usual.

Besides the Sultanate, new independent Muslim states sprang up all over the country throughout the fifteenth century. In all of them feverish architectural activity was carried on with the help of local slaves. At the centre, Sultan Sikandar Lodi is credited with constructing mosques in almost all important cities including Lahore, Karnal, Hansi, Makanpur (District Kanpur) besides many in Delhi and Agra.

In addition to the tombs in Lodi Gardens in Delhi, there are also so many other nameless tombs belonging to the Lodi period. Sikandar Lodi, like Firoz Tughlaq before him, is credited with constructing a canal in 1492-93 and a Baoli in Rajasthan. In 'Mathura and other place' like Allahabad and Banaras he turned temples into mosques, and established Muslim Sarais, colleges and bazars in Hindu places of worship. Like Firoz Tughlaq, Sikandar was also a great repairer and conserver of old Muslim monuments. An inscribed frieze at the entrance doorway of the Qutb Minar credits him with repairing this edifice in 1503 (909 H).

We have spoken about only some of the architectural works of just five sultans of Delhi-Aibak, Iltutmish, Alauddin Khalji, Firoz Tughlaq and Sikandar Lodi-and noted that thousands and thousands of slaves were required for their construction. It is unnecessary to repeat that all Muslim rulers were great builders and the number of slaves engaged on building cities, mosques, Sarais, tombs of every sultan and noble and Sufi Sheikh in Delhi and other cities of the Sultanate ran into thousands. Same was the case with the buildings of the provincial and independent kingdoms into which the Sultanate of Delhi broke up.

'There was a strain of artistic feeling which ran through the successive generations of the ruling Mughal house in India,' observed E. Maclagan in 1932. This artistic feeling found its greatest manifestation in their architecture. And those who built had unbounded command of both money and slaves. Babur writes that '680 men worked daily on my buildings in Agra' only; while 1491 stone-cutters worked daily on my buildings in Agra, Sikri, Biana, Dulpur (Dholpur), Gwalior and Kuil (Aligarh). In the same way there are numberless artisans and workmen of every sort in Hindustan.' Some workers were wage-earners, for says he at another place, 'Gifts were made to the stone-cutters, and labourers and the whole body of workmen in the way customary for master-workmen and wage-earners of Agra.' But as discussed elsewhere slaves were preferred to servants and wage-earners, and the *Korrah* was the surest leveller of artisan, handicraftsman, servant and slave. From the days of Babur to those of Shahjahan during whose 'august reign, when' lovely things reached the zenith of perfection,' money in millions and slaves in thousands were employed on erecting the hundreds of huge Mughal buildings still extant.

The example of kings was universally imitated by their principal nobles. The opulent grandees in the provinces esteemed it an honour and obligation to adorn towns and cities of the regions under their control with magnificent buildings. The law of escheat encouraged them to spend lavishly. Pelsaert perhaps has the last word on it. 'I have often ventured to ask great lords,' says he, 'what is their true object in being so eager to amass their treasures, when what they have gathered is of no use to them or to their family (because of escheat)' I have urged they would share it with the poor, who in this country are hundreds of thousands, or indeed innumerable [including of course the slaves]' Their answers have been based on the emptiest worldly vanity. 'Buildings they constructed with great zest-gardens, tombs, and palaces' 'they build them with so many hundreds of thousands'. Once the builder is dead, no one will care for his buildings, but every one tries to erect buildings of his own, and establish his own reputation alongside that of his ancestors. If all these edifices were attended to and kept in repair, the lands of every city, and even village, would be adorned (covered) with monuments; but as a matter of fact the roads leading to the cities are strewn with fallen columns of stone.'

In short, the Turkish and Mughal sultans and nobles were ever busy on a budding spree without any thought of preserving the edifices. The strain of their artistic feeling was borne by the blood and toil of the silent slaves.

In the Army

Another cadre which absorbed the services of large number of slaves from the beginning of Muslim rule was the Army. Without a strong army there could be no conquest, no Muslim rule in India. Ziyauddin Barani declares that 'Kingship is the army and the army kingship,' that is, the one was concomitant to the other. Extension of Muslim rule in India was not possible without conquest and so the Sultanate was, by its very nature, committed to maintaining a large army.

Soldiers in permanent service and the king's bodyguards called Jandars, were largely drawn from his personal slaves *ghilman* and *mamalik*. Foreign slaves were purchased from all countries and nationalities. There were Turks, Persians, Seljuqs, Oghus (also called Iraqi Turkmen), Afghans, Khaljis etc., in the army of Ghaznavids and Ghaurids.

'To sustain the new principalities, slaves, imported as youths from peripheral regions were trained at the court of their masters to be a fighting and administrative elite loyal to them alone and thus comrades in arms.' This tradition of obtaining slaves by all methods and from all regions, was continued by Delhi sultans. These foreign slaves may be called, for the sake of brevity, by the generic term Turks and Afghans. Mohammad Ghauri in his last expedition brought ten thousand Afghan horsemen with him. In the time of Iltutmish, Jalaluddin Mangbarni of Khwarism, fleeing before Chingiz Khan, had brought contingents of Afghan soldiers. In course of time many of them took service under Iltutmish. Balban appointed three thousand Afghan horse and foot in his campaigns against the Mewatis, and thousands of others for garrisoning difficult forts like Gopalgir, Kampil, Bhojpur, Patiali and Jalali. In his royal processions hundreds of Sistani, Ghauri, Samarqandi and Arab soldiers, with drawn swords, used to march by Balban's side. Like the Afghans, the Mongols (again a generic term ethnically), were enslaved or persuaded to join the forces of the Khaljis. They were called neo-Muslims under Alauddin Khalji. Persian element in the rank of officers and men was also prominent. Purchased Abyssinian slave-soldiers and officers became prominent under Raziyah. By the time of Firoz Shah Tughlaq indigenous slaves began to replace foreigners. As an example, 'when the Sultan went out in state the slaves, accompanied him, in distinct corps-first the archers, fully armed, next the swordsmen, thousands in number (*hazar hazar*), the fighting men (*bandgan-i-aword*), the *bandgan-i-mahili* riding on male buffaloes, and slaves from the Hazara, mounted on Arab and Turki horses, bearing standards and axes. All these thousands upon thousands, accompanied the royal retinue. About 40,000 were everyday in readiness as his personal guards. Under Saiyyad and Lodi rulers, Afghans of all tribes and clans flocked into India like ants and locusts.

Indian slaves were obtained as presents, part of tribute from subordinate states, or enslaved during campaigns. Once broken and trained into loyalty and service they were easily drafted into the army. Most Hindus belonged to the infantry wing and were called Paiks. Some of these were poor persons who joined the army for the sake of securing employment. Others were slaves and war captives. In war small boys were preferred as captives and they were the easiest to capture. For instance, in his campaigns in Katehar, Balban massacred mercilessly, sparing boys only of the age of eight or nine. The age factor is significant. As these boys grew up, they could hardly remember their parentage or nativity, and remained loyal only to their master. In other cases also the situation was about the same. The slave was usually a prisoner of war, and according to Islamic usage his life was at the mercy of his captor. So when a conqueror or invader chose to spare the life of a slave and take him in his employment, it was an act of special benevolence for which the slave felt obliged to him. Many other Paiks were recruited from the open market. Prince Alauddin Khalji, as governor of Kara, recruited 2,000 Paiks with the revenue he was supposed to send to Delhi, and marched with them on an expedition to Devagiri (1296).

The Paiks were allotted sundry duties to perform. They fed, groomed, and looked after the horses of the cavalrymen who had a superior status. Alauddin Khalji had 70,000 cavalrymen besides other ranks. Thousands of slaves were needed to look after them. Similar was the case with elephant stables. These pilkhanas had thousands of elephants and *mahouts,* and *ghulams* and Paiks were on duty to feed and nourish them. The number of slaves for maintaining them and other animals can only be imagined.

During a campaign, the slaves cleared the jungles and prepared roads for the army on march. During halts and on arrival at the destination the slaves and Paiks set up the camp and fixed tents, sometimes on land the total circumference of which was twelve thousand five hundred and forty six yards (about ten kilometre square). They built Gargach and Sabat. Gargach was a covered platform on wheels for reaching the base of the fort under protection. Sabats were platforms raised from the ground to reach the top of the fort during assault. War drums and standards were placed in front of tents of load-carrying slaves who were kept under protective surveillance by mounted soldiers.

The Paiks were often so stationed as to bear the first brunt of the enemy's attack, but they could not leave their posts because 'horses are on their right and left' and behind (them) the elephants so that not one of them can run away.' But the Paiks were also great fighters. That is how Alauddin's army of invasion of Devagiri (1296) had 2000 Paiks. Most Persian chroniclers write about Paiks as being good soldiers lending strength to the Muslim army in Hindustan. Duarte Barbosa, a Portuguese official in India, writing in 1518 says this about them: 'They carry swords and daggers, bows and arrows. They are right good archers and their bows are long like those of England' They are mostly Hindus.' Their most important weapon was Dhanuk or Dhanush. During the time of the Khaljis (1290-1320), the Paik element had become prominent in Alauddin's army because he had wrested political power from the Turkish slave-rulers and could not entirely depend on Turkish soldiers. When Sultan Alauddin was about to encounter the Mongol invader Qutlugh Khwaja, Malik Alaulmulk, the Kotwal of Delhi, tried to dissuade him from taking any precipitate action and one of his arguments was that 'our army is composed principally of the soldiery of Hindustan.' Their presence in large number was disliked by the fanatical Alim and historian Ziyauddin Barani who was against the recruitment of non-Muslims in the army. Indeed among the Hindus there were sometimes such high officers as Malik Naik. According to Amir Khusrau it was under Malik Naik, the Akhurbeg-i-Maisara (Master of Horse of the Left Flank), a 'Hindu *banda*', that thirty thousand horsemen were sent against the Mongols-All Beg, Tartaq, and Targhi. Alauddin's greatest general was Malik Kafur Hazardinari. Later in the day we come across names like Bahadur Nahar, Sarang Khan, Shaikha Khokhar and Mallu Khan, probably all converted Hindu warriors.

Loyalty of the Paiks

In an atmosphere of intrigue, suspicion and treachery, in which kings were overthrown and dynasties subverted by Turkish slaves or slaves turned nobles, the Paiks were known for their devotion and loyalty. Whether captured as small boys or grown ups in war or directly recruited as troopers, the Paiks in all situations remained mostly loyal to their masters. The foundation of this loyalty was the attachment of man to man, first by the relationship of the chief to his captive whose life had been spared, and if the warrior master succeeded in conquest and setting up a dominion, by the relation of suzerain to vassal. This adherence of loyalty to salt is a basic fact of Hindu tradition. There are many instances where the Paiks came to the rescue of their masters when danger threatened the latter's lives. For example, when Sultan Alauddin was marching to attack Ranthambhor (1301 C.E.), he halted at Tilpat for a few days during which Sulaiman, also known as Ikat Khan, planned to assassinate him. Ikat Khan had thought that just as Alauddin had obtained the throne by murdering his uncle Jalaluddin, so he could also kill his uncle and occupy the throne. That is why he had attacked the king. But the latter's loyal Paiks hedged around him from all sides and in their native shrewdness began to lament aloud that the Sultan was dead. The foolish and inexperienced Ikat Khan, partly because he was unable to lay hands on the Sultan and partly because he was in a hurry to seize the throne, readily believed the welcome wailings of the Paiks and dashed off towards the Camp and seated himself on Alauddin's throne. In the meantime, Alauddin's personal bodyguard Paiks dressed his wounds and he regained consciousness. He arrived in the Camp posthaste, ascended an eminence, and showed himself to the people. And Ikat Khan was beheaded.

After Alauddin's death, his favourite slave, General and Wazir, Malik Kafur, wished to gather all power in his own hands and towards that end began to order the execution of one prince after another. He sent four Paiks by the names of Mubshir, Bashir, Salih and Munir to blind the Sultan's son Mubarak Khan. But when the Paiks approached him in his prison cell Prince Mubarak reminded them of their loyalty and duty which they owed to the sons of the late king. Impressed by Mubarak's appeal they not only left him untouched, but also murdered Kafur and thus facilitated Mubarak Khan's ascension to the throne. Similarly, Rai Bhairon Bhatti, the personal attendant of Firoz Shah Tughlaq, came to his rescue when his own kith and kin made plans to murder the Sultan. But there was no hard and fast behavioural pattern. The king was supreme but if the Paiks developed loyalty towards a nobleman who was inimical to the sultan, they could as well kill the king. That is how Sarwar-ul-Mulk, the Wazir of Sultan Mubarak Shah Saiyyad (1421-34), got the latter killed with the help of a group of Paiks. On the other hand, the loyalty of Hindu officers and soldiers has become legendary.

In short, Indian slaves in the Muslim army performed all and sundry duties. They served as servants to cavalrymen. They cleared the jungles and laid roads during campaigns. They manufactured weapons, they fought in battles for their masters. Even so they were ever kept reminded of their inferior status so far as their remuneration was concerned. And this was determined according to Islamic law. In the booty collected during war, the State's share was one-fifth, while four-fifth went to the combatants, but the share of a horseman was twice that of a footsoldier. As a Zimmi, the Hindu Paik had no share in the booty. Zimmi women and children cannot wage *jihad* and they too had no claim. But they were all to be paid something 'in order to encourage them to fight and inferiority of their station be rendered manifest to them.'

Employment in Karkhanas

Large numbers of slaves were drafted to work in the royal Karkhanas. The Karkhanas (literally workshops) of the Delhi sultans and Mughal emperors were both manufactories and storehouses where articles of delicacy were produced, sometimes in bulk, and imports from far off regions and foreign countries like China, Iraq and Alexandria, were received and stored. Shams Siraj Afif gives a detailed account of the Karkhanas of Firoz Shah Tughlaq although such workshops existed during the reigns of former as well as later sultans also.

According to J.H. Krammers, 'Industrial production in Muhammadan countries had developed in a particular way; it was chiefly characterized by being completely under the control of the rulers' and by its organization of the craftsmen in guilds. At the time of Islamic prosperity it had made possible a development of industrial skill which brought the artistic value of the products to an unequalled height. In the first place should be mentioned the products of the textile industry'?

Under Firoz Tughlaq (1351-88) there were thirty six Karkhanas *directly under the Sultan*. In these were manufactured and stored articles of gold and silver and brass and other metals, textiles, wines, perfumes, armours, weapons, horse and camel saddles and covers of elephants, leather goods and clothes. But the Karkhanas also looked after 'the elephant, horse and camel stables, the kitchen, the butlery, the candle department, the dog-kennels, the water-cooling department and other establishments' the wardrobe, the '*Alam-khana* or insignia, the carpet stores, and the like' About two lakhs of tankahs were expended in the carpet department, and 80,000 *tankahs* on the 'Alam Khana.' Each of these departments was under the charge of a senior Amir or Khan and lakhs of *tankahs* were sanctioned as recurring and non-recurring expenditure for each of the Karkhanas.

Thus some sort of capital investment was there and the guilds were formed by slaves trained as artisans (*kasibs*) by expert mechanics and handicraftsmen. 12,000 slaves worked in the Karkhanas of Firoz Tughlaq and were given a salary from 100 to

10 *tankahs* according to each one's competence. These slaves formed some sort of guilds and produced excellent articles. 'There was no occupation in which the slaves of Firoz Shah (or for that matter any other sultan) were not employed.' We cannot and need not study about all the departments in detail. Here we will confine ourselves to a brief account of two departments, those of wardrobe and weapons. These will suffice to give an idea of the institution of Karkhanas which employed a very large number, if not the bulk, of the royal slaves.

Textiles and Robes

According to Shahabuddin Al Umri 'every year the Sultan (Mohammad Tughlaq) distributes 200,000 complete dresses: 100,000 in spring and 100,000 in autumn (among nobles)' Dresses are also distributed to the monasteries and hermitages (*khanqahs* and *dargahs*). The Sultan keeps in his service 500 manufacturers of golden tissues, who weave the gold brocades worn by the wives of the Sultan, and given away as presents to the amirs and their wives.' Ibn Batuta's list of the presents he carried from Mohammad bin Tughlaq to the Mongol emperor of Cathay also helps us appraise the development of textile industry in India manned by slaves.

These presents comprised 100 pieces of cotton fabric called *bairami*, of matchless beauty priced at 100 *dinars* per piece; 100 pieces of silk called *juz* of variegated tints; 104 pieces of *Salahiya*, 100 pieces of *Shirinbaf*, 100 pieces of *Shanbaf*, 500 pieces of *muraz*, a kind of woollen fabric of various colours, 100 pieces of *Katan-i-Rumi*, 100 gowns without sleeves, a tent with six pavilions, four golden candlesticks and four embroidered with silver, four gold basins and six of silver, and ten dresses of honour embroidered. Also sent were ten quivers one of which was studded with pearls, and 10 swords the scabbard of one of which was inlaid with pearls and jewels. Ziyauddin Barani's list of such items of textiles also indicates their prices under Alauddin Khalji, that of Abul Fazl under the Mughals.

Slaves as Makers of Weapons

Slaves also manufactured weapons and their accessories including armour for men and covering of gilded iron for elephants. As is well known, the most important element in the army was heavy cavalry. Mounted soldiers were armed with the bow for engaging in combat from a distance and with one or more weapons for hand to hand fighting, like the lance, the spear, the mace, the lasso. Fakhr-i-Mudabbir gives primacy to the bow and the sword as the most effective weapons of the horseman. Both these weapons were of different varieties. Among them all, the Hindu sword was the best and most lustrous (*gawhardartar*). Their export to such distant areas as Ummayad Spain and Seljuq Anatolia too is attested. He also declares that there is no better lance than the Indian. From the time of Iltutmish to that of Firoz Shah great development had taken place in the manufacture of weapons and engines of war like Arrada, Manjniq and Maghrabi. These were stone and missile throwing machines. Haqqaha were rockets. The *Sirat-i-Firoz Shahi* mentions some very interesting 'equipments, outfits and instruments for waging war'. In the midst of a hotchpotch of assortment of items like traps, nets, noose and snare, 'we find a brief reference to such instruments as' Bandiqa (venetian crossbow for throwing stone balls); Faraqha Falakun (slings made of rope for throwing stones); Kaman Guruha (large mounted crossbow); Harf-i-Kilk (arrow with inverted sharp points); Julahiq (balls of stone thrown by balists); Zand-i-Atish (incendiary fire-steel) etc. All these weapons and equipments were manufactured by hundreds and hundreds of slaves, and were kept stored in the royal Karkhanas.

Work in Palace and Court

For invaders and conquerors, the establishment of a regular government takes some time. It is achieved through an evolutionary process. Its set up is completed in the course of decades. In medieval times this process was delayed by dynastic upheavals and arrival of fresh conquerors. But not too much. Most Muslim law-books and administrative manuals were ready when the Turks conquered Hindustan and stayed on to rule over it. And as in the case of construction of edifices and service in the army, slaves were required in large numbers for the working of the administrative machinery. Slaves were the hewers of wood and drawers of water in every sphere of life.

The government departments which needed the largest number of slaves were the Diwan-i-Wazarat, Diwan-i-Arz, Diwan-i-Insha, the Diwan-i-Rasalat. The detailed list of ministries, departments and offices is too large to mention. Thousands of slaves were required in the Revenue Department, thousands of others in the Postal Department as carriers of official communication and still others as spies. For shortage of space and paucity of detailed information about the employment of slaves in the households of nobles and other important Muslim elites, we shall confine our study of this aspect only to the Sultan's palaces for they 'are exclusively occupied by the Sultan, his wives, concubines, eunuchs, male and female slaves and *mamaliks*'.

How many slaves were on duty in the King's palace? It is difficult to surmise. One can only say-in thousands and thousands. At the gate there was the *nawbat* or the royal band played by a large number of instrument players in relay service-trumpets, drums, flagesletters, pipes etc. Hundreds were needed for carrying royal *alams* or standards, for wielding of fans to keep away flies from the royal person and wafting breeze, for carrying of *Chatr* (parasol) and *Durbash* (royal baton), and for attendance near the throne. The head of the Household staff, *Sarjandar* and *Sarsilahdar* or Commander of the Royal Bodyguard and head of the Royal Armour-bearer, required other hundreds of slaves to help them carry out their assignments.

Among other officials in charge of domestic attendance were *Sar-abdar* (or *Aftabchi* of the Mughals) who looked after the washing and toilet arrangements of the Sultan, the *Kharitadar* who looked after the royal writing case and *Tahwildar* who looked after the purse. Each of these officials had subordinate slaves and servants. The *Chashnigir* (the predecessor of the *Bakawal* of the Mughals) supervised the royal kitchen with hundreds of subordinate slaves working under him. *Sar-Jamadar* was in charge of the royal wardrobe, the *Saqi-i-Khas* of wines and other drinks. The *Mashaldar* supervised the lighting arrangements of the palace, and the provision of lamps, candlesticks, lamp-stands etc. All these functionaries had a regular staff of subordinates comprising mainly of slaves.

The scores of subordinates or slaves required to 'run' the Muslim government in India ran into hundreds of thousands. The Muqti and later the Subahdar lived like a miniature king, the paraphernalia of his court and household was patterned on that of the King. The Iqtadars and subordinate officers tried to emulate the higher nobles and the number of slaves continued to rise.

In the heyday of the Sultanate period, Shihabuddin Al Umari has this to say about the time of Mohammad bin Tughlaq. At the cost of this prince there are maintained 1,200 physicians; 10,000 falconers who ride on horseback and carry birds trained for hawking; 300 beaters go in front and put up the game; 3,000 dealers in articles required for hawking accompany him when he goes out hunting; 500 table companions dine with him. He supports 1,200 musicians excluding his slave musicians to the number of 1,000 who are more especially charged with the teaching of music, and 1,000 poets of all the three languages, Arabic, Persian and Indian. According to one informant who based his account on the report of the royal cook, 2,500 oxen, 2,000 sheep, and other animals and birds were slaughtered daily for the supplies of the royal kitchen. How many slaves were required to cater to all these services and amusements can easily be conjectured. In the Mughal times the number of slaves as part of the ever-expanding paraphernalia went on growing. Some numbers are available but details are not possible to give.

The number of men employed in connection with sports and amusements was in aggregate very large. A numerous staff was employed specially for hunting and shooting, another for hawking, another for pigeon-flying. All Muslim rulers and nobles had pigeon-boys-Alauddin Khalji alone had 50,000 of them. Provision was made for training the fighting instincts of a variety of animals 'down to frogs and spiders.' The stables swarmed with animals and men. The number of animals in the stables may be judged from the fact that Sher Shah employed 3,400 horses for royal postal communications in the Kingdom, and maintained about 5,000 elephants on an average. An elephants in the royal use had seven men to attend on it. Terry tells how Jahangir assigned four attendants to each of the dogs brought to him as presents from England.

Slaves and Servants

The imperial camp employed between 2000 and 3000 servants in addition to a guard of cavalry; there was one tent in particular which required 1000 men for a week for its erection.' As I have said elsewhere, in Akbar's time 'each camp establishment required for its transport 100 elephants, 500 camels, 400 carts and a hundred bearers. It was escorted by 500 troopers. Besides, there were 100 *farrashes*, 500 pioneers, 100 water carriers, 50 carpenters, tent makers, and torch bearers, 30 workers in leather, and 150 sweepers.' Akbar's '*zanana* contained more than 5000 ladies, each of whom had separate apartments; they were attended by an adequate staff of servants, and watched in successive circles by female guards, eunuchs' and porters'.

The Emperor set the standard in such matters, and everyone who occupied or aspired to a position at Court followed that example so far as his means allowed. Ten to twelve servants were attached to every lady of importance. Some princesses had as many slave-girls as a hundred. Supplies for the Royal Household were obtained from distant sources, apparently regardless of the amount of labour expended. Wherever the Emperor might be, water for his use was brought from the river Ganga, a practice prevailing from the time of Mohammad Tughlaq if not earlier. Ice came daily by post carriages and by runners from snowy mountains.

Fruit was supplied regularly from Kashmir and Kabul, and even from more distant places, such as Badakshan and Samarqand. Relay service on all these and many other such items required hundreds and thousands of slaves. The Emperor's personal officers modelled their establishments on similar lines, 'one employing 500 torch-bearers, another having a daily service of thousand rich dishes, and so on'. Each fighting man of any consequence in the Turki and Mughal army had in the field an average of two or three servants. That the fashion was not confined to the entourage of the Emperor is shown by della Valle's statement that at Surat servants and slaves were so numerous and so cheap that 'everybody, even of mean fortune, keeps a great family, and is splendidly attended'. Pyrard says that the Zamorin of Calicut travelled with about 3000 men in his train, and that on the coast generally the prominent men had always a large following. He tells of the state maintained at Goa by the Bijapur envoy, who was accompanied about the town by a crowd of servants, pages, bearers, grooms, and musicians, and adds that all the great men of the Deccan indulged in similar display. Thevenot, writing of a later period (C. 1667) gives a corresponding description of the life in Golkunda. About North India in Jahangir's time, Pelsaert writes, 'Peons or servants, are exceedingly numerous in this country, for everyone-be he mounted soldier, merchant or King's official-keeps as many as position and circumstances permit. Outside the house, they serve for display, running continually before their master's horse; inside, they do the work of the house,' like the *bailwan*, the *farrash*, the *masalchi*, the *mahawat* etc. 'it will be understood,' writes W.H. Moreland, 'that the profusion of servants, which attracts attention in India at the present day (early twentieth century), is no modern phenomenon, but is in fact an attenuated survival of the fashions prevailing in the time of Akbar and doubtless dating from a much earlier period,' indeed from the time of Qutbuddin Aibak when every Muslim householder or soldier began to possess a number of slaves. Such exploitation in the Mughal period provided droves of *khidmatgars* to British officers and men when they established and ran their Raj in this country.' They found its impoverished people, ready to be used as Coolies to be sent abroad and exploited this nation as smartly as the Turks and Mughals had done in the medieval period.

Slave Trade

It is nowhere mentioned in medieval chronicles how slaves, captured in war, were sorted out and separated for the purpose of being sold, drafted into the army, given as gifts to princes and nobles or set apart for domestic service. All that is known is that slaves were disposed of on all these counts and many more. It appears that the sorting was done on the basis of the looks of the females, physical fitness of the males, intuition of the master, as well as the specific work that a slave was deemed fit to do. An early example is about the capture of Brahmanabad by Mohammad bin Qasim. Of the prisoners captured a selection was made from the slaves and other spoils, 'in order to detach the usual one-fifth share of the State. The number of the selected slaves came to about 20,000. The rest were distributed among the troops.' But the criterion of selection has not been specified. Another instance is about Amir Timur who invaded India in 1399, and took a large number of prisoners. He writes 'I ordered that all the artisans and clever mechanics, who were masters of their respective crafts, should be picked out from among the prisoners and set aside, and accordingly some thousands of craftsmen were selected to await my command. All these I distributed among the princes and *amirs* who were present, or who were engaged officially in other parts of my dominions (to take care of them). I had determined to build a *Majid-i-Jami* in Samarkand, the seat of my empire, which should be without rival in any country; so I ordered that all builders and stone-masons should be set apart for my own especial service.' But such details are not available in most cases.

Sale of Slaves

The majority of Indian slaves comprised captives made during wars. These slaves formed property of the State. At the time of Mohammad bin Qasim's invasion of Sindh the head of the State was the Caliph and prisoners taken in Sindh were regularly forwarded to him. Kufi, the author of the *Chachnama,* rightly sums up the position. Out of the total catch, four-fifths was the share of the soldiers, 'what remained of the cash and slaves was' sent to Hajjaj (the Governor of Iraq)' for onward transportation to the Khalifa. In such a situation any special acquisition had to be paid for in cash. Mohammad bin Qasim who wished to possess Raja Dahir's wife Ladi, avers the *Chachnama,* 'purchased her out of the spoils, before making her his wife.' But the price he paid is not mentioned. Similarly, when Hajjaj sent 60,000 slaves captured in India to the Caliph Walid I (705-715 C.E.), the latter 'sold some of those female slaves of royal birth', but again their price has not been specified.

Mahmud of Ghazni carried away large numbers of captives from India in every campaign and sold most of them. Jayapala the defeated Hindu Shahiya King of Kabul was publicly exposed at some slave market in Khurasan by the order of Mahmud who 'commanded that he might be ransomed for the sum of eighty *dirams*'. Raverty suggests that 'the word 'thousand' must have been left out. If not, Mahmud did not set much value on his captive.' As Jayapala was old, the price he could fetch in open auction probably could not be more than 80 *dirhams*. Or, as Hodivala points out, the object of exposing Jayapala to public derision was evidently to compel him into surrendering to his victor's demands and purchase his release on his captor's own terms, which was fixed at '200,000 golden *dinars* and 250 elephants; and the necklace taken from Jaipal was valued at another 200,000 gold *dinars*.' Therefore, 80 *dirhams* as the price of an old king signifies nothing.

In one instance specifically Al Utbi gives an idea of the gain from the sale of captives. According to his narrative, Mahmud, after his campaign in Mathura, Mahaban and Kannauj (1018-19), returned to Ghazni with, besides other booty, 53,000 captives and each one of these was sold for two to ten *dirhams*. From this statement it would be safe to infer that the lowest price at which an Indian captive was sold was two, and the highest ten *dirhams*.

It would also be safe to conclude that slaves were captured by invaders to be sold to make money; for Utbi adds that 'Merchants came from different cities to purchase them so that the countries of Mawarau-n-nahr, Iraq and Khurasan were filled with them'. Earlier, in the expedition to Thaneshwar (1015), according to Farishtah, 'the Muhammadan army brought to Ghaznin 200,000 captives, so that the capital (Ghaznin) looked like an Indian city, for every soldier of the army had several slaves and slave girls'. Similarly, in the Kashmir Valley (1014 C.E.), according to Utbi, the captives taken 'were so plentiful that they became very cheap'? But he does not say how cheaply they were sold.

The mention of price at one place is hardly sufficient to estimate the money value of Indian slaves sold in foreign lands in the eleventh century. What was the value of two to ten *dirhams* in those days is also not known. Abul Fazl traces the history of *dirham* from the time of Caliph Umar, but his detailed and rather confusing account only shows that the earliest *dirhams* of the Ghaznavid period were struck at Ghazni and Lahore. It was a silver coin of great variations in weight and value as was the case with the *dinar*, a gold coin. Yet, the sale of thousands of slaves after every campaign, as the figures of captives carried away by Mahmud shows, brought good profit to the invader. No wonder that besides treasure, captives also used to be regularly carried away from India during the Ghaznavid occupation of Punjab for making extra money through their sale. This lucrative business continued, and a scion of the house, Sultan Ibrahim (1054-1099), once carried away one lakh captives to Ghazni.

During the first hundred years of Muslim rule, that is, under Aibak, Iltutmish and Balban (1206-1290), slaves of both sexes were captured in droves during military expeditions, but they were mostly distributed among kings, nobles and soldiers for sundry duties. Large number of workers were needed by these early sultans for clearing jungles, making roads, as auxiliaries in the army, for construction of buildings, as errand runners by administrators, tent fixers and workers in camp establishments. Slaves were needed for arranging supplies for households of all kinds of foreign Muslims from kings and nobles to commoners, constructing small residential dwellings or grand and imposing State buildings etc. Slave girls were needed in plenty for providing pleasure and other services. All this work was done by captives turned slaves. It appears that because of their being detailed on these jobs, very few slaves were left available for sale. That is why there is no specific mention of their sale during this period, But sale of captives was a common practice. For example, it is mentioned that Sultan Nasiruddin, son of Iltutmish (1246-66), had no 'purchased' (*laundi va khadima*) slave girl, that his wife cooked for him and he earned his livelihood by selling copies of Quran written by himself. 'This story, however, is very stale indeed,' adds Raverty, 'as stale as the days of one of the early Khalifas', for this very sultan could present *forty head of slaves* to his nobleman Minhaj Siraj for being sent to his dear sister in Khurasan.

During the reign of Sultan Alauddin Khalji the Sultanate grew strong (1296-1316). He conquered extensively and in every campaign slaves were captured in large numbers. These were sold in various ways-on the Spot, in the markets of Delhi, and of other cities. Sometimes even women and children of Mongol invaders were captured and sold like Hindu slaves in Delhi and other cities of India.

Sale Price of Slaves

Alauddin Khalji's Market Control has become famous in medieval Indian history. He fixed the price of every commodity, including slaves. The sale price of slaves was like this. The standard price of a working girl was fixed at from 5 to 12 *tankahs*, and that of a good looking girl suitable for concubinage from 20 to 30 and even 40 *tankahs*. The price of a man slave (*ghulam*) usually did not exceed 100 to 200 *tankahs*. The prices of handsome boys were fixed from 20 to 30 *tankahs*; the ill-favoured could be obtained for 7 to 8. The price of a child slave (*ghulam bachchgan naukari*) was fixed at 70 to 80 *tankahs*. The slaves were classified according to their looks and working capacity. In the case of bulk purchases by traders who had ready money and who had the means to carry their flock for sale to other cities, prices were fixed accordingly.

Who got the profit form such sales? If Alauddin Khalji followed the example of contemporary rulers in West Asian countries, then the profit went to him, that is, the sultan or the government. This was also customary. It is stated by Isami in his *Futuh-us-Salatin* that when Mahmud of Ghazni defeated Raja Jayapala of the Hindu Shahiya dynasty, he 'carried him to the distant part of the kingdom of Ghazni and delivered him to an agent (*dalal*) of the *Slave Market* '(and) at the command of the king Mahmud they [the Brokers of the Market, *muqiman-i-bazar* in the original] sold Jaipal as a slave for 80 Dinars and deposited the money realised by the sale in the Treasury'.

Hodivala adds that 'it would be difficult to get better evidence than this of the ruler making the profit. In some of the West Asian countries in the Middle Ages, according to Ira Marvin Lapidus, the rulers used to take over wholesale trade, in grain and also probably in other commodities, so that profits from sale accrued to them rather than to the private traders. Ibn Khaldun also says that 'the slave merchants bring them to Egypt in batches' and government buyers have them displayed for inspection and bid for them, raising the price above their value.' It was equally true of Alauddin. He treated the merchants themselves as slaves. As per his orders, no middlemen or brokers were allowed to visit the slave-market and examine the 'goods', so that the profits of the traders were curtailed while those of the Sultan swelled. No wonder then that at his demise the Sindhi (Multani) merchants took out processions to rejoice at the death of Alauddin.

No rule about the sale price could be laid in special cases when the catch was big or a very beautiful slave ('man or woman/ boy or girl') of very high price, say 1000 to 2000 *tankahs* was brought for sale in the market. Sometimes it created a very piquant situation as nobody dared to buy him/her, lest the king should come to know that so and so was rich enough to pay so high a price for a slave/concubine. Even then slaves were sometimes purchased for high amounts. The poet Badr Chach claims to have bought a slave named Gul-Chehra (Rose Face) for 900 *tankahs*.

The title Hazardinari (of a thousand gold coins) for Malik Kafur shows that a skilled slave could have cost anything. It may therefore be contended that except in the reign of Alauddin when prices were fixed, prices of slaves and concubines were uncertain, varying according to fortunes of war and famine, looks of the person, bargaining talent of the auctioneers, shrewdness of the buyer and fluctuations in the market through influences of demand

and supply. For instance, when Mohammad Ghauri and Qutbuddin Aibak mounted a combined attack on the Khokhars of the Salt Range (Koh-i-Jud), 'great plunder was taken and many captives, so that five Hindu [Khokhars] captives could be bought for a *dinar*'. Captives were so plentiful that they were also sent 'to sell in Khurasan, not long after.' On the other hand, if the supply was short and demand great, the prices went shooting high. Narrating the events of the reign of Sultan Qutbuddin Mubarak Khalji (1316-20), the son and successor of Alauddin Khalji, Ziyauddin Barani says that the strict regulations of Alauddin were all thrown to the winds by the new Sultan, and Qutbuddin and his nobles gave themselves up to a life of debauchery and licence. In such circumstances the 'demand for beautiful girls and beardless boys made them a scarce commodity, and their prices rose to 500 and sometimes even to one thousand and two thousand *tankahs*.' So, in the early fourteenth century the lowest average price of a slave mentioned by chroniclers was about eight *tankahs*, the highest 2000 *tankahs*. Slaves in Hindustan were cheap during the Khalji period because of the price-control of Alauddin Khalji and also because coined money was in short supply. So that, writes Ziyauddin Barani, 'a camel could be had for a *dang* (small copper coin), but wherefore the *dang*'? In view of this some sort of barter should have been practised.

Low Price of Indian Slaves

Ziyauddin Barani reckons regulations regarding sale of 'horses, slaves and quadrupeds' under one category. T.P. Hughes quoting the *Hidayah* says that slaves, male and female, are treated merely as articles of merchandise, and 'very similar rules apply both to the sale of animals and bondsmen.' A milch buffalo cost 10-12 *tankahs*., a working girl was cheaper. The price of a good quality horse was 90-120 *tankahs*, that of a *ghulam* was 100 on an average. A handsome boy could be had for 20 to 30 *tankahs*. It is therefore a matter of some satisfaction that under the Khaljis the value of humans in terms of price was not less than that of horses and buffaloes.

The contemporary chronicler Barani boasts that the cheapness of prices in Alauddin's time was not witnessed after his reign. But the trend towards low prices was universal and spread over a long period. Writing about the days of Sultan Mohammad bin Tughlaq

(1325-51), Shihabuddin Al-Umari writes: 'The Sultan never ceases to show the greatest zeal in making war upon the infidels'. Every day thousands of slaves are sold at a very low price, so great is the number of prisoners' (that) the value at Delhi of a young slave girl, for domestic service, does not exceed eight *tankahs*. Those who are deemed fit to fill the parts of domestic and concubine sell for about fifteen *tankahs*. In other cities prices are still lower'? Probably it was so because Ibn Battutah while in Bengal says that a pretty *Kaniz* (slave girl) could be had there for one gold *dinar* (or 10 silver *tankahs*). 'I purchased at this price a very beautiful slave girl whose name was Ashura. A friend of mine also bought a young slave named Lulu for two gold coins.' It is very difficult to establish a relationship between the prices of Delhi market and those of the provinces. Umari continues, 'but still, in spite of low price of slaves, 20000 *tankahs*, and even more, are paid for young Indian girls. I inquired the reason' and was told that these young girls are remarkable for their beauty, and the grace of their manners.'

The cheapness of price of young slaves is indirectly attested to by Ibn Battutah also. Such was their influx that at one place he writes, 'once there arrived in Delhi some female infidel captives, ten of whom the Vazir sent to me. I gave one of them to the man who had brought them. My companion took three young girls, and I do not know what happened to the rest.' Thousands of slaves were captured in the minor yearly campaigns of Firoz Tughlaq and obviously sold, for, says the contemporary chronicler Shams Siraj Afif that 'in places which are sacked and looted the captives are selected as per royal regulations. Those fit for royal service (alone) are sent to the court.' The others were sold. It was under such a system that one of Firoz's slaves Bashir Sultani could buy with money 4,000 slaves (*mal kharida*) for his personal service.

From the fifteenth century onwards, we have some more information about the sale of slaves and their prices at home and abroad. Babur writes in his Memoirs that 'there are two trade-marts on the land-route between Hindustan and Khurasan; one is Kabul, the other, Qandhar. (Route to Kabul was from Lahore, to Qandhar from Multan)' Down to Kabul every year 'from Hindustan, come every year caravans' bringing slaves (*barda*)' and other commodities, and sell them at great profit. 'In Kabul can be had the products of Khurasan, Rum, Iraq and Chin (China); *while it is Hindustan's own market* (emphasis added).' There was also barter prevailing with regard to the disposal of slaves. For example, William Finch writing at Agra in about 1610 says that 'in hunting the men of the jungle were on the same footing as the beasts' and whatever was taken in the game was the king's *shikar*, whether men or beasts. 'Men remain the King's slaves which he sends yearly to Kabul to barter for horses and dogs.' Many other writers tell it besides Finch. Barter was in vogue not only in the days of Jahangir but it was practised throughout the medieval period.

The Ain-i-Akbari

The *Ain-i-Akbari* and other similar works giving data about the wages of servants and labourers, in consequence indirectly giving the value of slaves as a market commodity. W.H. Moreland observes that some of the men employed on various works were free, while others were slaves, but the functions assigned to the two classes were to a great extent interchangeable and, therefore, for our purpose it is relevant to treat them as a single group, and the price of slaves may be estimated on the basis of wages paid to the free labourer. In Mughal India, in the reign of Akbar (sixteenth century), and as seen by Bernier (seventeenth century), 'Freemen were hired at rates which sufficed for a little more than a bare existence' a servant with no special qualifications cost about 1½ rupees monthly at Akbar's court, and perhaps 2 on the west coast' Pyrard puts the price of a slave-girl at the equivalent of about 50 rupees in Goa, which was a very busy market for such commodities, but the rate must have varied between very wide limits, depending as it did partly on the qualities of the individual and partly on fluctuations in the supply.' This price of 40 to 50 rupees for a slave paid by the English was the average, 'the earlier reference shows that the Dutch demand had raised prices to about this level from the former standard of Rs. 15 to 20.'

The wages of free men, that is, labourers and not slaves, were equally low. But the proportion of slaves, who were valued as property, was more considerable than that of servants, who can be computed only as an expense. It was more to the interest of rulers, nobles, merchants and manufactures to purchase than to hire their workmen. In the countryside, slaves were employed as the cheapest and most laborious instruments of agriculture. But medieval slavery was more necessary for urban service. So rural populations were made captives and brought for work in cities.

Rural slaves and servants were not bought on the market but reproduced themselves through demographic increase. In the cities themselves there was no dearth of them. Pelsaert and so many other foreigners noted that men stood in the market to be hired and 'most of the great lords reckon 40 days to the month, and pay from 3 to 4 rupees for that period.' 'Akbar sanctioned the following daily wages for workers and artisans-2 *dams* (copper coins, 140 to the *Rupia*) for ordinary labourers, 3 to 4 *dams* for superior labourers, 3 to 7 *dams* for carpenters and 5 to 7 *dams* for builders.' In several instances the lowest grades of servants were entitled to less than two rupees monthly, 'while the bulk of the menials and of the ordinary foot-soldiers began at less than three rupees?

The minimum for subsistence at the Court is probably marked by the lowest grade of slaves who were allowed one dam daily, equivalent to three-quarters of a rupee monthly in the currency of the time? These instances appear to justify the conclusion that early in the seventeenth century foreigners could secure capable servants for somewhere about three rupees a month. What this represents in real wages is uncertain (but) the rates struck the Europeans as extraordinarily low'?

The inescapable conclusion deduced from the wages of labourers and applied to the prices of slaves is that these were very low throughout. There are not many references available about the actual price of slaves and therefore this section is closed with the information that 'in the month of November (1947), Hindu and Sikh girls brought by Pathan raiders from Kashmir were sold in the bazars of ghulam,' for rupees 10 or so each in the wake of the partition of the country, 1947-48.

Import of Foreign Slaves

As compared to Hindu slaves, who were often captured and sold in droves, the price of foreign slaves was high. They used to be Muslims, were always considered as talented, and in some cases essentially an item of luxury.

Foreign slaves were purchased from merchants coming from lands beyond the river Sindh for as much as 500 to 1000 dinars. Both in the *Hidayah* and the *Fatawa-i-Alamgiri* the price of a slave repeatedly mentioned, although in the form of examples, is mostly 1000 dirhams. For example Qutbuddin Aibak purchased two accomplished Turkish slaves for one lakh *jitals* or 2,000 *tankahs* (at 48-50 copper *jitals* to one silver *tankah*).

Similarly, Iltutmish purchased Qamaruddin Timur Khan for 50,000 *jitals* or 1000 *tankahs*. And the transaction was concluded after great haggling and bargaining. In this context the sale of Iltutmish to Qutbuddin Aibak makes an interesting and instructive reading. As seen earlier, a slave merchant Jamaluddin Mohammad had brought Iltutmish to Ghazni to sell him to Sultan Muizzuddin. 'At that period, no Turk superior to him in comeliness, commendable qualities' intelligence and sagacity, had they brought to that capital.' The Sultan inquired about his price.

The merchants or their brokers mentioned the price of two slaves together-one Iltutmish and another Ibak, as the 'sum of a thousand *dinars* of pure Rukni gold for each.' But the merchant Jamaluddin Mohammad declined to sell Shamsuddin for that amount. An angry Sultan then commanded that no one should purchase him, and that the sale should be prohibited. Jamaluddin Mohammad took Iltutmish back to Bukhara, which was a renowned centre of slave trade in the Middle Ages.

When he returned to Ghazni after four or five years, Qutbuddin Aibak showed an inclination to buy Iltutmish and requested Muizuddin for permission to do so. The Sultan replied: 'Since a command has been issued that he should not be purchased at Ghaznin, let them take him to the city of Delhi and there he can be purchased.' The merchant accordingly brought him to Delhi and Iltutmish and the other slave were bought by Qutbuddin Aibak for the sum of one hundred thousand *jitals*.

Haggling and bargaining was possible in individual cases. In bulk purchases price was settled for the whole lot at one go. Merchants from Turkey, Syria, Persia and Transoxiana used to approach Muslim kings with their consignments. Foreign slaves of both sexes were in great demand in India. Males were needed for heavy duties, females for concubinage and keeping surveillance on other harem inmates. Niccolao Manucci writes that when in 1661-62 an embassy was sent by the king of Balkh, 'the envoys brought several Tartar and Uzbeg women with them for sale. Aurangzeb purchased some of them. They were placed in the list of numerous Kashgar, Qalmaq, Pathan and Abyssinian women. They were chosen because they are warlike and skilful in the use of lance, arrow and sword,' and therefore could serve as efficient guards of the harem. For concubinage fair women from East European countries were preferred. For example, Udaipuri-Mahall, the concubine of Aurangzeb, was a Georgian slave girl.

Importation of foreign slaves went on right up to the eighteenth century. In the fifteenth century, the Ottoman capture of Constantinople in 1453 gradually diverted the immense flow of slaves from the Crimea, the Balkans and the steppes of western Asia to Islamic markets.

Later on, the southward expansion of Russia, culminating in the annexation of Crimea in 1783, gradually shut off the supply of white slaves to the Islamic markets. As Africa became almost synonymous with slavery, the world forgot the eagerness with which Tatars and other Black Sea peoples had sold millions of Ukrainians, Georgians, Circassians, Armenians, Bulgarians, Slavs and Turks. In Africa, in the nineteenth century in the Sudan region there were farms that specialized in breeding black slaves for sale like cattle or sheep. Other enterprising merchants in upper Egypt reaped large capital gains by purchasing prepubescent boys at a price of about three hundred piastres apiece, having them castrated by Coptic monks, and then selling them as eunuchs for one thousand piastres each. 'Islamic civilization did indeed practise castration of slaves on an unprecedented scale.

Several cities in Africa were real factories of eunuchs; they were an expensive commodity as only 25% of the victims survived the operation.' In short, black or white, castrated or otherwise, the price of foreign slaves was high as, besides other factors, it also covered the cost of their transportation.

Slavery was recognised by Prophet Mohammad. It was considered lawful in Islam. Regular trade in slaves began with the Ummayad Caliph Muawiya in the days of the Abbasid Caliphs it gained in impetus and extent. Slave trade spread so rapidly that no one was safe from being enslaved in the heyday of Muslim power, and black and white slaves were traded throughout the Muslim world. Brigandage was commonly resorted to in order to obtain slaves.

'The *Hudud al-Alam* (a tenth century Persian document) describes the Sudan (the land south of the desert separating it from the Maghreb) as follows: no region is more populated than this. The merchants steal children there and take them away. They castrate them and take them to Egypt, where they sell them. *Among them [the Sudanese] there are people who steal each other's children to sell them to the merchants* when they come.' Turks, Negroes, Ethiopians, Abyssinians, Berbers, Slavs and many others were sold in 'thousands'. White slaves were costlier than the black.

Egypt and Syria supplied a large number of them and Italian ports formed transit points for export. In the tenth century the most valuable commodity that was carried from Volga to Central Asia was slaves. They were brought to the Oxus region, more particularly Samarkand. There the best were put in the market for sale, and the trade was very profitable.

T.W. Arnold's observations on this slave-taking in East European and African countries is relevant in the Indian context. He writes that 'though the lot of many of the Christian captives was very pitiable one, others who held positions in the households of private individuals, were often no worse off than domestic servants in the rest of Europe. As organised by the Muhammadan Law, slavery was robbed of many of its harshest features, nor in Turkey at least does it seem to have been accompanied by such barbarities and atrocities as in the pirate states of Northern Africa'.

The condition of the Christian captives naturally varied with the circumstances of their own capabilities of adapting themselves to a life of hardship; the aged, the priests and monks, and those of noble birth suffered most, while the physician and the handicraftsman received more considerate treatment from their masters, as being servants that best repaid the money spent on them. The galley slaves naturally suffered most of all.' In East Africa the Arabs were 'given up wholly to the pursuit of commerce or to slaves-hunting'. Naturally the feeling of both chiefs and people was hostile to the Muhammadans, who were hated and feared as slave-dealers.' For the Muslims, on the other hand, slaves were stolen through acts of violence and then converted into commodities. 'Slave is the most fundamental form of property.'

Slave trade was carried on both by sea and land routes. Import of slaves from Africa and Western Asia was of substantial importance. 'In the centuries preceding the year 1500 Arabs and Persians had acquired a position of predominance in the sea-borne trade of the whole of Indian Ocean from Mozambique to the

Straits of Malacca.' They had settlements at seaports on both sides of India, and we meet with Muslims at practically every Indian seaport. One of the commodities in which they traded was slaves.

They sold these slaves to Indian rulers and nobles in such large numbers that the complexion of the government looked foreign. Indian sultans imported slaves throughout the medieval period for service in many fields, more particularly in administration and army and saving their kingdoms from indigenous popular risings, for, as Moreland remarks, even 'Akbar's court was essentially foreign, and even in his later years the Indian element, whether Hindu or Moslem, constituted only a small proportion of the whole.'

Abyssinians were in much demand, and we read of them frequently in the chronicles of the times. A regular traffic existed in the inhabitants of Mozambique, and there was also an import trade from Persia and countries lying beyond. Not only the sultans of Delhi or the Mughal emperors, but even the sultans of the Deccan states imported slaves to keep their rule established. Golkunda was connected with three great ports of Goa and Surat on the west coast and Masulipatam on the east.

For northern India, the land route was equally important if not more. There were slave markets in all important Muslim cities in the medieval world. It may be pertinent to recollect that Subuktigin had been purchased by Alptigin at Bukhara and Qutbuddin Aibak had been purchased by Qazi Abdul Aziz Kufi in the slave market of Nishpur.

All rulers of Delhi and Agra used to import foreign slaves. Sultan Shamsuddin Iltutmish once sent a Muslim merchant to Samarqand, Bukhara and Tirmiz to bring some slaves from those places. The trader purchased for the Sultan one hundred slaves and Balban was one of them. Chinese traders also once brought forty slaves and presented them to the Sultan. The list of Shamsi slaves given by Minhaj Siraj mostly comprised purchased slaves.

Internal Trade

In India the Muslims established a number of slave trade centres. Besides Delhi and cities in Bengal there is mention of Badaon in Uttar Pradesh and Mandor in Rajasthan. But of course from the narrative of the chroniclers it appears that slave markets existed in almost all important places in the country, for slaves were also sold in fairs held in major cities. In this inhuman business the Hindus were not interested. Firstly, they were themselves at the receiving end, they themselves were the victims.

And secondly, as W.H. Moreland points out, 'We may infer from della Valle's statements that the principal Hindus at Surat-perhaps the most humane people that ever lived-disapproved entirely of slavery.' Now few people are as good traders as Gujaratis. They would have excelled if they had taken to slave-trading.

But catching and selling of slaves did not fit in with the Hindu psyche. Although, commenting on the statement of della Valle, Moreland says, 'but I do not think that this remark can be extended to Hindus generally' though in Akbar's time at least it did not secure the approval of all Hindus? The existence of slavery is testified to by the travellers Abdur Razak, Conti and Barbosa.

It would be safe to presume that it prevailed in the Deccan, because it prevailed farther north in the country whence the Deccan dynasties had sprung and we may believe Nikitin's statement that in his time there was a trade in 'Black people' in Bidar.'

But the trade was carried on by Muslims and not Hindus, for Moreland adds that in 1643, 'a Nayak, or chief, rejected a Dutch request for leave to buy up to 1000 slaves yearly on the ground that the sale of human being was not only a scandal but a sin.' All accounts point to the fact that Hindus, otherwise great traders and merchants throughout India's history, did not indulge in slave trade.

But the Portuguese in this matter followed the custom of the Muslims. 'Linschoten recorded that they never worked, but employed slaves, who were sold daily in the market like beasts, and della Valle notes that the 'greatest part' of people in Goa were slaves.'

The Portuguese not only employed Indian slaves for domestic and other duties, but they also regularly brought slaves from Abyssinia and Mozambique for sale at good price in Goa and Surat. They dominated the Indian seas where they pirated non-chalantly, captured slaves and sold them in the markets of Hugli, Tamluk, Pipli, St. Thome, Ceylon and Goa. Pyrard (1608-11) observed that goods of all the world must pass Ormuz and pay tribute to the Portuguese.

It so happened that their Governor in Hugli, Manoel Travers, infuriated Shahjahan when as a prince, he was in rebellion and in a helpless position.

Travers seized some of the prince's richly laden boats and carried away some of Mumtaz Mahall's slave girls. When Shahjahan became king he ordered the Mughal governor of Bengal to chastise the Portuguese. After a sanguinary battle on the famous river port Hugli in 1632 they were expelled from Bengal. As a matter of fact the people of India hailed the other European adventurers as liberators from Portuguese tyranny, their forcible conversions and their obnoxious slave trade.

The Dutch also indulged in slave trade. In this regard the views of Coen, the great Dutch Governor-General, are worth noting.

In 1623, he advised his successor, not merely the prosecution of Asiatic trade, ' but the investment of all available capital in principal means of production ('many thousands of slaves')' so that the returns for our native country be made out of the gains of the inland trade and the ordinary revenues'.

From about 1620 the Dutch requirements from India were, first, a large initial supply of slaves, and then a steady stream of reinforcements to make good the losses. For example, Dutch families in the Spice Islands needed a sufficient number of slaves, 'mostly of Indian origin' besides those who had experience of working on the spice fields.

Many imported slaves, 'Bengalders, Arakandars, Malabars, etc.,' were greatly affected by sickness owing to the change of climate on arrival in the Islands and losses had to be made up. 'There is nothing to suggest that the Dutch merchants practised either force or fraud, and we find them buying regularly from Indian dealers after obtaining the permission of the authorities.'

In 1661 a ship belonging to the Sultan of Golkunda carried 300 slaves to Achin and slave trade was regarded by Muslims as well as the Dutch, 'precisely as any other branch of commerce'.

The Portuguese and the Dutch were followed by the British. The export of slaves and indentured Indian labour by the British to various parts of the British Empire when it was in the making, is beyond the scope of this study. But the genesis of endeavours and achievements of the European nations in the field of making and exporting Indian slaves was a continuation of the practice by the Muslims in medieval times. It is even said that the profits accruing to the Muslims from slave trade tempted many foreign nations to join in the race.

However, in contrast to the foreign imported slaves, whose market price was rendered high by cost of transportation and deaths in transit, the price of Hindu slaves, sold abroad remained low. For example, Hindu Kush (Hindu-killer) mountain is so named because thousands of enslaved Hindus died in crossing it. But their numbers were so large that the price of survivors remained low in foreign markets.

4

Rise of Urban Economy, Trade and Commerce

The available evidence suggest that the urban economy on the eve of the Ghorid conquest waq on a low ebb. The towns were fewer in number and smaller in size in the centuries preceding the establish'ment of the Delhi Sultanate. D.D.Kosambi shows that even the capital was a camp city on the move. The higher ruling class wandered from place to place along with the army while the lower ruling class was almost completely ruralized. This view of urban decline has been supported by R.S. Sharma who has cqnvincingly reasserted his theory of urban decay with the help of enormous archaeological data painstakingly collected.

This theory of decay of towns is further corroborated by the evidence of sluggish trade: The near complete disappearance of gold and silver currencies and the almost total absence of foreign coins in the Indian coin-hoards of the period are indicators that the foreign trade was at a very low scale. Moreover, the fact that not even the coins of various regional dynasties are found in the coin-hoards of other regions, suggests that inland commerce was not widespread. All this scenario changed almost immediately with the establishment of the Delhi Sultanate. The archaeological and numismatic evidence corroborate the literary evidence of growth of towns and increase in commerce.

Growth of Towns

Before discussing the evidence of increase in number and size of towns, we must first understand what we mean by town. There are two simple definitions of a town : (a) the usual modern definition of a settlement of 500 or above, and (b) a settlement where an overwhelming majority of population (say above 70%) is engaged in occupations other than agriculture.

Economy of Delhi Sultanate

While the archaeological evidence available for earlier period is not forthcoming from the 13th-14th centuries owing to the much less attention paid to medieval archaeology, the literary dvidences testify growth of urbari centres. Lahore was a big town but decayed after the Motlgol invasion in the 13th century. However, in the 14th century it flourished again. While not even a guesstimate of the population of any town is available in our sources there are reliable indications to assume that at least some of these were cities big enough by contemporary standards. Ibn Battuta, who visited Delhi in 1330,. deseribes it as of enormous extent and population, the largest city in the Islamic East in spite of the fact that Mohammad Tughluq had shifted much of its population to Daulatabad. He describes the latter too, as large enough to rival Delhi in size. Some new towns were established during the period, such as Jhain (Chhain) in Eastern Rajasthan that was named 'Shahr Nau' during Alauddin Khalji's reign (1296-1316).

Factors for Urban Expansion

Five strength of the invader, of course, lay in combination and not in dispersal in an unfamiliar land and, thus, in initial stages, it was but natural for the members of the ruling class to prefer to stay at their iqta headquarters along with their cavalry. These iqta headquarters having the concentration of cavalry, its hangers-on and the retinue and household of the rnuqti thus emerged in the early phase as camp cities.

Most of the 13th century towns are infact defined as iqta headquarters in our sources; for example, Hansi, Kara, Anhilwara, etc. These towns were to be fed and provided for. In the beginning, the troops had to go for realising khar & j/mal by plundering the surrounding villages; but gradually by the 14th century, as pointed out by Moreland, cash nexus developed. The revenue was realised in cash from the peasants who were thus forced to sell their produce at the side of the field. The merchants catered to the needs of towns giving risk to what we will discuss below as-induced trade'.

The ruling class coming from a different cultural milieu had needs of leisure and comforts of a different type; they wanted songs in Persian and dances of a different style, books, silk to wear and arcuate light architecture (not !he stone edifices). Out of the resources that were indeed enormous by contemporary standards at its command, the new rulers naturally. Wanted to get luxuries and comforts of their taste which encouraged immigration from Islamic culture area. These immigrants were not only soldiers, but craftsman, artisans, singers, musicians, dancers, poets, physicians, astrologers and servicemen as described by Isami.

Urban Manufactures

It seems that the urban craft production received a twofold impetus with the establishment of the Delhi sultanate. First, the Sultanate ruling class remained town-centred and spent the enormous resources it appropriated in the form of land revenue mainly in towns, either on buying services or procuring manufacturers. Even the money spent on the service sector partly went to help the urban craft sector through multiplier effect. While the nobility created demand for high-priced skill-intensive luxury items, its hangers-on in all likelihood created a mass market for ordinary artisanal product.

The second factor that contributed to urban manufacturers was the introduction of a number of technological devices that reached India with the invaders. (You will learn, about them in detail in the next Unit). In the luxury sector, silk weaving expanded and carpet-weaving came from Persia. The other notable urban manufacture was paper making. Perhaps a major sector of urban employment was building industry. Baranl says that Alauddin Khalji employed 7b,000 craftsmen for his buildings. One may well be justified in saying that there was considerably more masonary per acre of occupied space in the towns of 1400 than in those of 1200.

Organization of Production

It is indeed important to know how production was organized. Whether the town artisans carried out production under the 'domestic system', that is, they owned their tools, raw material and the end product and also sold their product themselves; in other words, whether they were self employed or while tools were their own and they worked at their homes, raw material was provided to them by the merchants, that is whether they worked under the 'putting-out system'. The contemporary sources shed little light on these aspects. One can, however, legitimately assume that since the tools of production even after the introduction of new devices were still simple and mainly of wood and little of iron should have remained cheap. The artisan wish thus master of his own tools, though varied forms of labour organization seem to be prevalent. Certain artisans hawked or hired out their services such as cotton-card & who with a bow-string on his shoulder, went door to door selling his services as is evident from the account given in Khair-ul Majalis. Spinning was done usually by women staying at their homes.

The weavers too usually worked at their own looms at home weaving' cloth for sale, out of the yam bought or spun by the plosives. They also worked on wages to weave yarn supplied to them by customers. But if the raw material was expensive such as silk or gold of silver thread, etc. and the products were luxury items, the craftsmen were to work in karkhanas under supervision. We have definite information about the Sultans and high nobles maintaining these karkhanas where the production was to cater to their own needs and contrary to D.D.Kosambi's assumption was not for market. Shahabuddin al Umari records in his Masalik-ul Absar that in Mohammad Tughluq's karkhanas at Delhi, four thousand silk workers worked as embroiderers. According to Afif, Feroz Tughluq's karkhanas produced cloth and carpets in a big way. While there is no suggestion in our sources, we may only conjecture that perhaps merchants also maintained karkhanas where production was for sale.

Trade And Commerce

We have seen that there emerged some considerably big flourishing towns as well as numerous townships during the 13-14th centuries. These towns naturally needed to be fed and supplied raw material for craft production. At the same tinye, there was growing practice of lad revenue realization in cash. By the time of Alauddin Khalji, the cash-nexus came to be well developed and the-ruling class tended to claim almost the entire peasant suhlus by attempting to reduce the share of rural intermediaries, as we have seen in the previous Unit.

Both these factors were conducive to the development of inland trade. To pay the land revenue in cash, the peasantry was forced to sell its surplus produce while merchants had a market in newly emerged towns for agricultural products. This trade resulting from the compulsions of land revenue system is termed as 'induced trade'

Inland Trade

The inland trade developed at two levels : (a) the short distance village-town trade in commodities of bulk, and (b) long distànce inter-town trade in high value goods. The village-town trade, as already explained, was a natural consequence of the emergence of towns of land revenue in cash. The urban centres were dependent for supply of food gardens and raw material for manufactures from the surrounding villages whereas the villages had to sell the agricultural products to receive cash for meeting the land revenue demand. The peculiar nature of this trade was the one-way flow of commodities. While the towns received grains and raw material from the villages in the vicinity they had no need to send their products in' exchange to the villages which were by and large self-sufficient. This one-way trade was owing to the land revenue demand imposed upon villages which naturally led to a continuous drain on rural sector and made the towns dependent on villages. The turnover of this trade was high in terms of volume but was low in terms of value. The commodities were food grains, that is wheat, rice gram, sugar cane, etc.

The inter-town trade was mainly in luxury articles and was thus high value trade. The manufactures of One town were taken to another : for example Barani reports that Delhi, the capita] itself, received distilled wines from Kol (Aligarh) and Meerut Muslin (fine cloth) from Devagiri and striped cloth from Lakhnauti (Bengal) while, according to Ibn Battota, ordinary cloth came from Awadh and betel-leaf from Malwa (twenty-four d!ays journey from Delhi). Candy sugar was supplied to Multan from Delhi and Laholie and ghi from Sirsa (in Haryana)., The long distance inter-town trade also carried goods coming from other countries exit-points.

Foreign Trade : Seaborne and Overland

During the Sultanate period, overland and overseas trade were in a flourishing state.

Seaborne Trade

The Khalji annexation of Gujarat must have enlarged trade religions between the Delhi Sultanate and the Persian Gulf and the Red Sea Gujarat was connected with the Persian Gulf as well as the Red Sea.

Hormuz and Basra were the chief ports for the ships passing through the Persian Gulf, while the ports of Aden, Mocha and Jedda along the Red Sea were important for Gujarat. Through these ports, commodities moved on to Damascus and Aleppo, on the one hand, and Alexandria on the other. Aleppo and Alexandria opened upto the Mediterranean Sea with linkages to Europe. Merchandise of Gujarat were also carried towards the East-the port of Malacca situated at the Malacca straits and Bantam and Achin in the Indonesian archipelago.

A European traveller Tome Pires, who came to India in the first decade of the 16th century, comments on the trade of Cambay as follows : "Cambay chiefly stretches out two arms : with her right arm she reaches out towards Aden, with the other towards Malacca...." Pires further says :

"Malacca cannot live without Cambay, nor Cambay without Malacca, if they are to be very rich and very prosperous. If Cambay were cutoff from trading with Malacca, it could not live, for it would have no outlet for its merchandise." The main export from Gujarat to Malacca was the coloured cloths manufactured in Cambay and other Gujarat towns. These cloths were in demand in these places. In exchange, the Gujarati merchants came back with spices grown there. This pattern of "spices for coloured cloths" continued even after the Portuguese advent in the Asian waters.

Varthema, an Italian traveller, who came to India during the first decade of the 16th century says that about 300 ships (annually?) of different countries come and go from Cambay. He adds that about 400 "Turkish" merchants resided at Diu. The Khanid court historian Wassaf reports that 10,000 horses were annually exported to Cambay from Persia.

The Broach coin-hoards containing the coins of the Delhi Sultans along with the gold and silver coins of Egypt, Syria, Yeman, Persia, Genoa, Armenia and Venice further testifies to largerscale overseas trade.

The Major Seaports

13th-15th Centuries, Imports and Exports

Ri of Urban Economy and Trade and Commerce

The two principal items of import were :

(a) horses-that were always in demand for cavalry since superior horses were not bredi? India and Indian climate was not wellsuited to Arabian and Central Asian horses. They were primarily imported from Zofar (Yemen), Kis, Hormuz, Aden and Persia;

(b) precious metals viz gold and silver, especially silver that was not at all mined in India but for which there was a high demand not only for metallic currency but also for fashioning luxury items.

Brocade and silk stuffs were imported from Alexandria, Iraq and China. Gujarat was the major centre from where the luxury articles from Europe used to enter. The Sultanate India mainly exported grain and textiles. Some of the Persian Gulf regions totally depended on India for their food supply. Besides, slaves were exported to Central Asia and indigo to Persia along with numerous other commodities. Precious stones like agates were exported from Cambay.

The Portuguese Advent

In spite of brisk trading activities, Indian merchants' share in the overseas trade was negligible. Only a small section of Gujarati Banias, Chettis of the South and domicile Indian Muslims used to take part in this large trading activity. Trade was mainly in the hands of the Arab Merchants. With the landing of the Portuguese at Calicut in A.D. 1498 after the rounding of the Cape of Good Hope, a new dimension was added to the Indian seaborne trade, that is, the 'element of force'. On account of better ships armed with cannons, the Portuguese soon imposed their commercial hegemony over the trading world of Asia, included the Indian seas, especially in Western part. This curtailed the Arabs' share of the Indian trade, though they survived in the Eastern part, especially at Malacca along with the Indian merchants. The Portuguese took Goa in 1510 which became their headquarters, Malacca fell in them hands in 1511. Hormuz in 1515; and Bassem and Diu In 1534 and 1537 respectively. Goa, under their patronage, soon developed as a major centre for import and export. The Portuguese well understood the strategic importance of Goa, which in their opinion, was essential to the maintenance of their position in India.. But the Portuguese possession of Goa was unfavourable to other Western Indian ports. Tome Presh ad rightly observed that the Muslim rulers of the Deccan and Gujarat had "a bad neighbour in Goa". Many ports on the west coast fell into decay during the hundred years of the Portuguese domination In the Indian waters.

Commercial Classes

Two types of merchants are mentioned in the sources of the Delhi Sultanate : the karwanis or nayaks and Multanis. The merchants specialising in carrying grains were designated by Barani as karwanis (a Persian word meaning those who moved together in large numbers). The contemporary mystic, Nasiruddin (Chiragh Delhi) calls them nayaks and describes them as those "who bring food grains from different parts to the city (Delhi)-some with ten thousand laden bullocks, some with twenty thousand" It can be said with a degree of certainty that these karwanis were the banjaras of succeeding centuries. As is clear from the Mughal sources, these were organised in groups and their headman called nayak.

The other important group of merchants mentioned in our sources was that of the Multanis. Barani says that the long distance trade was in the hands of these merchants. They were engorged in usury and commerce. It appears that the sahas and Multanis were rich enough to give loans even to nobles, who, according to Barani, were generally in need of cash. The sahas and Multanis were generally Hindu, but at least some Muslims also were among the Multani merchants: merchant). Besides these well defined merchant groups, others who had p chosen could take to trade : thus a Sufi (mystic) from Bihar became a slave-merchant trading between Delhi and Ghazni, and a number of pious men from Central Asia came to Delhi and became merchants.

Another important commercial class that emerged during the Sultanate period was that of the dallals ink between the buyer and the seller and took commission from both the parties. Barani says that they were the 'masters of market' (hakimnn bsenr) : they were instrumental in raising prices in the market. Alauddin Khalji used to conduct them about the cost of production of every article in the market in order to fix prices. But by Feroz Tughluq's reign, they seem to have regained their position.

Sads were yet another ambient group whose economic role was no less important than the brokers money changers, they were most sought after by the merchants, especially the foreign ones who came to India with their native coins. The sarapus tested the metallic party of the coins (indigenous and foreign) and established the exchange-ratio. They also issued bills of exchange or letters of credit, thereby acting as "bankers". The introduction of paper by the Turks into India accelerated the institution of bill of exchange. For all these troubles, the sarraf naturally charged his commission. Thus, both the brokers and the sarrafs occupied pivotal position in the commercial world of their period; they were the custodians of several basic economic institutions. Indeed, no merchant could have dispensed with their services.

Transport

It appears that the goods we transported both by pack animals and on bullock-carts. Perhaps the share of the pack animals was more than the latter. Ibn Battuta mentions 30,000 mans of grains being transported on the backs of 3,000 bullocks from Amroha to Delhi. Bullock-carts were also used, according to Afif, for carrying passengers on payment. The pack-oxen were of course a cheap mode of transport travelling slowly, grazing as they went and moving in large herds, thus reducing the cost of transport specially along the desert routes. Ibn Battuta describes that highways ran through the empire marked by minarets spaced at set distances. On the testimony of Shahabuddin a Umari, the author of the kasalik ul Abser, we may infer that efforts were made to create conditions conducive ko trade. Inns were built at each stage (mruudl). In Bengal, Iwaz Khalji built long embankments to safeguard from floods. Boats were employed for riverine routes to carry bulk goods, while large ships used for seabrone trade.

Industry and Trade

Hindus occupied an important role in foreign, as in domestic, trade, although foreign Muslim merchants, known as khurasani, also had a large share of it. The rulers of the coastal kingdoms in the Deccan accorded to foreign merchants certain extra-territorial rights and special concessions, in consideration of the heavy taxes which they paid to the treasury. An organized class of brokers handled the business on the coast and inside the country. The imports consisted mainly of certain luxury items for the upper classes, and a general supply of all kinds of horses and mules, in which India was deficient. Hindus had never attached any importance to cavalry, but seeing the success of the Muslim horsemen, they started to substitute horses for elephants. The exports included large quantities of food-grains and cloth. Among the agricultural products were wheat, millet, rice, pulses, oilseeds, scents, medicinal herbs, and sugar. Some of the countries around the Persian Gulf depended on the subcontinent for their entire food supply. Cotton cloth and other textiles were especially important items of export, particularly to Southeast Asia and East Africa, although some reached Europe. They were carried by the Arabs to the Red Sea and from there found their way to Damascus and Alexandria, from where they were distributed to the Mediterranean countries and beyond.

Many industries of considerable size and importance developed during this period, the most important of which were textiles, various items of metal work, sugar, indigo, and in certain localities, paper. The Indian textile industry is very old, but the variety of cloth produced was originally limited. Taking advantage of the local talent, the Muslims introduced a number of fine varieties of textiles, most of which had Persian or Arabic origin. Bengal was the main centre of this industry, but Gujarat rivalled it as a supplier of the export trade during the sultanate period. Next in importance were a number of industries connected with metal work: the manufacture of swords, guns, and knives, as well as household needs such as trays and basins. Manufacture of sugar was also carried on a fairly large scale, and in Bengal enough was produced to leave a surplus for export after meeting the local demand. Paper-making was a minor industry, of which little is known except that Delhi was the centre of a considerable market.

These industries were mainly privately owned, but the government equipped and managed large-scale karkhanas, or factories, for supplying its requirements. The royal factories at Delhi sometimes employed as many as four thousand weavers for silk alone. The example of the sultan of Delhi was followed by the rulers of the regional kingdoms, and the contribution of the state to the development of the industry was not a minor one.

In certain aspects of social life, the Hindus had virtual autonomy during the sultanate. This was in accordance with the established axiom of Islamic law that while Muslims are governed by the Shariat, non-Muslim zimmis are subject to their own laws and social organization, but it was also a product of the Indian situation. The Muslim rulers from the days of the Arab occupation of Sind accepted the right of the village and caste panchayats to settle the affairs of their community. This meant that the Hindu villages remained small autonomous republics, as they had been since ancient times, and in commerce and industry the Hindu guilds were supreme. This position continued throughout the Muslim rule, but during the sultanate, when the provincial administration had not been properly organized, Hindu autonomy outside the principal towns was particularly effective.

It is often forgotten—and Muslim court chroniclers were not anxious to mention it—that a large number of independent or quasi-independent Hindu chiefs remained after the establishment of the sultanate. Some of them were rajas, or kings; others were only petty chieftains, controlling a few villages. Many of them belonged to old families, but new principalities grew up even after the establishment of Muslim power at Delhi. Rajputs often found new kingdoms for themselves in remote, easily defended areas in Rajputana and the Himalayas. From such movements during the sultanate come also some of the large landed estates still held by Rajputs in Oudh and in Bihar. In these predominantly Hindu areas the old religion was fostered, and its cultural expressions kept alive even in the periods of greatest Islamic power.

Learning, Literature, and the Arts

After the sack of Baghdad in 1258, Delhi was perhaps the most important cultural centre in the Muslim East. Heir to the traditions of Ghazni and Lahore, its importance increased when the Mongols destroyed the cultural centres of Central and Western Asia, and the poets, scholars and men of letters from these areas took refuge in Muslim India. Balban, who gave high offices of the state only to persons of good families, welcomed these distinguished refugees, and many illustrious families of Muslim India trace their origin to this period. This influx bore fruit in a large number of works, many of which are lost, but the contemporary historians attest to their worth. During the reign (1296–1316) of Alauddin Khalji the general prosperity engendered by his conquests enabled the nobles, and not just the sultan, to become literary patrons. This probably explains why Barani could devote fourteen pages to an account of the scholars, poets, preachers, philosophers, physicians, astronomers, and historians who thronged Delhi in the days of Alauddin Khalji. If the surviving poetry of Khusrau, the historical works of Barani, and the table talk of Hazrat Nizamuddin Auliya are any indication of the cultural vitality and richness of the age, one can well understand why Amir Khusrau and others felt that Delhi was the metropolis of the Muslim East.

Yet despite the cultural eminence of the capital, it cannot be claimed that the sultanate is a period marked by that solid scholarship and study of sciences which distinguished Baghdad and Cordova. The reason is obvious. Learned and gifted men had come to India, but without their libraries. Those who were escaping with their lives could not be expected to carry heavy loads of books over long distances. We get a glimpse of this in the case of Fakhr-i-Mudabbir, who fled from Ghazni without even his family papers, and had to wait for an opportunity to go back to reclaim them. The result was that only those cultural activities gained prominence which, like poetry, belles-lettres, local history, architecture, and music, were not dependent on accumulated stores of knowledge.

Probably for the same reason—the lack of libraries—great educational institutions of the kind found in Baghdad and Cairo did not develop in India. There were, however, schools and colleges in Delhi and all the important provincial capitals.

In Muslim society, teaching and the promotion of educational enterprises are regarded as necessary marks of religious vocation, and the Muslim state is expected to facilitate this by providing teachers with ample means of subsistence. This was the procedure generally adopted during Muslim rule in India, and the official in charge of religious endowments, the sadr-i-jahan, arranged for the grant of tax-free lands to Imams, Qazis, and other religious groups who provided education, particularly in Islamic subjects. This education was usually on the elementary level, but the system also provided for the maintenance of scholars who had specialized in different branches of learning. We find even nobles and distinguished men of affairs teaching subjects in which they had become proficient. Hazrat Nizamuddin Auliya, for example, studied under Shams-ul-Mulk, who became the wazir of Balban. The children of nobles were taught at their own residences by private tutors, whose guidance was often available for other students also.

For advanced students Madrasas, or colleges, were set up by pious and public-spirited rulers, and this activity received special attention during the early period. Two major Madrasas called Muizziya and Nasiriya were established during the beginning of Muslim rule at Delhi. Details about these Madrasas are lacking, but probably one of them was the college built by Iltutmish and repaired a century later by Firuz Tughluq. Similar steps to establish educational institutions were taken by Muslim rulers in the distant provinces, and we read of Mohammad Bakhtiyar Khalji setting up Madrasas at Devkot and other places in Bengal. Firuz Tughluq was unusual in that he looked after the institutions established by his predecessors; probably most of these establishments fell into decay when the original founders passed away, and the grants made for the Madrasas were diverted to other purposes.

Historians give little information about the staff or the curriculum of Madrasas, but some details are available for one founded by Firuz Tughluq near Hauz-i-Alai in Delhi. Barani has given a lengthy account of the beautiful building and gardens which provided a centre around which people built their houses. Both Barani and Mutahar, a well-known poet, praise the comprehensive knowledge of Maulana Jalauddin Rumi, the head of the institution. The main subjects taught seem to have been religious (interpretation of the Quran), hadith (tradition), and fish (jurisprudence). The intellectual activity of the schools owed much to the refugee scholars from Central Asia, Persia, and Iraq who came to Delhi in the thirteenth century.

After this influx had ceased and the Mongols had established their rule in the northwestern borderland, communication between Central Asia and northern India became difficult. It appears that in the Deccan, where contact was maintained with Iran by the sea route, intellectual activity during the later centuries encompassed a wider range than was the position in the north. In northern India, apart from religious subjects, literature, history, mysticism, and ethics were the principal subjects studied. In the Deccan, scientific subjects also received attention. The great Bahmani king, Firuz (1397–1422), for example, encouraged botany, geometry, and logic. He was interested also in astronomy, and in 1407 started work on an observatory near Daulatabad. The untimely death of Hakim Hashim Gilani, the astronomer who was to supervise the observatory, put an end to the project. When Sayyid Gisu Daraz, who has left a large number of books on mysticism and who was famous for his knowledge of religious subjects, reached the Deccan, Firuz went to meet him. The historian Firishta records that the sultan found the saint lacking in solid scholarship, and made no secret of his disappointment. The fact that Firuz was not alone in intellectual pursuits is evident from the account of a prince who used to teach students mathematics (including Euclid), theology, and rhetoric. Promotion of learning in the Deccan was largely the work of Persian statesmen and scholars whom the rulers had attracted from Iran, and an interesting monument to the age is the ruined college of the Bahmani minister, Mahmud Gawan, in Bidar. It was a magnificent building, as can be seen from its beautiful minarets and facade, but it was badly damaged during the wars of the Deccan kings with Aurangzeb.

The one scientific subject that received considerable attention in the schools was medicine. The earliest work on medicine, of which an imperfect manuscript copy has survived, was written about 1329 in the reign of Mohammad bin Tughluq. Its author, Zia Mohammad, went to the Deccan under the orders of the sultan. His book, Majmua-i-ziai, based on Arabic and Indian sources, gives local counterparts for Arabian medicines as well as the prescriptions of Hindu physicians. Following this work, other writers combined Greek and Indian works. The history of Indo-Islamic medicine has not yet been carefully studied, but it is reasonably certain that in the books written in India during the sultanate one sees the blending of the three streams of Greek, Arabic, and Hindu medical knowledge. The most famous of these works is the Tibb-i-Sikandari, written by the court physician Mian Bhuwa about 1512. It draws freely on the classical Sanskrit writers, and it long remained a standard textbook for followers of the indigenous medical systems.

Of the purely literary works of the early period, very few have survived. This is especially true of poetry, for barring the works of major poets like Amir Khusrau and Hasan, only those poems have been preserved which, because of their topical nature, were included in general histories. Examples are the poems of Sangreza on the arrival of Iltutmish's patent of sovereignty from the Abbasid caliphate and his verses on the accession of Iltutmish's son or Ruhani's poem on Iltutmish's conquest of Ranthambhor. While these poems have the usual limitations of occasional poetry, they indicate high poetic skill.

The early men of letters represented a trans-Indus tradition. Most of them had received their education beyond the border, and although they had settled down in Islamic India, an indigenous literary tradition was slow in developing. The two most important representatives of the early tradition were Mohammad Aufi and Mohammad bin Mansur Qureshi, generally known as Fakhr-i-Mudabbir. Aufi a native of Bukhara who lived in Lahore and Delhi, was the author of the earliest extant collection of biographies of Persian poets, Lubabul-Albab. He also completed the voluminous encyclopedia of anecdotes, Jawami-al-Hikayat, which, apart from its literary interest, is a mine of curious and interesting information relating to this and earlier periods. The major work of Fakhr-i-Mudabbir, who lived in Lahore at the beginning of the thirteenth century, was a study of statecraft; this has already been discussed in Chapter VII.

The first Persian poet of eminence who was born in India was Reza, or, as he was sometimes known, Sangreza. He was Iltutmish's secretary. The most distinguished writer of the early sultanate, however, was Amir Khusrau. His father, a junior Turkish officer under Iltutmish, had married a daughter of Rawat-i-Arz, Balban's famous minister. Khusrau showed literary promise at an early age, and, after spending some time at the provincial court of Oudh, became attached at first to Prince Bughra Khan, the governor of Samana and later of Bengal, and subsequently to Prince Mohammad, the heir-designate of Balban, who maintained a magnificent court at Multan. The prince lost his life in a skirmish with the Mongols in 1285, and the poet went to Delhi. Balban's successor, Kaiqubad, was Khusrau's first royal patron. In all, seven rulers were to be his patrons, but it is doubtful whether he was greatly concerned by the kaleidoscopic changes of royalty.

Apart from lyrics, Khusrau wrote poems relating to contemporary events. Qiran-us-Saadain, completed in 1289, gives an account of the historic meeting of Bughra Khan and Kaiqubad on the banks of the river Sarju, and contains an interesting description of the Delhi of those days. Miftah-ul-Futuh (1291) is a versified account of the exploits of Jalal-ud-din Firuz Khalji; in Ashiqa (1315) is an account of the romance of the Gujarati princess Deval Devi and Prince Khizr Khan, son of Alauddin Khalji.

The latter's conquests are the subject matter of Khazain-ul-Futuh (1311), an ornate prose work, while Nuh Sipihr, completed in 1318, celebrates the reign of Qutb-ud-din Mubarik Shah. In this book Amir Khusrau challenged the poets of Iran and sang of his native land, its hoary past, its love of learning, its flowers, and its fair, intelligent people. Tughlaq Nama describes the successful expedition of Ghiyasuddin Tughluq against the usurper Khusrau Khan. Khusrau was also among the earliest writers of Hindi poetry, and though the origins of the Hindi poems attributed to him are doubtful, he referred to his Hindi verses in the introduction to one of his Persian diwans. He also played a major role in the development of Indian music, as noted below.

The work of Hasan, a friend of Khusrau, was praised by Jami, the great Persian poet, a rare distinction for an Indian writer. He wrote prose as well as verse, and his Fawaid-ul-Fuad, a record of the table-talk of his spiritual guide, Nizamuddin Auliya, is a literary classic. Equally interesting, though not so well known, was Ziya Nakhshabi, who was a master of simple and eloquent prose. His Tuti Nama (The Book of the Parrot) was based on a Sanskrit original. It has been translated into Turkish, German, English, and many Indian languages. His other translations include the Kok Shastra, a Sanskrit text on erotics.

While there were many distinguished names in poetry, perhaps the most important literary contribution during the sultanate was in the field of history. Since classical Hindu culture produced almost no historical literature, the Muslim works are of special significance for Indian historiography. Written by contemporaries who had taken part in the events they describe, these histories are of enormous value for an understanding of the period. They are marred, however, by certain defects which their very excellence tends to conceal. One is that many of the chronicles were written specifically for certain rulers and nobles whom the historians glorified at the expense of rivals; another is the tendency to picture the conquerors as actuated by unselfish and religious motives. These peculiarities of method can generally be discounted, however, and the historians do not seem to have falsified historical facts even when they were writing panegyrics.

The number of historical works of the sultanate period which have reached us is not large, but the works possess rich variety. The historians of the period, many of whom have already been mentioned, include Barani, Fakhr-i-Mudabbir, Hasan Nizami, Minhaj-us-Siraj, Aufi, Khusrau, Yahya, and Isami. Most of them occupied high official positions and wrote from personal knowledge. Barani is the most interesting, but he is not very particular about dates (normally the strong point of the Muslim historians), and this detracts from the value of his book, Tarikh-i-Firuz Shahi. But he wrote history as an artist, selecting and carefully arranging his material so that his book, instead of being a chronicle of events, emphasized the characteristics of various rulers and different reigns. He does not confine himself to the kings, but gives details about the political philosophies of different monarchs and leading men of the times, the literary and the religious history, the prices in the market, and other matters of concern to the ordinary people. Even more interesting is the gallery of portraits which he has brought to life by a skillful analysis of personalities and by providing those significant small details which most Indian historians omit.

As already noted, the rise of regional kingdoms in the fifteenth century played an extremely important role in the dissemination of Islamic culture. One significant feature of this disintegration of the central authority, with its dependence on Persian as the official language, was the rise of regional languages. Hindu kings had given their patronage to Sanskrit as the language of religion and the classics; Muslim rulers felt no such compulsion, and supported the common languages of the people. It was Muslim rulers, therefore, who were responsible for many of the first translations of the Sanskrit classics into the provincial languages. The Muslim rulers of Bengal engaged scholars to translate the Ramayana and the Mahabharata into Bengali. Maladhar Vasu translated the Bhagavata Purana into Bengali under the patronage of Sultan Husain Shah, and Chuti Khan, governor of Chittagong, employed Srikara Nadi to translate parts of the Asvamedha Parva of the Mahabharata into Bengali. In Kashmir, Hindu literature and philosophy were studied enthusiastically at the court of Zain-ul-Abidin (1420–1470). Rajatarangini, one of the few histories written in Sanskrit, was translated into Persian, with a supplement to bring the account up to date. Other works on music and mathematics were composed by Hindu scholars at the Kashmir court. In the south the Muslim rulers of Golkunda and Bijapur employed Hindus as ministers, and maintained the state records in the Marathi language. Cultural histories of the various provincial governments are yet to be written, but a similar process was at work at all places.

Among the nonliterary arts, music, rather than painting or sculpture, underwent important developments during the period of the sultanate. As already noted, Indian music had made an impact on the Arab systems as early as the conquest of Sind, and the interchange between the two forms was even more fruitful when the rich heritage of Persia and Central Asia was added. The result was the creation in North India of a new type of music, quite different from traditional Indian music which maintained its hold in South India.

Credit for this important work of synthesis is given to the poet Amir Khusrau, whose fame helped to give prestige to the new music, which had as its rival in the Delhi court the musical modes favoured by the Turkish rulers. The interest of the Chishti Sufis in "Hindustani" music and its practical cultivation by them further ensured its popularity. The next stage was reached during the establishment of the independent Muslim kingdom at Jaunpur, not far from Benares, and Kannauj, the old centres of Hindu arts. Here music received special attention, both at the royal court and in the Sufi monasteries. The two most important Indian Muslim musicians of the day were Sultan Husain Sharqi, the last king of Jaunpur, and the contemporary saint, Pir Bodhan of Barnawa. The saint's dwelling became a rendezvous for musicians from Delhi, the Deccan, and Jaunpur. The contribution of Sultan Husain to the development of Indian music was much more specific. He is regarded as the original founder of the khiyal (or romantic) school of music, which slowly matured and took its final shape in the days of the later Mughals, particularly under Mohammad Shah. Related to a Hindu devotional form that dealt with the love of Krishna for the milkmaids, the khiyal transformed the devotional theme to thinly veiled invocations of human love and romance.

Another regional kingdom where music was highly cultivated after the breakdown of the sultanate was Gwalior. Here the ruler, Raja Man Singh, was a Hindu, but the chief musician at his court, Nayak Mahmud, was a Muslim. Under his leadership a band of musicians systematized Indian music in the light of the changes it had undergone since the advent of the Muslims. This resulted in the compilation of Man Kautuhal, which contains almost all the airs introduced by the Muslim musicians.

Probably the greatest artistic achievement of the sultanate was neither literature nor music, but architecture. As with the musicians, the creativity of the Muslim architects was nourished by the mature styles of both the existing Islamic and Hindu traditions. The Muslims brought to India the experience gained in the great buildings of Cairo, Baghdad, Cordova, and Damascus, and they were able to draw upon the skill of Indian stonemasons. The result was a profusion of mosques, palaces, and tombs unmatched in any other Islamic country.

In the same year in which Delhi was occupied, the foundation of the mosque of Quwwat-ul-Islam was laid by Qutb-ud-din Aibak to commemorate the capture of Delhi and, as the name implies, to glorify the power of Islam. Aibak however spent most of his brief reign at Lahore, and adornment of the new Muslim capital was essentially the work of his successor, Iltutmish. He more than doubled the size of the Quwwat-ul-Islam mosque, built the Qutb Minar, one of the world's loveliest towers, erected the buildings for Nasiriya Madrasa, and, to meet the needs of the growing population of Delhi for water, excavated the great water reservoir, the Hauz-i-Shamsi. He also changed architectural methods. Previously material from Hindu buildings had been used for constructing mosques, but in 1230, when he extended the Quwwat-ul-Islam mosque, he used stone especially quarried for the purpose. This gave the addition a more Islamic appearance.

In architecture, as in other spheres of culture, the Indo-Islamic society was enriched by the dislocation in Central Asia and Persia caused by the Mongol invasion. Not only scholars but artisans as well came to Delhi as refugees, and they found a ready market for their skills in the expanding Muslim state. One important result was that the indigenous Indian artistic element ceased to be dominant in Delhi during this period. By the time of Alauddin

Khalji, Muslim traditions had become firmly established on Indian soil, with the result that methods of construction were revolutionized and ornament became an integral part of the scheme, rather than a quasi-independent accessory, as was the case in the earlier buildings. The Jamaat Khana mosque, constructed in the reign of Alauddin, is the earliest surviving example in India of a mosque built wholly in accordance with Muslim ideas.

In the provincial capitals, however, the influence of the refugee artisans was slight, and the indigenous styles remained important. In Bengal the Muslim rulers decorated their buildings with carving which is obviously the work of Hindu craftsmen, and in Gujarat they adapted the local style to Muslim needs to create some of India's most beautiful buildings. Yet even where most was owed to native Indian skills and tradition, the peculiar Muslim architectural characteristics of spaciousness and graceful forms are present. Furthermore, the Muslims made full use of concrete and mortar, which were known but scarcely used before their arrival in India. "Thanks to the strength of their binding properties, it was possible for the Muslim rulers to span wide spaces with their arches, to roof immense areas with their domes, and in other ways to achieve effects of grandeur such as the Indians had never dreamt of."

The Tughluqs in the fourteenth century introduced a new and austere phase in architecture. Mohammad Tughluq, who shifted his capital from Delhi to Daulatabad, had no interest in the old city. The many buildings erected in Delhi during the reign of his successor Firuz show a severe simplicity, possibly due as much to the need for economy as Firuz's own strict orthodoxy. Hindu influences were reduced to the minimum, and Tughluq buildings are lacking in elegance and refinement. Under the Lodis there re-emerged a vigorous and catholic spirit of design, replete with creative energy and imagination. The explanation is probably that with the conversion of the Mongols to Islam and the reduction of chaos in Central Asia, inspiration from Persia was now available in architecture as in literature. The Lodis were soon replaced by the Mughals, under whom Persian influences became even more dominant.

5

The Administrative System of the Sultanate

A rapid survey of the three-hundred-year history of the Delhi Sultanate is likely to leave the reader with two impressions. One is of a political structure in which violence, based on a powerful fighting force, was the only support of a ruler's government; the other is that anything like a coherent political philosophy was completely lacking. What is becoming increasingly plain, however, as the period is studied in more depth, is that the sultanate under its abler rulers had a quite sophisticated administrative structure. In addition, the Turkish sultans were heirs to a tradition in which political theory had been considerably evolved, and there were many scholars in Islamic India who had given thought to both the general principles underlying government and the techniques of public administration. We know of the works of some of these writers only from casual references in other books, but a number which have survived suggest the background of thought against which the sultanate's actual administrative structure developed.

Political Theory

The earliest work of importance for the history of political thought of Muslim India was probably intended to be a blueprint for the first Muslim government at Delhi. It was written by a contemporary of Iltutmish, Fakhr-i-Mudabbir, who had spent a considerable part of his life at Lahore, where he met Sultan Mohammad Ghuri and Sultan Qutb-ud-din Aibak, to whom one of his works, a book on genealogies, was presented in 1206. The historical introduction to this work has been translated into English, but his more important work, variously styled *Adab-ul-Muluk wa Kifayat al Mamluk* (Rules for the Kings and the Welfare of the Subjects) or *Adab-ul-Harab wal-Shujaat* (Rules of Warfare and Bravery), has not yet been published in its entirety. It was undoubtedly intended to be a guide for rulers and administrators. The first part of this book deals with the privileges and responsibilities of kings, with separate chapters giving the qualifications and functions of different officers of state. The rest of the book is a manual dealing systematically and in some detail with the art of war. The work was presented to Iltutmish and, as the contemporary histories show, the government organization set up by him corresponded very closely to the structure visualized by Fakhr-i-Mudabbir.

Another early work, of which only an incomplete copy has survived, belongs to a different category. This is *Fatawa-i-Jahandari* (Rulings on Government) by Ziya-ud-din Barani (1285–1357), the greatest of fourteenth-century historians of Muslim India. A political phantasy consisting mainly of a number of discourses purporting to have been addressed by Sultan Mahmud of Ghazni to his successor, it was written after Barani had retired from the royal court in disgrace. It reflects Barani's bitterness against recent trends, his extremism, and his acute class-consciousness. He is bitter not only against the Hindus but also against the Muslim lower classes who, he believed, should not be "taught reading and writing, for plenty of disorders arise owing to the skill of the low-born in knowledge ... For on account of their skill, they became governors, revenue collectors, auditors, officers and rulers." If the teachers disregard this edict, and it is discovered that "they have imparted knowledge or taught letters or writing to the low-born, inevitably the punishment for disobedience will be meted out to them."

Fatawa-i-Jahandari represents an individual's views, and made no impression on the course of Indo-Muslim history or political thought. Indeed, it is not referred to by any later writer or historian, and is not included in the fairly full list of Barani's works given by his contemporary, Amir Khurd. The importance of the book is partly personal, as an insight into the mind of Barani, and partly topical, as it gives his views in the context of the political and social situation then prevailing. In spirit and sentiments, *Fatawa-i-Jahandari* is in complete contrast with Fakhr-i-Mudabbir's book, which is throughout inspired by practical idealism, moderation and good sense.

Barani dealt at length with political philosophies of early Muslim rulers, statesmen, and religious leaders in his great historical work, *Tarikh-i-Firuz Shahi*. The long discourses on political affairs and statecraft contained in his book are dramatizations and expansions by an eloquent historian who is also a creative artist. Among the most interesting of these discourses are Nur-ud-din Mubarik Ghaznavi's advice to Iltutmish on the responsibilities of a Muslim "Defender of the Faith" (Din Panah); Balban's views on kingship, and his long lecture to his son, Bughra Khan, the governor of Bengal, on the relationship between the central and the provincial governments; Ahmad Chap's advice to Jalal-ud-din Khalji; Kotwal Ala-ul-Mulk's discourses at Alauddin's consultative assemblies; and Qazi Mughis's views on major political and legal problems of the day. They are presumably coloured by his own predilictions, and should not be treated as verbally authentic, but the views attributed to different rulers and dignitaries are so distinct and so much in character that they may be taken to represent generally the individual views of the persons to whom they are attributed.

To turn from theory to practice, the first comment that should be made on the Islamic state in India is that it was not a theocracy, as sometimes has been suggested. Aside from the question of the relevance of the concept of a theocracy to a society that does not recognize a priesthood, by the time the Delhi Sultanate was established the religious function of the caliph had ceased to be of much significance for the outlying Islamic world. It is true that a few of the Delhi rulers obtained formal recognition of their titles from the caliph, but this pious legal fiction did not alter the reality. The temporal authority of the caliph at Baghdad dwindled to a mere shadow even within his own territories, and the actual reality of the Indian links with the caliphate may be judged by the fact that occasionally a caliph would have been dead for years before Delhi became aware of the event. The patents obtained by the rulers meant so little that at one time a caliph sent patents simultaneously to both rulers of Delhi and Bengal.

In any case the policy adopted by the early sultans under the stress of circumstances with which they were confronted could scarcely permit the growth of theocracy. Iltutmish, recognizing the essentially secular nature of the sultanate saw that under the conditions prevailing in India, it was not possible for him to be a "Defender of the Faith" except in limited spheres. Balban went even further. In spite of his courtesy to the leading ulama and his personal observance of religious practices, in matters of administration he was guided by the needs of the state, not Islamic law. Alauddin Khalji followed the same policy. "When he became sultan," Barani records, "he came to the conclusion that polity and government are one thing, and the rules and decrees of Islamic law are another. Royal commands belong to the sultan, Islamic legal decrees rest upon the judgment of the qazis and muftis." It was under the Tughluqs, particularly under Firuz, that Muslim jurists gained some recognition, but by then the pattern of Muslim rule in India had become firmly established.

The early ulama, realizing the complexity of the Indian situation and the need for strengthening the Muslim government, accepted Iltutmish's policy. Their lack of power may be judged by the fact that Raziyya ascended the throne of Delhi although Muslim legal opinion is firmly opposed to female rulers; it was left to a much later scholar, Shaikh Abdul Haq Muhaddis (1551–1642), in the more legalistic days of the Mughals, to criticize the selection of Raziyya and express surprise at the action of the contemporary jurists and Shaikhs in confirming it. There was an equally glaring departure from the correct legal position in Qutb-ud-din Aibak's acceptance as sultan before his manumission. In general, then, the position was that so long as a sultan undertook to safeguard the honour and the observances of Islam, did nothing in open defiance of the principles of shariat, appointed qazis and made arrangements for religious education and observance of religious practices, the ulama did not interfere in the affairs of the state.

The use of the title "sultan" in itself indicates the transition from the quasi-theocratic caliphate to a secular institution. Although the process was implicit in the establishment and administration of the Umayyad caliphate, it was strengthened by the Persian belief in the divine right of kings. This idea, which had become dominant in Baghdad under the later Abbasids, was even more marked at Ghazni. At Delhi, in the early days of the Turkish rule, there was some opposition to it in orthodox Muslim circles, and Iltutmish was almost apologetic about his kingly role. The position completely changed with Balban, who was an advocate of Persian ideas, modelled his court after the Persian style, assumed the title of *zillullah,* and introduced Persian etiquette, court ceremonial, and festivities. With him Persian ideas of monarchy became dominant. The process was facilitated by the fact that the Hindus regarded a king as a representative of divine powers.

These theories gave medieval rulers powers which occasionally were used arbitrarily, but a number of checks remained on the absolute exercise of authority by the sultan. For one thing, the Islamic theory curtails the law-making power of a ruler, and although there was nothing to stop an autocratic ruler from becoming a law unto himself, he could do so only in defiance of the system which gave him power. Even the autocratic Alauddin Khalji admitted that administration of justice was the concern of the Muslim jurists.

Equally important was the opinion of the nobility. The sultans consulted their chief nobles and the routine affairs of the state were left to them. Minhaj refers to a dignitary, Amir-i-Majlis, whose duty was to arrange meetings of the sultan's closest associates. Important questions were discussed freely, and some favourite royal schemes (such as Alauddin's proposal to establish a new religion) were ruled out. Together with the influence of public opinion and the natural desire of the sultan to maintain his position, the nobles in this way exercised a check on the theoretical absolutism enjoyed by him.

According to Muslim theory, held particularly by the Sunnis who formed the bulk of the Muslim population in India, election was the accepted method for selecting the ruler. This was rarely observed anywhere, and both Turko-Iranian and Hindu conceptions of sovereignty were opposed to it, but a form of limited election or acceptance was generally followed at Delhi. The oath of allegiance taken by the governors of the provinces, the principal nobles of the capital, and the chief theologians was taken as a symbol of the indirect consent of the mass of the people.

Structure of Government

Fakhr-i-Mudabbir lists the principal dignitaries of the state as follows: wazir, *wakil-i-dar, amir-i-dad, amir-i-hajib, mushrif, mustaufi,* and *sahib-i-barid.* The *wakil-i-dar* (noi to be confused with the wakil-i-sultanat of the Sayyid dynasty and the wakil-i-mutliq of the

Mughals) was the controller of the household. The *amir-i-dad* (literally lord of justice) was the most important judicial dignitary. The *amir-i-hajib* is often designated as the chief chamberlain, but this does not fairly describe the functions and duties of this officer. He was the master of ceremonies at the court; no one could enter the royal presence without being introduced by one of his assistants, and all petitions were presented to the sultan through him. The post, therefore, was one of great prestige and was reserved for trusted nobles. One holder of this post, Balban, was the most powerful noble of his day. The *mushrif* was the accounts officer responsible for income, and the *mustaufi* for expenditure. The *sahib-i-barid* was in charge of communications and intelligence.

The chief minister of the sultan was called the wazir. Fakhr-i-Mudabbir considered the wazir a "partaker in sovereignty" and recommended that in his own technical domain he must be left free by the monarch. He describes the normal functions of the wazir in the following passage: "The kings know well how to lead expeditions, conquer countries, give rewards, and shine in the assembly or battlefield; but it is the domain of the wazir to make a country prosperous, to accumulate treasures, to appoint officials, to ask for accounts, to arrange for the stock-taking of the commodities in the karkhanas, and the census of horses, camels, mules, and other animals, to assemble and pay the troops and artisans, to keep the people satisfied, to look after the men of piety and fame and to give them stipends, to take care of the widows and the orphans, to provide for the learned, to administer the affairs of the people, and to organize the business of the state." This was the position in early days, when the wazir was in charge of the entire government, both the civil and the military departments and the functions which were later entrusted to Sadr-i-Jahan, but this arrangement underwent drastic changes in the light of practical experience. In view of the importance of the office, and to illustrate the administrative experiments that were carried on under the sultanate, it will be useful to sketch the history of the *wizarat* [=vazir-ship].

Although few details are known about administrative arrangements during the brief rule of Qutb-ud-din Aibak, presumably the practice of combining civil and military offices (which was introduced by the Ghaznavids at Lahore, and was continued under the Ghuris) remained in operation. This was also the position under Iltutmish. His first wazir, Nizam-ul-Mulk Junaidi, was in charge of all sections of the government, and in addition to his civil duties, was occasionally entrusted with military commands. During the troubled reign of Raziyya and her successors, Khwaja Muhazzab-ud-din used his influence with the weak rulers and his own capacity for intrigue to consolidate his position by taking all power out of the hands of the nobles. An attempt was made to curb the wazir's powers by the creation of the post of naib (deputy of the realm), but this was unsuccessful and the wazir continued to be all-powerful. Muhazzab's opponents, therefore, joined forces and had him assassinated.

His death marks the close of a period in the history of the wizarat. The provincial governors and other administrative officers would not permit an individual selected for his ability in office to obtain so much power. His successors were selected for their docility. Balban, even before he became deputy, was more powerful than the wazir, and when he became sultan, he took away the military functions of the wizarat. The *rawat-i-arz* (the muster-master, who was originally in charge of the finances and records of military personnel) was made independent of the wazir.

Some fifty years later, Ghiyas-ud-din Tughluq made an even more interesting experiment. He created a board of three ex-wazirs, with the senior having the high title of malik-ul-wuzara (chief minister). Ghiyas consulted them in all important matters, but the routine work of the wizarat was carried on by Malik Shadi, his son-in-law.

With the general policy of the Tughluqs to approximate standard Muslim practice in all matters and with Mohammad Tughluq's preference for Arab and Persian ways, we notice a reversion to the earlier character of the wizarat. Khwaja Jahan, though essentially a civil servant, was occasionally entrusted with military duties. This change is more marked under Firuz, whose wazir fulfilled the Arab notion of an all-powerful wazir. Khan Jahan, a Hindu from Telingana who had accepted Islam at the hands of Hazrat Nizamuddin Auliya, exercised both civil and military powers. His position may be judged by Firuz's frequent remark that Khan Jahan was virtually the sultan of Delhi. After his death in 1372, his son became wazir and followed his father's ideas for a long period, but this led to jealousy, and in 1387 he was killed in a quarrel with a noble. This also marked the end of

Firuz Tughluq's power and the decline of the dynasty. Khwaja Jahan Sarvar-ul-Mulk, the wazir (1390–1394) of Mohammad Shah, exercised authority both in civil and military spheres, but realizing that the sultanate was tottering, he had one of the military leaders made wakil-i-sultanat, and he himself left for the eastern provinces, where he carved out a kingdom for himself in Jaunpur.

With the accession to power of the Lodi dynasty, the wizarat lost some of its importance, for Buhlul Lodi, with his tribal conception of kingship did not establish an organized wizarat. Sikandar Lodi, however, saw the impossibility of applying this tribal conception to a huge territory and had a regular diwan and a wizarat. His wazir, however, seems to have confined himself to civil work.

The developments that took place under the Mughals will be described later, but essentially their wizarat was based on Balban's model, with the holder of the office confined to civil duties. This meant that the wazir in the Indian Islamic state had less power than that assigned to him by Muslim political theorists, but the system worked fairly well. Indian tradition and the needs of the Islamic rulers favored strong monarchs. It is probably true that the people, insofar as they had a preference, preferred an absolute monarch to an absolute wazir.

Revenue

The financial arrangements of the sultanate were in accordance with the normal Islamic theory and practice as inherited from the Ghaznavid predecessors, but they were modified in the light of local needs and usages. Land revenue was, as in Hindu India, the mainstay of the government. Sultan Qutb-ud-din Aibak, the first Muslim ruler, fixed the state demand (*kharaj*) at one-fifth of the gross produce. In land revenue, as in other spheres, Balban laid down the administrative pattern for the sultanate. According to W. H. Moreland, one of the most careful students of Indian economic history, Balban "had grasped the main principles of rural economy in an Indian peasant-state, at a period when the environment afforded little scope for individual advance; he aimed at a peaceful and contented peasantry, raising ample produce and paying a reasonable revenue; and he saw that it was the king's duty to direct the administration with this object in view." Under Alauddin Khalji, because of the need to build up a large army, the state demand was raised to one-half of the produce, the uppermost limit allowed by Muslim law. In the following reign the heavy demands were lowered. The scale of demand in the reign of the first Tughluq king has been a matter of dispute. According to R. R. Tripathi, Ghiyas-ud-din Tughluq fixed the demand at 10 percent of the produce; according to Moreland, the relevant reference in the contemporary history refers to the limit of increase being 10 percent. I. H. Qureshi, on the other hand, holds that except for a few areas the general charge on land was a fifth of the produce, which was maintained from the earliest days of the sultanate until the end of Firuz Shah's reign. Under the Mughal rulers who followed Timur's precedent in charging a third of the produce as land revenue, the scale was raised and Sher Shah, who had seen the increase in the state demand under Babur and Humayun, followed their example.

Apart from the land revenue there were a number of local imposts imposed on various occasions. Orthodox Muslims considered them illegal, and the two monarchs who made an attempt to run the state in accordance with Islamic law, Firuz Tughluq and Aurangzeb, abolished these taxes. These imposts were of ancient origin, however, and most sultans permitted them. And when the rulers abolished them, they were realized by corrupt officials or even by panchayats. A tax which gained importance during Firuz's reign was the charge levied for use of canal water. Firuz was not the first to dig canals, but he was the first monarch to ask Muslim jurists whether an irrigation tax was lawful. The jurists' reply was in the affirmative, and so a 10 percent addition was made to the land revenue in cases where canal water was used for irrigation.

During the early period, when the subcontinent was being conquered and new areas were being occupied, the *ghanimah* (the spoils of war) provided an important source of state income. According to Islamic law, all booty should be collected and a fifth set apart for the state, the rest being distributed among the soldiers. Later the practice was reversed and four-fifths of the booty was appropriated by the state treasury. Firuz's ulama considered it illegal, and Firuz ordered the restoration of the old rate as fixed by the law.

The taxes which had a special religious significance in an Islamic state—zakat and jizya—have been the subject of much controversy, both as regards their nature and their actual imposition during Muslim rule in India. Zakat was imposed only on Muslims; it is not, strictly speaking, a tax in the normal sense, since its payment was an act of piety. Contemporary historians do not record that zakat was levied by the sultans of Delhi, and their silence has been taken to mean that the procedure, common to all Islamic states, was followed. There were, at any rate, arrangements for the receipt of zakat, paid voluntarily by Muslims as a religious duty, and *Fiqh-i-Firuz Shahi* mentions a separate treasury for zakat. Toward the end of the sultanate, Sikandar Lodi abolished the zakat on grain and it was not renewed by any subsequent sultan.

The question of jizya is even more complex, not only because of the lack of clarity in the contemporary records but also because of the strong emotional reaction that has been aroused in discussion concerning it. Under Islamic law, jizya was a tax levied on non-Muslims. This action can be interpreted as an equitable arrangement, since only Muslims had to pay zakat; and, in addition, they alone were liable to military service. From this point of view it was, in the words of a modern historian, a poll tax levied on non-Muslims "in return for which they received protection of life and property, and exemption for military service." In the Quran jizya is used in the same sense as kharaj, meaning simply a tax, and the fact that early Muslim writers in India preserve this usage without attaching any technical significance to the term suggests that it was not levied during the first conquests. However it was later levied as a poll tax. As such it was borrowed from Persia, where it was called *gezit.* The failure of the historians to indicate when jizya was paid cannot be taken as an indication, as has been sometimes suggested, that some rulers, notably Alauddin, did not levy jizya because they refused to accord the Hindus the status of zimmis, or protected peoples. The reason jizya is not more definitely mentioned in the records is probably that for the sake of convenience in rural areas, where the population was overwhelmingly Hindu, jizya and kharaj, the land tax, were realized as a consolidated tax. In the early days of the sultanate the rulers had not built up an elaborate organization, and tax farming—through Hindu middlemen—was the normal means of recovery. It appears unlikely that apart from a comprehensive demand made on a village or a territory, separate or specific realization of jizya was feasible. Where jizya was recovered it was charged in three categories. The wealthy paid four dinars per head per annum, the middle groups two dinars, and the poor, one dinar. Women, children, and those on a bare subsistence level were excused.

Nothing better illustrates the practical approach of the early Muslim rulers to administrative problems than the cautious evolution of their coinage system. Mohammad Ghuri has usually been pictured as an ardent Muslim, zealous in the destruction of Hindu idols and the establishment of Islamic religion. Yet of the three of his coins which are extant, two are mere imitations of earlier Hindu coins, with even the figure of the goddess Lakshmi reproduced, the only distinguishing element being the sovereign's name inscribed in Indian characters. The third coin, though based on the dinar of the Muslim countries, bears a Devanagri legend and the figure of a horseman, much in the tradition of the Hindu coins. This evidence suggests that Muslim rulers, faced with the problem of establishing a new currency among a people unacquainted with the Muslim coinage system, much less with Arabic, disturbed existing usages and practices as little as possible. Not until sixty years after the conquest of Delhi did Balban finally complete the process, begun by Iltutmish, of replacing the Hindu device of the bull and horseman with the sovereign's name in Devanagari characters.

In the early days of the sultanate, the jital, an adaptation of the old dehliwala current before Muslim rule, was the token coin in use. Iltutmish introduced the silver tankah (which was replaced by the rupiah of Sher Shah and Akbar), but even this innovation, in addition to its indigenous name, was linked to an Indian weight standard. Once the monetary system was established, the rulers introduced changes and improvements in the designs and legends of their coins and made them approximate to the normal Muslim coinage in legend and appearance. Apart from Mohammad Tughluq's unsuccessful effort to introduce token currency of mixed metals, the coins were made of pure metal and the state took precautions to maintain their purity and weight.

The Army

An effective army was a vital feature of the administrative structure of the Islamic state in India; it is significant that Fakhr-i-Mudabbir's book on government was largely a war manual. Good generalship, disciplined troops, and sound knowledge of warfare techniques had been responsible for the conquest of India, and the ablest of the sultans were aware that continuance of power depended upon these same factors.

The steps taken by Balban to keep his troops in good trim, and by Alauddin Khalji to raise and maintain a large standing army, have been described by Barani. The cavalry was the backbone of the army, but the sultans did not confine their organization to the traditional pattern. They soon began to employ elephants on an extensive scale, and Balban considered a single war elephant to be as effective in battle as five hundred horsemen. The foot-soldiers (payaks) were mainly Hindus of the lower classes. The military grades were organized on a decimal basis: a *sar-i-khail* had ten horsemen under him; a *sipah salar* commanded ten sar-i-khails; an *amir* ten sipah salars; a *malik* ten amirs; and a *khan* ten maliks.

The use of naphtha and Greek fire was known from early times. Incendiary arrows and javelins as well as pots of combustibles were hurled against the enemy. The Delhi army used grenades, fireworks, and rockets against Timur, but although there are references to a crude form of cannon, and in the provincial kingdoms of Gujarat and the Deccan this weapon was properly developed, the sultanate of Delhi had not made much progress in the use of artillery. It was the neglect of this weapon which turned the scales against the Delhi forces in the battle of Panipat in 1526.

For maintaining the army, the important functionary within the central government was the *ariz*. Although Fakhr-i-Mudabbir, writing at the beginning of the sultanate, does not emphasize the office of ariz, possibly because it was directly under the wazir, by the time of Balban the position was independent of the wizarat. With the expansion of the empire and the growth of the military side of the government, the importance of the *ariz* increased. Not only did he function sometimes as the general of the forces, but he also acted as the chief recruiting officer and fixed the salary of each recruit. The commissariat was under him, and his office, *diwan-i-arz,* disbursed salaries to the troops. Even the poet Amir Khusrau and the other court officials who held a military rank received salaries from this office. Thus already under the sultanate we can see the beginnings of the Mughal system of placing all public servants on the army pay-list and giving them mansabs.

The *ariz-i-mumalik* was not the commander-in-chief, or even the senior general—the sultan named the generals for different campaigns—but it is not difficult to see in contemporary accounts the power and the importance of the head of the *diwan-i-arz*. Jalal-ud-din Khalji held this post before he ascended the throne, and the part played by Shaikh Farid, who held the corresponding position of Mir Bakhshi under Akbar, in securing the accession of Jahangir is well known.

Justice

The administration of justice received attention quite early in the sultanate, and here as elsewhere traditional Islamic practice was modified to suit the peculiar problems of India. Four types of courts were normally recognized in Islamic society: the *diwan-i-mazalim*, the court of complaints, presided over by the ruler or his representative; the Qazi's court, which administered the Holy Law of Islam; the courts of the muhtasib, or censor, which dealt with public morals and offenses against religious ordinances; and the *shurta*, or police courts. In India the third type of court gained in power and prestige under the Tughluqs, and later under Aurangzeb.

The first important judicial dignitary of the sultanate at Delhi to whom a reference is found in contemporary records was the *amir-i-dad*, or chief magistrate. He was a layman, and the office was usually reserved for a leading noble with special aptitude for judicial work. Fakhr-i-Mudabbir suggested that only a member of the royal family, or a nobleman known for piety and learning, should be appointed to this post. A large salary was to be paid to him, as he might have to try complaints against governors and high commanders. In the absence of the sultan, who functioned as supreme judge throughout Muslim rule, the *amir-i-dad* presided over the court of complaints, but his office had many other functions. He controlled the police, was responsible for public works, including the maintenance of the city walls, kept copies of documents registered with the Qazi, and forbade covenants which transgressed the law. If he felt that there had been a miscarriage of justice he could either draw the attention of the Qazi to the fact or delay the execution of the decision until the matter was reconsidered by a fuller or a higher court; he also ordered the arrest of criminals, dealt with breaches of law, and tried cases, where necessary with the assistance of a Qazi who functioned as a legal adviser.

While the system of dispensation of justice by the sultan or his representative continued, administration of justice by the qazis grew in importance and became a prominent feature of the Tughluq rule. The main concern of the Qazi was civil disputes among Muslims, although later his jurisdiction was widened to include the supervision and management of the property of orphans and lunatics. Appointed by the central government, he was completely independent of the provincial governors. The office of the *Qazi-i-mumalik*, or chief judge, was normally held by the head of the ecclesiastical department, who was generally known as the *sadr-i-jahan*. It is not certain whether he heard appeals against the judgments of the qazis. He was also the sultan's legal adviser in matters relating to shariat, the holy law of Islam. With the monarch retaining the powers of appointment of the chief Qazi, though the enlightened opinion and books on Muslim statecraft emphasize the importance of appointing only honest, pious, and well-qualified qazis in the realm, the sultan had the final say in the framing of the judicial structure.

Public opinion was critical of the appointment of chief qazis for considerations other than those of merit, and most of the kings took steps to uphold the prestige of the judiciary. The manner in which on one occasion Mohammad Tughluq appeared like an ordinary plaintiff in the court of a Qazi and saluted him may be nothing more than a theatrical gesture, but such episodes built up the prestige of the courts and enabled the general public and the legal profession to realize what was expected of the judges. Although under a despotic monarchy there were obvious limitations to the role which an individual could play, the jurists generally acted with courage and independence. When Jalal-ud-din Khalji wanted Sayyid Maula, who was accused of high treason, to vindicate himself by walking through fire, the jurists vetoed the idea by contending that fire did not distinguish between the innocent and the guilty. The sultan bowed to their decision, though he later connived at Sayyid's murder. Similarly, in spite of Alauddin Khalji's reputation for ruthlessness, Qazi Mughis-ud-din did not fail to criticize his actions, and in spite of this condemnation, he rewarded the Qazi. The sanctity attached to the office of Qazi, as an expert in Islamic law, and the pressure of public opinion, encouraged an honest and independent judiciary, the need for which was universally recognized.

An important development during the sultanate was the crystallization of the Indo-Muslim legal tradition. The first important figure in the legal history of the Delhi Sultanate was Sayyid Nur-ud-din Mubarik, originally of Ghazni (d.1234). He was held in high regard by Sultan Mohammad Ghuri, and he maintained his position even though he was extremely critical of court etiquette and the mode of living adopted by Muslim rulers. He wanted Iltutmish to deal firmly with non-Muslims, and he condemned not only all heresy but also the study of philosophy. Barani often puts some of his own ideas in the discourses which he attributes to important personalities, but the puritanical, ascetic approach which he attributes to Nur-ud-Din Mubarik appears typical of the early days of Muslim India, when simplicity and piety found favour with the jurists and the ruling monarch.

A different type of personality, and one whose policy left a great mark on the history of Islamic law in India, was Qazi Minhaj-us-Siraj, the most important historian of the Slave dynasty. A native of Ghazni, he came to the subcontinent during the reign of Iltutmish and received many important assignments. In the days of Iltutmish's successors, including Nasiruddin Mahmud, he held the important office of the chief Qazi of the realm. It is said that the *sama* (ecstatic dances performed by groups similar to the "whirling dervishes") to which most orthodox lawyers objected, became prevalent in Delhi when Minhaj was Qazi. A contemporary of Minhaj thought that he was not fit to be a Qazi, but should have been the principal Sufi Shaikh. These statements give a clue to his policies, for as he himself has recorded, he was so unpopular with other ecclesiastics that once they even attempted to have him assassinated.

In the light of these observations it is reasonable to infer that Minhaj was not rigid in the application of Islamic law, and that his long tenure as chief Qazi contributed toward the evolution of a suitable modus operandi for the new Muslim government. His views on Islamic law in fact appear to have been in agreement with those of Balban. Although personally punctilious in his religious observations, and careful about showing formal courtesy to religious leaders, Balban attached no importance to the views of ulama in political and administrative matters. He used to say that these things had to be decided in accordance with political considerations and not the views of jurists. According to Barani, "he would order whatever he considered to be in the interest of the realm, whether it was or was not sanctioned by Islamic law." Balban's practice and Minhaj's theory united to provide the flexibility needed by Islamic law if it were to operate in the peculiar conditions created by the existence of a tiny Muslim ruling class and a vast Hindu populace. The tradition of strong common sense and a realistic approach to problems built up by Minhaj was maintained by his daughter's son, Sadr-ud-din Arif, who was a deputy to the chief Qazi for a long time, and whom Alauddin Khalji promoted early in his reign. According to Barani he was not distinguished for scholarship, but he was a strong executive officer who understood the temperament of the people, so that "in spite of the freed slaves who overran Delhi, it was not possible for anyone to resort to swindling, deception, or trickery before his court."

The man who most directly influenced the course of Indo-Muslim legal history was not a high official, as was Minhaj, but a scholar who introduced the systematic study of Islamic law into India. This was Maulana Burhanuddin, who brought with him to India from Balkh the *Hidaya*, the great legal textbook. This remained the basis of Muslim law for centuries, and was finally translated into English by officials of the East India Company. So great was Burhan-ud-din's reputation as a teacher that Balban, accompanied by his entire royal retinue, visited him after Friday prayers. Despite his orthodoxy, he was not particularly rigid in his application of Islamic law. On the crucial question of *sama*, the ecstatic dances, which remained the major legal controversy of the day and generally provided the dividing line between the mystics and the ecclesiasts, his practice was not different from that of the more tolerant Minhaj. "I have not committed any major sin in life," he said, "except hearing of *sama*, which I have heard and want to hear again, if I have an opportunity." The popularity of *Hidaya* and other textbooks from Central Asia ensured that in legal affairs, as in much else, Muslim India followed the traditions of Central Asia. These books, which were brought to India mainly by refugees during Balban's reign, were in Arabic. With the efforts made by Firuz Tughluq to run the government according to Islamic law, it became necessary to have summaries and abstracts of Islamic law in Persian, the court language of Muslim India. We accordingly see a large number of manuals prepared in his reign, usually based on the compilations of the lawyers of Central Asia. In addition more substantial efforts for compilation of books on Islamic law in Persian and Arabic were made. The earliest of such compilations prepared in India was in the time of Balban and was dedicated to him. Others were prepared during the Tughluq period but the most comprehensive digest compiled in Muslim India prior to the compilation of *Fatawa-i-Alamgiri* in Aurangzeb's reign was the *Fatawa-i-Tatar Khania,* named after the pious nobleman, Tatar Khan, who sponsored the compilation. Prepared by a committee of ulama, it consisted of thirty volumes. It attracted attention ouside the subcontinent, and a summary was prepared by Shaikh Ibrahim, the imam of the mosque of the Ottoman sultan, Mohammad the Conqueror, in Istanbul.

Provincial Administration

Although contemporary historians give meager details about the provincial governments, it seems a fair inference that the provincial administrative structure did not crystallize until the days of Sher Shah and Akbar. It is possible that this development was facilitated by the establishment of regional kingdoms in the original iqtas (regions) of the Delhi Sultanate. From the earliest period governors were appointed for large *iqtas* which later became provinces, but their responsibilities were mainly the maintenance of peace, establishment and extension of the authority of the government, and recovery of tribute from the Hindu chiefs and others. The observance of state laws and the maintenance of order depended on the ability and the interest of the individual governor, and in some areas their authority must have been confined to main centers of administration and places easily accessible. The provincial boundaries were shifting and vague, and it was a long time before the territorial units took a stable form. Even the powers of all the governors were not identical. Governors in charge of bigger or more important areas or with special personal claims exercised wider powers than ordinary *muqtis* [=holders of *iqtas*] and were referred to as *walis.*

Before Balban's time, the governors were often semi-independent military chiefs of the territories conquered by them or by their ancestors, but even then many functions remained outside their domain. They were not given authority in religious and judicial affairs, nor were the local intelligence officers under their control. The governor's main concern was military control and revenue collection. With Balban the wizarat became more organized at the center and the provincial diwans were posted from Delhi, and a close check was exercised by the central government over the recovery and transmission of revenue. The provincial *sahib-i-diwan* was appointed by the sultan on the recommendation of the wazir, and submitted detailed statements of provincial accounts to the capital. On the basis of these statements the wazir's department settled the accounts with the *muqtis*. Even in the military sphere the powers of the provincial governors came to be regulated by the presence of the provincial *ariz* who was under the chief ariz at Delhi.

Balban had asserted the authority of the central government over the provincial chiefs, and Alauddin Khalji tried to introduce system and uniformity in the administration of the Doab (the fertile area between the Ganges and the Jamna), the most dependable source of state revenue. Ghiyas-ud-din Tughluq, who had a long experience of provincial administration in the Punjab, tried to improve the administration, but details of his provincial administration have not been recorded. Under his son, Mohammad Tughluq, we get details of the hierarchy of provincial officials, and this possibly follows a pattern introduced earlier. The empire consisted of twenty-four provinces divided into a number of *shiqs*, or rural districts. The next smallest unit after the shiq was the *pargana*, or group of villages. In a pargana and in the villages the old Hindu organization continued. The head of each pargana was a *chaudhari*, while a *Muqaddam* or a *mukhiya* was the head man of the village. The most important feature of Muslim administration in India was the acceptance of the local autonomy enjoyed by rural areas. This policy had been followed by Mohammad ibn Qasim in the earliest days of Muslim rule in the Sind and was maintained by the sultans of Delhi. Qutb-ud-din Aibak, who originally handed back Ajmer to a son of Prithvi Raj, first adopted the policy of appointing Hindu officers for the administration of the country. "The Hindu chief played such an important role in the rural life of the period that to many he was the government, whereas the sultan was almost a mythical figure."

The position of the nobility and the officers was so dominant in the early period that Minhaj, the historian of the period, devotes more space to an account of the principal officers of the realm than to the sultans. The existence of this bureaucracy made possible a large degree of stability in administration, and even in the periods of decline the succession of dynasties at Delhi was not usually reflected in changes of government at the local level.

Emphasis on administrative stability during the sultanate should not be taken as an indication that the period was peaceful or that normal judicial processes were always respected by either the sultans or their officials. Maintenance of control in a conquered area requires force, and, in addition, the ceaseless struggle for power that went on made violence commonplace. The smallest incident could be turned into a pretext for the drawing of the sword and the shedding of blood. Nor was violence confined to the cruel and heartless. Rulers such as Balban were not deficient in a sense of justice or in political ability, but these qualities did not deter him from severe punishments and free spilling of blood. At times a sense of justice and concern for the public welfare seemed to militate against human kindness. Once the deterrent theory of punishment was adopted and carried to extremes, all other human considerations gave way before it. In vain did the religious lawyers and intellectuals try to curb the extreme punishments inflicted by the sultans. Qazi Mughis argued before Alaud-din Khalji that his punishments were unauthorized and opposed to Islam, and the historian Barani told Mohammad bin Tughluq that human life could be taken only for eight specific crimes, but the autocratic sultans listened unmoved.

Not only was human life held in little esteem, but there were abhorrent cases of torture and mutilation. In this Mohammad bin Tughluq, who was a highly educated monarch and enjoyed the company of intellectuals and philosophers, was the worst offender. Some of the punishments meted out by him—for example to his cousin Gurshashp—are truly revolting. The Moorish traveller Ibn Battuta wrote of him: "Notwithstanding all his modesty, his sense of equality and justice, and his extraordinary liberality and kindness to the poor, he had immense daring to shed blood. His gate was hardly ever free from the corpse of a man who had been executed. And I used to see frequently a number of people killed at the gate of the royal palace and the corpses abandoned there. ... The sultan used to punish all wrongs whether big or small and he would spare neither the men of learning and probity, nor those of high descent. Every day hundreds of people in chains with their hands fastened to the neck and their feet tightened were brought into the council hall. Those who were to be killed were killed and those who were to be tortured were tortured and those who were to be beaten were beaten. ... May God save us from calamity."

It is true that these punishments were reserved for treason, and it is also true that conditions in the medieval ages in other parts of the world were not very much better, but the position in Muslim India in this respect seems to have worsened distinctly during the hundred years or so following the death of Iltutmish. Possibly the instances of brutality and cruelty during the sultanate in the thirteenth and fourteenth centuries reflect the impact of the Mongols; certainly the extremes of ruthless severity associated with Mohammad Tughluq or even with Balban and Alauddin Khalji, did not exist in the days of Mohammad ibn Qasim, Aibak, and Iltutmish.

6

Trade and Commerce under Vijayanagara and its Offshoots

The rulers of the Vijayanagara empire maintained the well-functioning administrative methods developed by their predecessors, the Hoysala, Kakatiya and Pandya kingdoms, to govern their territories and made changes only where necessary. The King stood as the ultimate authority, assisted by a cabinet of ministers (Pradhana) headed by the prime minister (Mahapradhana). Other important titles recorded in inscriptions included the chief secretary (Karyakartha or Rayaswami) and the imperial officers (Adhikari). The government required all high ranking ministers and officers to have military training. A secretariat near the king's palace employed scribes and officers to maintain records made official by using a wax seal imprinted with the ring of the king. At the lower administrative levels, wealthy feudal landlords (Goudas) supervised accountants (Karanikas or Karnam) and guards (Kavalu). The palace administration divided into 72 departments (Niyogas), each having several female attendants chosen for their youth and beauty (some imported or captured in victorious battles), trained to handle minor administrative matters and to serve men of nobility as courtesans or concubines.

The empire had been divided into five main provinces (Rajya), each under a commander (Dandanayaka or Dandanatha) and headed by a governor, often from the royal family, who used the native language for administrative purposes. A Rajya divided into regions (Vishaya Vente or Kottam), and further divided into counties (Sime or Nadu) themselves subdivided into municipalities (Kampana or Sthala). Hereditary families ruled their respective territories and paid tribute to the empire while some areas, such as Keladi and Madurai, came under the direct supervision of a commander.

On the battlefields, the king's commanders led the troops. The empire's war strategy rarely involved massive invasions; more often it employed small scale methods such as attacking and destroying individual forts. The empire emerged among the first in India to use long range artillery commonly manned by foreign gunners. (Gunners from present day Turkmenistan had been considered the best). Army troops consisted of two types: The king's personal army directly recruited by the empire and the feudal army under each feudatory. King Krishnadevaraya's personal army consisted of 100,000 infantry, 20,000 cavalrymen and over 900 elephants. That number constituted only a part of the army numbering over 1.1 million soldiers, a figure that varied as an army of two million has also been recorded along with the existence of a navy as evidenced by the use of the term Navigadaprabhu (commander of the navy). The army recruited from all classes of society (supported by the collection of additional feudal tributes from feudatory rulers), and consisted of archers and musketeers wearing quilted tunics, shieldmen with swords and poignards in their girdles, and soldiers carrying shields so large that they fought without armour. The horses and elephants wore full body armour and the elephants had knives fastened to their tusks for maximum injury in battle.

The capital city depended completely on the water supply systems constructed to channel and store water, and to ensure a consistent supply throughout the year. The remains of those hydraulic systems have given historians a picture of the prevailing surface water distribution methods in use at that time in South India's semiarid regions. Contemporary inscriptions and notes of foreign travellers describe how labourers constructed huge tanks. Excavations have uncovered the remains of a well-connected water distribution system existing solely within the royal enclosure and the large temple complexes (suggesting exclusive use of royalty, and for special ceremonies) with sophisticated channels using gravity and siphons to transport water through pipelines. The remains of large water tanks that collected the seasonal monsoon water and then dried up in summer except for the few fed by springs represent the only structures resembling public waterworks. In the fertile agricultural areas near the Tungabhadra River, labourers dug canals to guide the river water into irrigation tanks. Those canals had sluices that opened and closed to control the water flow. In other areas the administration encouraged the digging of wells monitored by administrative authorities. Royal patronage supported the construction of large tanks in the capital city while wealthy individuals funded smaller tanks to gain social and religious merit.

Economy

The empire's economy depended largely on agriculture. Corn (jowar), cotton, and pulse legumes grew in semi arid regions, while sugar cane, rice and wheat thrived in rainy areas. Betel leaves, areca (for chewing), and coconut constituted the principal cash crops, and large scale cotton production supplied the weaving centres of the empire's vibrant textile industry. Spices such as turmeric, pepper, cardamom, and ginger grew in the remote Malnad hill region, transported to the city for trade. The empire's capital city thrived as a business centre that included a burgeoning market in large quantities of precious gems and gold. Prolific temple-building provided employment to thousands of masons, sculptors, and other skilled artisans.

Owning land proved vital for creating wealth. Most of the growers worked tenant farmers, given the right of part ownership of the land over time. Tax policies encouraging needed produce made distinctions between land use to determine tax levies. For example, perfumers depended upon the daily market availability of rose petals, so cultivation of roses received a lower tax assessment. Salt production and the manufacture of salt pans received similar benefits. The making of ghee (clarified butter), sold as an oil for human consumption and as a fuel for lighting lamps, proved profitable. Exports to China intensified and included cotton, spices, jewels, semi-precious stones, ivory, rhino horn, ebony, amber, coral, and aromatic products such as perfumes. Large vessels from China made frequent visits, some captained by the Chinese Admiral Cheng Ho, and brought Chinese products to the empire's 300 ports, large and small, on the Arabian Sea and the Bay of Bengal. The ports of Mangalore, Honavar, Bhatkal,

Barkur, Cochin, Cannanore, Machilipatnam and Dharmadam received the heaviest trade.

When merchant ships docked, officials took the merchandise into official custody, assessing taxes on all items sold. The administration officials guaranteed the security of the merchandise. Traders of many nationalities (Arabs, Persians, Guzerates, Khorassanians) settled in Calicut, drawn by the thriving trade business. Ship building prospered. Ship builders constructed keeled ships of 1000–1200 bahares (burden) without decks by sewing the entire hull with ropes rather than fastening them with nails. Ships sailed to the Red Sea ports of Aden and Mecca with Vijayanagara goods sold as far away as Venice. Pepper, ginger, cinnamon, cardamom, myrobalan, tamarind timber, anafistula, precious and semi-precious stones, pearls, musk, ambergris, rhubarb, aloe, cotton cloth, and porcelain constituted the empire's principal exports. Ships carried cotton yarn to Burma and indigo to Persia. From Palestine, importers received chiefly shipments copper, quicksilver (mercury), vermilion, coral, saffron, coloured velvets, rose water, knives, coloured camlets, gold and silver. Cannanore served as the port of entry for Persian horses, followed by a two week land trip to the capital. Silk arrived from China and sugar from Bengal.

East coast trade hummed, with rice, millet, pulse and tobacco arriving from Golkonda. The weaving industry drew imports of dye crops of indigo and chay root. A mineral-rich region, Machilipatnam served as the gateway for high quality iron and steel exports. The Kollur region conducted active diamond mining. The cotton weaving industry produced two types of cottons, plain calico and muslin (brown, bleached or dyed). Merchants exported cloth printed with coloured patterns crafted by native techniques to Java and the Far East. Golkonda specialized in plain cotton and Pulicat in printed. Non-ferrous metals, camphor, porcelain, silk, and luxury goods comprised the main imports on the east coast.

Most information on the social life in Vijayanagara empire comes from the writings of foreign visitors and evidence that research teams in the Vijayanagara area have uncovered. The Hindu caste system prevailed, followed rigidly followed with each caste represented by a local body of elders who represented the community. Those elders set the rules and regulations implemented with the help of royal decrees. Untouchability constituted part of the caste system, leaders (Kaivadadavaru) representing those communities. The Muslim communities had representation by their own group in coastal Karnataka. The caste system failed to prevent distinguished persons from all castes from being promoted to high ranking cadre in the army and administration. In civil life, by virtue of the caste system, Brahmins enjoyed a high level of respect. With the exception of a few who took to military careers, most Brahmins concentrated on religious and literary matters. Their separation from material wealth and power made them ideal arbiters in local judicial matters, and their presence in every town and village had been a calculated investment made by the nobility and aristocracy to maintain order. The popularity of low-caste scholars (such as Molla and Kanakadasa) and their works (including those of Vemana and Sarvajna) indicated of the degree of social fluidity in the society.

The practice of Sati where wives threw themselves on the burning pyre of their dead husbands, had been common, though voluntary, and mostly practiced among the upper classes. Over 50 inscriptions attesting to that have been discovered in the Vijayanagara principality alone. Those inscriptions have come to be called Satikal (Sati stone) or Sati-virakal (Sati hero stone). Satikals commemorated the death of a woman by entering into fire after the death of her husband while craftsmen made Sati-virakals for a woman who performed Sati after her husband's heroic death. Either way, the woman raised to the level of a demi-goddess and proclaimed by the sculpture of a Sun and crescent moon on the stone.

The socio-religious movements of the previous centuries, such as Lingayitism, provided momentum for flexible social norms expected of women. By that time South Indian women had crossed most barriers, participating in activities hitherto considered the monopoly of men, such as administration, business and trade, and involvement in the fine arts. Tirumalamba Devi who wrote Varadambika Parinayam and Gangadevi who wrote Madhuravijayam stood among the notable women poets of the era. Early Telugu women poets like Tallapaka Timmakka and Atukuri Molla became popular during that period. The court of the Nayaks of Tanjore has been recorded patronizing several women poets. The Devadasi system existed, as well as legalized prostitution relegated to a few streets in each city. The popularity of harems amongst men of the royalty has appeared abundantly in records. Well-to-do men wore the Petha or Kulavi, a tall turban made of silk and decorated with gold. As in most Indian societies, men and women used jewellery, records describing the use of anklets, bracelets, finger-rings, necklaces and ear rings of various types. During celebrations, men and women adorned themselves with flower garlands and used perfumes made of rose water, civet, musk or sandalwood. In stark contrast to the commoners who lived modestly, the empire's kings and queens lived lives full of ceremonial pomp in the court. Queens and princesses had numerous attendants who dressed lavishly, adorned with fine jewellery, their daily duties being light.

Physical exercises had been popular with men, wrestling standing out as an important male preoccupation for sport and entertainment. Records even mentioned women wrestlers. Gymnasiums have been discovered inside royal quarters and records speak of regular physical training for commanders and their armies during peace time. Royal palaces and market places had special arenas where royalty and common people alike amused themselves by watching matches such as cock fights, ram fights and wrestling between women. Excavations within the Vijayanagara city limits have revealed the existence of various types of community-based activities in the form of engravings on boulders, rock platforms and temple floors, implying those places served for casual social interaction. People play some of those games today, others have yet to be identified.

Although the empire had been built to shield Hindu dharma from the onslaughts of the Mughal Empire and the Deccan sultanates, the Vijayanagara kings practiced tolerance of all religions and sects as writings by foreign visitors show. The kings used titles such as Gobrahamana Pratipalanacharya ("protector of cows") and Hindurayasuratrana ("upholder of Hindu faith") that testified to their intention of protecting Hinduism. The Empire's founders Harihara I and Bukka Raya I had been devout Shaivans (worshippers of Shiva), but made grants to the Vaishnava order of Sringeri with Vidyaranya as their patron saint, and designated Varaha (the boar, an avatar of Vishnu) as their emblem. The later Saluva and Tuluva kings declared the Vaishnava faith, but worshipped at the feet of Lord Virupaksha (Shiva) at Hampi as well as Lord Venkateshwara (Vishnu) at Tirupati. A Sanskrit work,

Jambavati Kalyanam by King Krishnadevaraya, called Lord Virupaksha Karnata Rajya Raksha Mani ("protective jewel of Karnata Empire"). The kings patronised the saints of the dvaita order (philosophy of dualism) of Madhvacharya at Udupi.

The Bhakti (devotional) movement had been active during that time, and involved well known Haridasas (devotee saints). Like the Virashaiva movement of the twelfth century, that movement presented another strong current of devotion, pervading the lives of millions. The Haridasas represented two groups, the Vyasakuta and Dasakuta, the former being required for proficiency in the Vedas, Upanishads and other Darshanas, while the Dasakuta merely conveyed the message of Madhvacharya through the Kannada language to the people in the form of devotional songs (Devaranamas and Kirthanas). Eminent disciples such as Naraharitirtha, Jayatirtha, Vyasatirtha, Sripadaraya, and Vadirajatirtha spread the philosophy of Madhvacharya. Vyasatirtha served as the guru (teacher) of Vadirajatirtha, Purandaradasa (Father of Carnatic music), Kanakadasa and King Krishnadevaraya who considered the saint his Kuladevata (family deity) and honoured him in many of his writings. During that time, another great composer of early carnatic music, Annamacharya composed hundreds of Kirthanas in Telugu at Tirupati in present day Andhra Pradesh.

The defeat of the Jain Western Ganga Dynasty by the Cholas in early eleventh century and the rising numbers of followers of Vaishnava Hinduism and Virashaivism in the twelfth century mirrored a decreasing interest in Jainism. Two notable locations of Jain worship in the Vijayanagara territory had been Shravanabelagola and Kambadahalli.

Islamic contact with South India began as early as the seventh century, a result of trade between the Southern kingdoms and Arab lands. Jumma Masjids existed in the Rashtrakuta empire by the tenth century and many mosques flourished on the Malabar coast by the early fourteenth century. Muslim settlers married local women; their children became known as Mappillas (Moplahs), actively involved in horse trading and manning shipping fleets. The interactions between the Vijayanagara empire and the Bahamani Sultanates to the north increased the presence of Muslims in the south. The introduction of Christianity began as early as the eighth century as shown by the finding of copper plates inscribed with land grants to Malabar Christians. Christian travellers wrote of the scarcity of Christians in South India in the Middle Ages, promoting its attractiveness to missionaries. The arrival of the Portuguese in the fifteenth century and their connections through trade with the empire, the propagation of the faith by Saint Xavier (1545) and later the presence of Dutch settlements fostered the growth of Christianity in the south.

Economy of Hoysala

The Hoysala administration supported itself through revenues from an agrarian economy. The kings gave grants of land as rewards for service to beneficiaries who then became landlords to tenants producing agricultural goods and forest products. Two types of landlords (gavunda) existed; gavunda of people (praja gavunda) lower in status than the wealthy lord of gavundas (prabhu gavunda). The highlands (malnad regions) with its temperate climate proved suitable for raising cattle and the planting of orchards and spices. Paddy and corn served as staple crops in the tropical plains (Bailnad). The Hoysalas collected taxes on irrigation systems including tanks, reservoirs with sluices, canals and wells built and maintained at the expense of local villagers. The state created irrigation tanks such as Vishnusagara, Shantisagara, Ballalarayasagara at their expense.

Importing horses for use as general transportation and in army cavalries of Indian kingdoms became a flourishing business on the western seaboard.

Hoysalas harvested the forests for rich woods such as teak, exporting through ports located in the area of present day Kerela. Sung dynasty records from China mention the presence of Indian merchants in ports of South China, indicating active trade with overseas kingdoms. South India exported textiles, spices, medicinal plants, precious stones, pottery, salt made from salt pans, jewels, gold, ivory, rhino horn, ebony, aloe wood, perfumes, sandalwood, camphor and condiments to China, Dhofar, Aden, and Siraf (the entryport to Egypt, Arabia and Persia). Architects (Vishwakarmas), sculptors, quarry workers, goldsmiths and other skilled craftsmen whose trade directly or indirectly related to temple construction also became prosperous due to the vigorous temple building activities.

The village assembly assumed responsibity for collecting government land taxes. The government included land revenue, called Siddhaya, in the original assessment (Kula) plus various cesses. Professions, marriages, goods in transit on chariots or carriages, and domesticated animals all had taxes levied on them. Village records note taxes on commodities (gold, precious stones, perfumes, sandalwood, ropes, yarn, housing, hearths, shops, cattle pans, sugar cane presses) as well as produce (black pepper, betel leaves, ghee, paddy, spices, palm leaves, coconuts, sugar). The village assembly could levy a tax for a specific purpose such as construction of a water tank.

Administration

In its administrative practices, the Hoysala Empire followed some of the well-established and proven methods of its predecessors covering administrative functions such as cabinet organization and command, the structure of local governing bodies and the division of territory. Records show the names of many high ranking positions reporting directly to the king. Senior ministers, called Pancha Pradhanas, ministers responsible for foreign affairs, designated Sandhivigrahi, and the chief treasurer, Mahabhandari or Hiranyabhandari conducted top level government affairs. Dandanayakas led the armies while Dharmadhikari served as the chief justice of the Hoysala court.

The kingdom divided into provinces named Nadu, Vishaya, Kampana and Desha, listed in descending order of geographical size. Each province had a local governing body consisting of a minister (Mahapradhana) and a treasurer (Bhandari) that reported to the ruler of that province (Dandanayaka). Under that local ruler, officials called Heggaddes and Gavundas hired and supervised the local farmers and labourers recruited to till the land. Subordinate ruling clans such as Alupas continued to govern their respective territories while following the policies set by the empire.

An elite and well trained force of bodyguards known as Garudas protected the members of the royal family at all times. Those servants moved closely yet inconspicuously by the side of their master, their loyalty being so complete that they committed suicide after his death. The government erected Garuda pillars, or Hero stones (virgal) in memory of those bodyguards. The Garuda pillar at the Hoysaleswara temple in Halebidu stood in honour of Kuvara Lakshma, a minister and bodyguard of King Veera Ballala II.

King Vishnuvardhana's coins had the legends "victor at Nolambavadi" (Nolambavadigonda), "victor at Talakad" (Talakadugonda), "chief of the Malepas" (Maleparolganda), "Brave of Malepa" (malapavira) in Hoysala style Kannada script. Their gold coin, called Honnu or Gadyana, weighed 62 grains of gold. Pana or Hana weighed a tenth of the Honnu, Haga a fourth of the Pana and Visa a fourth of Haga. Other coins existed, called Bele and Kani and people still use some of those terms such as Hana and Bele in the Kannada language today, meaning "money" and "cost" respectively.

The Rajas of Kolathunadu

This chapter sets about to analyse the political setup in pre-colonial Kolathunadu. I will argue that the political formation in this region was in many respects distinct from that of the other regions in South India in general and Kerala in particular. Hitherto, the studies on the political system in pre-colonial Kerala did not pay sufficient attention to the regional differences in process of state-formation. The heavy dependence of the scholars on the Brahmanical textual traditions often obscured the variations and gave the impression of the development of a homogeneous state-form throughout Kerala. The political system developed in medieval Kolathunadu exemplifies the regional variation in the political configuration of pre-colonial Kerala. For a better understanding of this regional political system, I will try to present my research in the framework of the academic debate on state-formation in pre-colonial Kerala.

The 'State' in Pre-colonial Kerala

The 'state' in pre-colonial Kerala is not a well-attended field of research. Although, K.V. Krishna Ayyar, the author of The Zamorins of Calicut, traced similarities between the naduvazhi system of Kerala and the feudal order in Europe long before D. D. Kosambi who introduced a 'feudal' model as an analytical concept in Indian historiography, he did not develop it as an analytical tool to study the pre-colonial Kerala states. His argument was that the naduvazhis of Kerala 'were similar to the tenants-in-chief of feudal England having more or less the same rights and obligations'. Similarly, O. K. Nambiar also attributed 'feudal' status to the Kunjalis of Calicut, hence sharing a common platform with Krishna Ayyar. Later, Kathleen Gough, borrowing from the study on medieval Ceylon by Edmund Leach, proposed the concept of 'hydraulic feudalism' to portray the political system in the region.

M. G. S. Narayanan's doctoral dissertation on the Cheras of Mahodayapuram can be considered as a breakthrough in Kerala historiography in terms of analysing the state structure in the early medieval Kerala. His attempt to construe a kingdom with a centre at Mahodayapuram (Kodungalloor) exercising control over the nidus across the region tallied well with the feudal perception of medieval Indian states. Similarly, although perceiving differences with the contemporary Chola-Pandya state organizations, Kesavan Veluthat also tried to highlight the feudal aspect of state in early medieval Kerala under the Chera rulers of Mahodayapuram.

One fact that seems indisputable is that the political formation in post-Chera Kerala was in many ways different from those in other parts of South India. The rise of an array of petty principalities in Kerala after the twelfth century has made it difficult for scholars to conceive and schematize the development within a broader theoretical framework. For many, medieval Kerala represents an odd case which is therefore often neglected in the general historiography of India. Dick Kooiman suggests that this negligence is due to 'the bewildering variety of numerous coastal kingdoms [which] does not seem to offer the historian a solid base for the construction of more enduring frameworks'. The easiest way to escape from such an academic predicament, which failed to encompass medieval Kerala in a pan-Indian, 'enduring' theoretical framework, was simply to omit it altogether from historical discourse. Notwithstanding this situation, recently some attempts have been made to look at the pre-colonial Kerala polities from new theoretical perspectives, deviating from that of the 'feudal' approach. Burton Stein's 'segmentary state' model found some reflection in Kerala historiography, though not without striking some sceptical notes. Dick Kooiman had this to say on the matter:

> As far as the character of the state on the Malabar Coast is concerned, there is much evidence to argue for an interpretation along the lines of the segmentary state model. Fiscality does not seem to have been a prominent aspect of internal relations, whereas

religious grants were a major source of power. However, the problem remains that the numerous states in this region had no single dominating centre. So we should ask ourselves whether the sacred memory of a former kingship in the old Chera days served the same purpose in Kerala as ritual deference to a living ruler in the Chola Empire did in Tamil Nadu.

Similarly, Hugo K. S. Jacob suggested using the 'segmentary state' model to analyse the political structure in early-modern Kerala, but he did further develop this argument. It is noteworthy that both these Dutch scholars were dealing principally with the political formations in the southern parts of Kerala—Venadu (Travancore) and Cochin. Their area of study obviously influenced their perception that 'ritual' and 'religious grants' were prerequisites necessary to acquire political power in Kerala.

The 'Little Kingdom' Model

Adopting the concept of the 'little kingdom', mainly from Nicholas B. Dirks, Margaret Frenz, modified it to suit the Malabar situation and made an attempt to give theoretical coherence to the analysis of pre-colonial Kerala polities. Although, another Dutch scholar, Mark de Lannoy already in 1997, suggested the 'little kingdom' model as a tool with which to analyse the state forms in early modern Kerala, it was Margaret Frenz who presented it as a full-fledged model in Kerala historiography. Frenz summarizes the 'little kingdom' model of Dirks as follows.

The State structure is depicted as pyramidal, with the great king positioned at the very top. His political and ritual might enables him to exercise supreme power over the little kings. The great king's range of power, however, continually decreases at the periphery of this 'catchment area'; there, it is the little kings who are more important, since they are actually on site. The little king legitimises and manifests his rule through political and ritual actions, which express the extent of his participation in power. This pattern is repeated on a smaller scale in the lower levels, right down to the foot of the pyramid to individual person's relations and family relationship.

Although this description depicts a close resemblance to the 'segmentary state' model of Stein, unlike him Dirks considers 'ritual and political forms were fundamentally the same', rather than separate entities. Dirks also recognizes military power as an important element of authority within a 'little kingdom', though the military system was 'organised around subordinate chieftains, connubial connections, and privileged landholding rather than on centralized or bureaucratically organized revenue collection and military rule'. The relationship between the 'great king' and the 'little king' is mutually beneficial, whereas the military might of the former did not play a decisive role. The 'great king' had to depend on loyal 'little kings' when he had conflicts to settle with other 'great kings' or rebellious little kings. In such a situation, the 'little king' enjoyed complete freedom within his domain. In brief, the relationship between 'little king' and the 'great king' remained largely 'symbolic'.

Frenz, albeit of her acceptance of the 'little kingdom' model as a useful tool with which to analyse the pre-colonial Malabar polity, Frenz criticised Dirks' model as too rigid and without any scope for further development. So, she tried to develop it to suit the medieval Kerala situation. For Frenz,

A little king is a ruler who has, within his territory, essential instruments of rule such as financial and military means at his disposal, and who legitimises his rule through political and ritual acts. Outwardly the little king must accept the rule of a great king who is superior to him in a ritual and political sense, and who can demonstrate this by military means if necessary. The little king also relies on the great king, since he can legitimise his rule internally over the great king by the system of ritual redistribution, thereby gaining a share of the great king's power. Conversely, the great king cannot, in the long term, assert his rule over the little kings by military means, since he requires the political and ritual support of the little kings for the legitimation of his rule.

In his model Dirks proposes a two-tier system, where the 'great king' and 'little kings' occupy the first and second positions. In preference to this, Frenz suggests a more flexible arrangement in Malabar and tries to put 'little kings' between the 'great king' and such minor chieftains as nauvazhis or desavazhis. Frenz strengthened her argument by claiming that 'in this way the little king is left with a far greater scope for political, ritual and military action, the struggle for power is more pronounced and the order of precedence is continually being rearranged'. But her attempt to form a three-tier political hierarchy to introduce the 'little kings' in Kerala forced Frenz to discover a 'great king' who actually was not present in the political context of the region. In the absence of this 'great king'; the concept of 'little kings' is simply nullified. As Dirks argued, 'little kingship could not be attained without great kings'. In her effort to solve this problem, Frenz introduces a 'virtual' 'great king'—the legendary 'Cheraman Perumal'—who occupies the apex in the ritual hierarchy of Kerala. It appears that Frenz was trying to 'fit' the 'little kingdom' model into the medieval Kerala political situation rather than to find a model to suit the polity she was dealing with.

It is true that most of the Kerala rajas putatively traced their authority and their legitimization to rule over their respective territories to the legendary Cheraman Perumal. But this was a common process throughout India where almost all the ruling dynasties tried to trace their origin to Puranic figures or dynastic lines such as Surya Vamsa, Chandra Vamsa and the like. The purpose remained the same—to legitimize and to enhance the prestige of the ruling authority in society—whether it is a matrilineal or a patrilineal society. Hence, introducing Cheraman Perumal as 'great king' does create 'little kings'. However, as a model, it fails to explain the social dynamics in pre-colonial Kerala in relation to socio-economic changes or even fails to explain the different levels of power relations among the 'little kings' or between the 'little kings' and the nauvazhis or desavazhis of Kerala. Instead of finding a place for a functionally inactive 'virtual' 'great king' in pre-colonial Malabar political system, it would, perhaps, be better to look at the ruling houses of Kerala in their historical contexts. It is more feasible to examine those known as rajas of Kerala as 'rajas' in their own right, whatsoever the term meant in the political context of pre-colonial Kerala.

The Swarupam Polity

After the disappearance of the Perumals or the Cheras of Mahodayapuram in the twelfth century, the political formation in Kerala took a different turn from the other parts of South India. The emergence of the institution known as the 'swarupam' as the focus of political power in Kerala after the twelfth century was a significant development in the history of Kerala. However, in spite of its importance in the political economy of pre-colonial

Kerala, only a limited number of studies are available about the swarupam polity. The literal meaning of the term swarupam—'self-figure or self-form'—does not seem to have any explicit political connotation and does not help us to expound this unique political system in any satisfactory way. The title swarupam was attributed to such major political houses of Kerala as the Kolaswarupam (Cannanore), the Nediyirippu Swarupam (Calicut), the Perumpadappu Swarupam (Cochin), the Venadu Swarupam (Travancore) and the like. It is probable that some of these houses had already attained political prominence during the Chera period. The Chera inscriptions mention the 'governors' (utaiyavar or vazhunnavar) of such nidus as Kolathunadu, Venadu (Travancore), Eralanadu (Calicut) and the like. Gradually, after the disappearance of the Cheras of Mahodayapuram, the houses of these nadu utaiyavars appeared as independent political houses or swarupams. This shows that some of the swarupams of Kerala had a long history of political standing, which may have strengthened their claim to political supremacy among the other minor swarupams after the twelfth century. This may also indicate the possibility that the term 'swarupam' was coined for these houses only after the Chera period. Besides those prominent swarupams which can trace their histories back to the Perumal period, new swarupams also came into existence in Kerala in the course of time.

In spite of their differences in the period of origin, all of these swarupams had a specific trait in common. They were powerful matrilineal joint families claiming hereditary political authority. In this respect swarupam closely resembled a taravadu. The taravadu is also a matrilineal joint family headed by a Karanavar. The Karanavar was usually the eldest male member of a taravadu, who succeeded to the position through the matrilineal line of succession. Property was owned jointly by the family members under the supervision of the Karanavar. Even though proprietary rights were traced through the female line, it does not seem that the women members enjoyed any crucial control over the actual use of the property. Bigger taravadus controlled extensive landed properties which helped them to gain political and judicial control over their vicinities. It is noteworthy that a taravadu which succeeded in establishing its dominance in a region could eventually claim the status of a swarupam. For instance, as revealed in a Mackenzie manuscript, the prominent land-owning Kudali

Taravadu in North claimed the status of a swarupam. This intimates that the political structure in pre-colonial Malabar was essentially flexible and that the demarcation between the status of a swarupam and a taravadu was very narrow.

Here it seems that the role of Brahmanism was crucial in delineating the superior political status of the swarupams in comparison with that of the other powerful taravadus in Kerala. The heads of the swarupams were generally honoured as 'rajas', mainly in Brahmanical narratives. It is also true that the consecration ceremonies of many of these 'rajas' of the Kerala swarupams were presided over by Brahmin 'priests'. Although, these factors indicate that Brahmanism influenced the conceptualization of swarupam kingship in Kerala, my argument is that, conceptualizing the state form in pre-colonial Kolathunadu cannot be drawn solely from the Brahmanical notion of 'ritual kingship'. It is also necessary to take the regional notion of cosmic power or sakti into consideration.

The Concept of Sakti

While analysing the indigenous cultural matrix of northern Malabar in his in-depth study on Teyyam worship in this region, J. R. Freeman noticed the existence of three distinct value-systems co-existing within the cultural matrix of the region. Firstly, there was the Brahmanical strand recapitulated in its purity-impurity dichotomy. The second was the political or 'royal' system which was founded on martial and material power. And thirdly, the strand drawing its strength from magical powers. All these three streams coalesced in or were absorbed into the regional cosmos of sakti (sacred power) embodying the local Dravidian culture and consequently formed an integral and indissoluble part of the regional cultural matrix. Freeman noticed the spatial factor which limited the ideological influence of Brahmanism over Dravidian ritual centres (temple/kavu). Therefore, the local worship centres lying closer to Brahmin temples tended to be more heavily influenced by the 'purity-impurity' concept, whereas this influence diminished in proportionate to the increasing spatial distance between the two.

Although there are indications of a compromise between these streams, Brahmanism never succeeded in dominating or substantially transforming the indigenous world of beliefs and practices. Instead, what we notice is a complex process in which various cosmological concepts interpenetrated to form a complex social ideology. What I have in mind is that the Nambutiri Brahmins in Kolathunadu gradually had to 'internalize' the local Dravidian sakti cults if they were to co-exist in the local social structure, instead of completely altering the existing systems after their perceptions.

Even in the case of the political elites of the region, the influence of Brahmanism and its emphasis on ritual purity were limited. This absence is conspicuous in the ritual practices which follow in the royal temples of the Kolaswarupam. For example, Maday Kavu, the oldest ritual seat of the Kolaswarupam, till recently performed blood sacrifices. The situation is no different in the cases of the bhagavati (goddess) worshipping centres like the Nileswaram Kavu (Mannanpurathu Kavu) and the Kalarivatukkal Temple, linked to the royal houses of the Alladam Swarupam (Nileswaram) and the Kolaswarupam respectively. Here animal sacrifices were carried out regularly as a part of sakti worship. There seems to have been attempts on the part of the Kolaswarupam to create a 'royal' priesthood, by reproducing the equivalent of the priestly class in Brahmin temples to serve in these temples. Pidarar, who served in these temples, followed the same ritual life as the Brahmins, except that they were regarded as sakteya Brahmins, practising blood sacrifices and drinking toddy as a part of their daily puja. Analogous to the Brahmin temples and different from the common local kavus, these swarupam temples performed daily pujas. It is probable that the Kolaswarupam was trying to create its own ritual system rooted in the local notion of sakti by appropriating some of the features of the functioning of Brahmanical temples.

This indicates that assuming 'ritual' authority as a separate entity is not enough to do full justice to the conceptualization of political power in Kolathunadu. In another sense, there was no real segregation of power into 'ritual' and 'political' realms. Both of them were the constituents of the concept of sakti. As Shelly Errington has commented, the presence of invisible cosmic power was inferred by people through visible signs such as wealth, status, influence and the like. The Zamorins, rulers of the nearby Calicut, carried pallimaradi in front of their army marching against Vellattiri, the rival ruler, because it visualized the presence of goddess 'Tirumandhamkunnu Bhagavati', which assured their victory over the enemy. Hence, the marching column resembled a ritual procession in honour of the glory of their goddess and the victory of the king over the enemy was the manifestation of the sakti of the goddess. A raja who controls material wealth and achieves military victories would implicitly mean that he possesses sakti or cosmic power. He embodies the invisible sakti through his material achievements. Accordingly, physical power and material affluence designate the presence of the invisible cosmic power which consequently legitimizes political power. Loyalty was gained and sustained through material means. The material prosperity of a taravadu or a swarupam was an expression of the cosmic power or sakti.

There was no fundamental difference between the sakti emanating from a raja or a god/goddess. Both of them were expressed through actions in the real world. Vanquishing the enemy and attaining material benefit were the two 'blessings' which a devotee expected from his/her tampuran—a term used to denote both a god and members of the local elite. Attaining swarga (heaven) or escaping from the cycle of births and attaining moksha (salvation) did not figure largely in the spiritual tradition of Kolathunadu. The sakti inherent in a man/woman was visible through earthly deeds; before and after death. After their death, they could be transformed into a teyyam (corrupted form of the Sanskrit daivam, which means 'god') and manifest their sakti through material means and express their visions and blessings through human medium (velichappadu). In this sense, ritual legitimation of political power in Kolathunadu and in Kerala generally was not very much different from the legitimation attained through material power. It is true that there were attempts on the part of the Nambutiri Brahmins to exalt the political dignity of the rajas of Kerala. The Kolathiris were praised as 'Vadakkan Perumals' (Perumals of the North) by the author of the Keralolpathi. However, unlike the neighbouring Chola kings who were able to manipulate the Brahmanical ideology to construct a royal cult in which the king, replicating such Puranic deities as Shiva, were transformed into the embodiment of power and the centre of authority, the royal cult creation in Malabar, particularly in Kolathunadu, achieved only limited success.

There appears to have been a significant discrepancy between the ideal type of polity presented in Brahmanical texts such as the

Keralolpathi, where the Kolathiri 'raja' is presented as the custodian of legitimized political power, and the actual working of power relations in the region. Conversely, there does not seem to have been a sharp distinction between the various power levels in Kolathunadu. The 'kingly' status attributed to the Kolathiris remained more or less a nominal one. The Kolathunadu society did not seem to have conceived of the position of the Kolathiris as being a fundamentally different entity from that of other 'men of prowess' in the region. The Kolathiri was usually referred to in local folklore as tampuran—a common term used to designate both local gods and members of the regional elite, including the Ali Rajas, indicating that they were thought to from the same cosmic category in the regional cosmos.

An examination of the state-formation process in medieval Kerala reveals that it did not present a picture of a homogeneous development throughout the region. Historical forces which shaped the fortunes of swarupams varied considerably in time and space. While Calicut presents the features of an 'early state' with perceptible centralization impulses and a successfully developed its own control mechanisms embedded in ritual practices, it was only by the middle of the eighteenth century that a kingdom (Travancore under Marthanda Varma) succeeded in organizing a state with a powerful centre and elaborate administrative and ideological apparatuses. In contrast, Kolathunadu presented a loosely knit political structure, in which the concept of 'rajaship' retained more of the nature of a ritual facade. Although there were attempts by the Brahmins to construct an ideological framework within which the political systems in medieval Kerala hypothetically functioned, in fact the region witnessed the development of state forms which were distinct from each other in many respects.

Houses by the Sea

The interpretation of the pre-colonial Malabar political organisation as 'houses by the sea' by Dilip M. Menon seems to show a close resemblance to the reality of the situation in Kolathnadu. Menon envisages a politically and economically decentralized state structure in pre-colonial Malabar which seems to have been far more loosely organized than the 'segmentary state' model of Burton Stein. While for Stein at least there was a royal court at the 'core' to symbolize the 'ritual' function of the state, Menon posits that taravadus or large households in the interior of Malabar functioned as independent politico-economic units without any 'ritual core' distinction between the swarupams and taravadus in Malabar. It is likely that he does not assume such a distinction to be significant in the actual functioning of political relations in Malabar. This transforms his rendering of Malabar polity as 'houses by the sea' into a useful model from which to analyse the political relations in Kolathunadu.

He argues that the concept of kingship in Malabar actually developed around large household formations on the coast, such as that of the Zamorins, which depended entirely on the 'flows of trade from the interior to the coast and beyond'. Menon pursues his thesis by arguing that in Kerala 'monarchy was the story of an ever-shifting coalition of merchants, naval powers and the emergent court' and assumes the existence of a political equilibrium in Kerala during the pre-Portuguese period. He states that, 'based on access to a wide frontier such as the ocean, centralizing impulses had never arisen' and logically the impulse for a drive towards political centralization in medieval Kerala arrived late, becoming visible in the wake of the European impact The Zamorins of Calicut and the Travancore kingship were the products of conflicts with the Portuguese, Dutch, and the English commercial powers. In a nutshell, a full-fledged concept of kingship never developed in medieval Kerala and 'in northern Kerala kingship remained a failed experiment'.

Although I agree with Menon that the state structure in pre-colonial Malabar was far more fluid compared to other parts of the Sub-Continent, it should not be assumed that there were no centralizing forces before the arrival of the Europeans. Nevertheless it cannot be denied that the possibilities of maritime trade played an increasing role in shaping the process of state formation in the region. This particularly holds true in the case of the political system as it developed in early modern Kolathunadu.

As discussed elsewhere, the geographical features of Kolathunadu did not guarantee a large-scale agricultural surplus. Shaped by the limited agrarian economy in Kolathunadu, the possibility of a centralized political structure to emerge was limited. The constricted opportunity to exploit the limited agricultural surplus obviously restricted the chances of the Kolathiris to exercise considerable influence over the people of the region. Instead, there emerged a fluctuating field of powerful taravadus exercising control over the resources from their respective landed properties and the dependent labour-service classes. The insufficiency in rice production may also have assisted the evolution of 'communities of subsistence', 48 under the command of influential taravadus controlling the limited wet-land paddy fields during the pre-colonial period in the region. The peculiar state structure in Kolathunadu in the seventeenth and the eighteenth century has to be analysed against this background of the economic and concomitant social relations in Kolathunadu.

The maintenance of political dignity through the orchestration of ritual practices and commanding obedience and loyalty by the exercise of force required control over substantial economic resources. The income derived by the Kerala rajas depended on various sources such as income from royal estates, tolls and taxes on trade, kazcha (gifts), ankam (dual), purushantaram (succession fee), changatam (fee for special protection), fee on conferring titles and other covert 'taxes'. The swarupam's landed property was called cherikkal. These cherikkal lands were divided among the different lineages (taivazhis or mother's lineages) and lineage segments (kovilakams) of each swarupam. The income from a particular cherikkal was allotted to a person occupying a particular position (stanam) in the swarupam. This stanam was decided according to the muppu (eldership) within the swarupam, encompassing its various lineages and lineage segments. Therefore, the order of seniority (muppumura) was crucial not only to determine the stanam of a person within the swarupam's power hierarchy, but also to control the income from a particular cherikkal.

The 'right' of a stani (one who occupies a stanam) in a particular cherikkal was limited only to collecting a share of the produce of the land. The cherikkal lands were usually leased out to cultivators (pattam). The actual cultivators of the land were known as adiyalar. In this system, the right to collect a share of the produce, at least among the higher ranks, was usually given to 'officials' appointed by the raja, who were entitled to a monthly allowance and a certain amount for their personal expenses. A share of the income from cherikkal was also spent on religious purposes. Consequently, the income from the cherikkal was distributed at different levels of production relations and the ruling members enjoyed only a limited share of the income from cherikkal. This is particularly important considering the fact that there was no systematic, centralized system of land revenue in Malabar until the last quarter of the eighteenth century, when this region came under Mysorean control.

Kerala rajas did not enjoy any kind of ideological support to promote themselves as the supreme owner of the land (bhupati). Even from the Nambutiri Brahmanical point of view, it was they, not the rajas, who were the ultimate authority on the land. In the swarupam kingship, the raja did not appear as the supreme head of a land system in which the land derived its political value from which the state could systematically extract the revenue. Instead, he was an embodiment of authority which bound various power centres through such accoutrements of sovereignty as receiving gifts, conferring titles on influential personalities and nobles, punishing violations of customary practices and the like. The raja exercised control over a network of power relations, operating through various people of stature, by a combined strategy composed of ritual and authoritative instruments. Obviously, under such a construction the raja derived only a limited income from the agrarian surplus. Likewise, the other sources of income to which the raja were entitled such as ankam, gifts, purushantaram and suchlike, albeit of crucial importance to the realm of political and ritual relations, were invariably inconsistent and unreliable. In this context that income from trade and commerce acquired paramount importance for the raja.

Given the culmination of all these circumstances, it is natural that the swarupams in pre-colonial Kerala appear as 'houses by the sea', as many of them depended on maritime trade as an important source of income. Consequently, maritime centres, such as Maday and later Cannanore appear as the political centres of the Kolaswarupam. However, the Kolathiris and other kingships of Kerala never succeeded in establishing a decisive control over the commodity movements within their realm. Toll (chunkam), levied on commercial goods, was collected by 'men of prowess' sitting at different nodes of inland trade routes. Available evidence points to the fact that swarupam lineages also participated in this sharing of the trade income from inland commodity movements. The upshot was that the rajas had to be content mostly with the tolls derived from the maritime trade centres. Invariably, fluctuations in maritime income had a significant influence on the political fortunes of maritime trade-oriented swarupams.

The economic resources of the rajas of Kerala did not permit them to maintain a regular standing army of their own. Employing the Nairs in military service placed a heavy economic burden on the shoulders of the rajas. During military operations, which demanded large-scale deployment of the Nairs, these people were paid on a daily wage basis. It was not an unusual occurrence that Nairs who had not been paid by their employers for a long time would take service under other lords. It is probable that there was a military labour market in Malabar, constituted mainly of the traditional Nair militia plus other armed groups as Tiyyas and Mappilas. This easy availability of armed service and the inability of the Kolathiris to monopolize the use of force in the realm on account of their weak economic position meant that the outward appearance of regal authority remained more or less nominal. The swarupam polity in Kolathunadu exhibited the character of a political authority with limited access to economic resources which they had to share among different echelons of the political elites of the society. The Kolathiris had to sustain their political dignity within the constraints set by the limits of their economic resource base. The logical consequence of this was a limitation in the scope of political power in Kolathunadu and a diminished chance of developing a centralized state form in the region.

Compounding the inadequate resource base, the organization of political power within a swarupam also weakened the possibility of the growth of a strong centralized power. Political power in a swarupam was diffuse in nature. As mentioned earlier, the swarupams of Kerala were branched into lineages and lineage segments. Theoretically, each of these small political units of a swarupam was qualified to make a claim to the 'rajaship' on the basis of muppumura or eldership. The eldest male member from the various lineages/lineage segments of a swarupam assumed the 'rajaship', but even in such a position he did not enjoy full command over political authority in a swarupam. Within a swarupam, the authority was divided into and conferred on different members according to muppu, that is, in a descending order. This was known as kuruvazcha. Usually the eldest member of the reigning house (muttakuru) assumed the 'rajaship', and the next junior the elamkuru was designated as the immediate successor to the 'rajaship'. The politico-economic powers within lineages and lineage segments of a swarupam were also divided in a similar manner. When the segmentation of a swarupam into lineages and lineage segments grew more complex, the determination of muppu concomitantly grew more complex. The almost inevitable consequence was the power struggles among various lineages and lineage segments.

Therefore, in pre-colonial Kerala, kingship never appeared as the ultimate, single source of power. Instead, political authority remained a collective entity and was unevenly distributed within the swarupam. This fragmented character of political authority in Kerala in general and in Kolathunadu in particular, was the main obstacle to the emergence of a powerful king.

The Co-sharers of Kolathunadu

By the seventeenth century, the Kolaswarupam had to share its political authority with two other lineages in North Kerala. The Nileswaram (Alladam) Swarupam and the Arackal Swarupam claimed independent political identity. Moreover, political power within the Kolaswarupam was also disseminated into different kovilakams. In the Keralolpathi there are four kovilakams sharing the political authority of the Kolaswarupam namely: Talora Kovilakam; Arathil Kovilakam; Muttathil Kovilakam; and Karipathu Kovilakam. According to the Keralolpathi Kolathunadu tradition, the Karipathu Kovilakam claimed some sort of superiority over the others. However, it was the Palli Kovilakam and the Udayamangalam Kovilakam, as apparent from the Dutch records, which dominated the political scene of Kolathunadu. Both these kovilakams had again branched into various kovilakams, thereby, creating a network of 'political houses' within the Kolaswarupam. This testifies that the Kolaswarupam was not an exception to the general situation that existed among the other ruling houses of Kerala. Power, consequently was not embodied in the raja, but appeared in its collective form—the swarupam.

The taravadu appears as the basic unit of political and economic life in Kolathunadu. Beyond its spatial existence as a household with control over landed property, the taravadu was a ritually significant unit. Each taravadu had its own family deity or paradevata. Ancestral worship was a part of the ritual life of a taravadu. This reveals that each taravadu turned out to be a micro-reflection of the cosmic power, sakti, exhibiting its own unique identity in the social order. In Kolathunadu these dynamic autonomous taravadus were not organized hierarchically, on the basis a systematized holistic socio-political ideology. Although the Kolaswarupam maintained a distinguished status among these taravadus, political power was not confined exclusively to it. Powerful taravadus, sharing cosmic energy with the Kolaswarupam, enjoyed political power in the respective territories under their control.

The Kolaswarupam appears to have been nothing more than a complex form of taravadu, having greater control over the landed properties and other sources of affluence. It seems that Kolathunadu was constituted of numerous taravadus sharing different levels of political power in the realm and their difference was only in dimensions of power or sakti expressed through their social relations. Consequently, the nature of the relationship between the Kolaswarupam and the taravadus in Kolathunadu and the relationship among each other were determined by the sakti or power they possessed. The political picture of Kolathunadu during the seventeenth and the eighteenth century in a way resembled the South-East Asian polity described by Shelly Errington as a form of unevenly distributed energy field with various nodes of concentration.

The energy exists everywhere in the field, but it is unevenly distributed: in some places it is quite thin; in others, densely concentrated. The energy is continuous-there are no boundaries and no empty spaces, but only thinner and thicker concentrations. The energy in this filed is distributed not only unevenly, but unstably. It is continually moving, waxing and waning from particular locations. Its flux is usually, though not always, gradual. In addition to currents of energy, numerous visible objects occupy this field. One of the differences between the objects and the currents of energy is that the objects are discrete: they have boundaries and surfaces. Thus houses have walls, and humans have skin. But if we could see the energy, or if we were in the habit of thinking of the world in this way, we would understand that the boundaries or surfaces of these objects are the least important things about them. The objects provide locations and nodal points at which the energy collects, though in differing degrees of concentration.

In this model, a boundary oriented conceptualization of the state gives way to a disseminated political structure in which the concept of 'space' or 'territory' is relatively unimportant. This model is able to contain individuals, institutions, houses and palaces as a part of this power field, but, with variations in the concentration of power. The potency of the individuals and institutions is invisible and it is, as seen earlier, manifested through such signs indicating its presence as material wealth and the numerical strength of the people under its command. Neither the raja nor the Brahmins had a monopoly on this potency, but it was unequally distributed. However, the rajas, powerful households, Brahmin gramams certainly did manifest their potency through their wealth and entourage which differentiated them from the less potential majority of society.

The concentration of power was not fixed but was in an incessant state of flux, with the inherent possibility of the emergence or expansion of new nodes of power and waning or contraction of others. However, the total disappearance of the power nodes does not appear to have been a common phenomenon in the swarupam polities of Kerala, since the prevalent practice of adoption helped save the swarupams and taravadus—at least nominally from total extinction—on many occasions. Besides, establishing a 'territorial' authority through conquest was not the ideal of political power in Kerala. Instead of total annihilation, it was considered fair to merely reduce the sakti of the opponent.

The Kolaswarupam attained a special status of power in the realm through a gradual process of transformation over centuries with considerable fluctuations in its fortunes. It appears that the Kolathiris never exercised a monopoly of authority in the realm. Authority was a decentralized, shared, and pluralistic entity. Though Brahmanism envisaged a highly structured idea of political power, this ideology never figured prominently in the swarupam polity of Kolathunadu. Crucial political decisions pertaining to the realm were, in all probability, taken not by the Kolathiri alone, but in a 'council' of influential persons. They later even played a significant role in succession issues in the swarupam. Judicial and political decisions at the micro-level were taken independently by local 'men of prowess'.

The Kolaswarupam claimed a kind of titular sovereignty over Kolathunadu. The Kolathiri was the primus inter pares among the members of his own swarupam. Similarly, the Kolaswarupam enjoyed a premier status among the other taravadus in Kolathunadu. Indubitably in such a system, there was no concentration of power within a single entity. Instead, power remained fragmented and dispersed throughout the realm. These micro politico-economic units in the form of religious institutions, powerful taravadus, royal lineages and suchlike performed under a loosely knitted umbrella composed of personal loyalties. These power centres remained as floating entities either recognizing Kolathiri or some other ruler as their titular sovereign, maintaining varying degree of relations, or claiming independent political status. The actual power, however, remained with them in their respective territories. In other words, Kolathunadu and the Kolaswarupam were neither identical nor interchangeable identities. Kolathunadu remained a geo-cultural zone with loose, open borders of identity, consisting of numerous power centres. It was not unusual at any given time that more than one swarupam claimed authority over Kolathunadu, ineluctably casting the concept of a 'kingdom' in Kolathunadu with fixed political borders and a central authority in perpetual doubt.

During the seventeenth and eighteenth centuries, the Kolaswarupam became a more or less authoritative symbol without power when new power centres claiming political clout began to emerge. Canter Visscher portrayed eighteenth-century Kolaswarupam as follows.

The royal family consists of four branches, of which the present representatives, both male and female, are so numerous that they live in great poverty for the most part, though it is true that the State is well managed and that it possesses a good army.

At first glance, this statement in which the rulers of a well-organized state are portrayed as poor and underprivileged may appear paradoxical. In spite of its segmentation into various kovilakams through the course of centuries, the resource base of the Kolawarupam did not expand proportionately to sustain the growth of the house. It is probable that the landed property (cherikkal) did not expand on a considerable scale either. The economic position of the Swarupam became precarious because it did not enjoy any sort of control over the resources of Kolathunadu. The new venues of resource accumulation provided by Indian Ocean trade was appropriated by the newly emerging Mappila trading communities and other petty 'men of prowess' along the coast. Gradually, by the end of the seventeenth century, the Kolathiri transformed into a muted symbol of authority, reduced to virtual impotence in Kolathunadu.

The scope for applying a centre-periphery concept in the political order in Kolathunadu seems fairly limited. As we have already seen, the authority of the Kolaswarupam was diffused throughout its lineages. Even if we consider the Chirakkal Kovilakam as a sort of 'centre', the influence exercised by the 'centre' on the peripheral area was not directly proportionate to the distance between them. The Arackal Swarupam, though spatially very close to the 'centre', enjoyed independent political status. Ritual relationships between different political nucleuses were also not determined by spatial factors. The Alladam Swarupam (Nileswaram), which was politically closer to the Kolathiris, maintained ritual relations with the spatially more distant Zamorins of Calicut. In spite of this, from a modern perspective, seemingly 'chaotic' political situation, Kerala society appears to have developed its own system of balance based on some 'codes of conduct' known under different titles as maryada, margam, or acharam. These codes of social ethics determined the social behaviour of the people in the group, including its political elites. Dutch observers interpreted this phenomenon in their own terms. In 1743 Commander Stein van Gollenesse commented,

> Although the king and princes exercise great authority over their subjects, affairs are so regulated by the laws of Cheraman Perumal that their rule can in no way be called despotic. Subjects obey their king ungrudgingly as long as he remains within the limits of the law, and even if a chief were to wrong a few individuals, the whole community would not take up the quarrel. However, if he were to issue orders calculated to injure the interests of the whole community, they would not be obeyed.

Van Reede found the Kerala polity neither democratic, nor monarchic, nor oligarchic, but a combination of all of three. He deemed it an ideal type of polity where the weak were protected against the strong. However, these codes of conduct or as they were known the 'laws of Cheraman Perumal', should not be interpreted as a fixed constitution or a social contract but merely as a highly contingent description of the rules and objectives of the political game.

Therefore the fluctuations in the political fortunes of swarupams need to be explored not in the 'ritual' realm, but in terms of the economic forces which shaped and re-shaped these political forms. Economic forces determined their position in the political hierarchy of Kerala in relation to other rajas or 'feudal lords' such as naduvazhis and desavazhis and other power nodes. The cause of the success or failure of these ruling houses has to be sought in their success or failure to accumulate resources to support their claims. It was in this context that maritime trade attained such overwhelming importance in the regional political economy.

Lords of the Horses

As discussed earlier, the political power and the limited economic resources of the Kolaswarupam were dispersed among its lineages and lineage segments. Though the land of Kolathunadu was not suitable to extensive paddy cultivation, geo-climatic features combined to help it to produce high quality pepper and such other spices as cardamom, ginger, and wild cinnamon, which were in great demand throughout the Indian Ocean. The emergence of a number of port towns along the coast of Malabar was one of the most palpable consequences of this great demand for Malabar spices throughout world markets. Pertinently, Kolathunadu covered the extensive coastal belt of North Malabar which was suited to the development of a number of maritime trade centres. Spices produced in the hinterland were mainly shipped across the seas from these coastal port towns of Kolathunadu. The possibilities to accumulate income from maritime trade, supplementing the land-based returns would have been the main attraction for the local political elites. From this point of view, it is not surprising that the political seat of the Kolaswarupam was transferred, moving with the shift in the focus of maritime trade in the region.

Ezhimala, which was the original seat of the Kolathiris, was an important hub of maritime trade from an earlier period. The ancient sea ports of the region, such as Ilangopatanam,

Achalapatanam, and Kachilpatanam, were located in and around the general area of Ezhimala. It would be logical to assume that the disappearance of these old trading centres and the silting up of the old royal port city of Maday contributed to the emergence of Cannanore as the main port of the kingdom. The loss of status of Ezhimala as a maritime commercial hub might have been the deciding factor in the shifting of the political centre from Ezhimala to Cannanore—an emerging port town in the kingdom.

The name of the port city of Cannanore emerged from obscurity to the limelight of history only by the end of the fifteenth century, when the Portuguese appeared on the scene. The rapid growth of this port city was probably linked with the developments in Vijayanagara State during the fifteenth century. The expansionist thrust of the Vijayanagara rulers all over South India and their concomitant continuous conflicts with the Bahmani Sultanate compelled the former to search for an easy access to the horse trade of the Arabian Sea. Cavalry played a vital role in the military successes of the Vijayanagara rulers. Saletore commented; 'the foreign policy of the [Vijayanagara] rulers was to a large extent governed by the necessity of securing for themselves a continuous supply of horses from Ormuz'. Firishtah claims that the Vijayanagara army in 1443 was constituted of no less than 80,000 horsemen. Because these horses which were imported from West Asia had a short span of life, a continuous supply of horses to the Empire had to be maintained in order to keep the cavalry force up to strength.

During the second half of the fifteenth century, the Empire suffered great setbacks at the hands of the Bahmani Sultanate. Their control over the Konkan Coast gradually slipped from the hands of the Vijayanagara rulers. The massacre of Muslim traders at Bhatkal—the most important port in Konkan which supplied horses to the Vijayanagara kings—carried out on the orders of King THE RAJAS OF

Virupaksha in 1469 and the subsequent loss of control over Konkan and Goa greatly curtailed the direct access of the Empire to the ports along the southwest coast of the Indian Sub-Continent where horses from West Asia were disembarked. Varthema reported horses were very expensive in Vijayanagara, 'because those kings who hold the seaports do not allow them to be brought there.' This political condition favoured the prospects of Malabar ports, which were free of the political turmoil in the rest of South India. There is cogent evidence to back the claim that, exercising its influence on a large portion of peninsular India, the Vijayanagara State was an important hinterland of Malabar ports. The thriving presence of West Asian traders along the Malabar Coast made it easier for the Vijayanagara rulers to gain access to the West Asian horses imported into Malabar ports.

The geographical features of the port of Cannanore made it suitable to the disembarkation of horses. In contrast to the earlier ports of Kolathunadu, the location of this port was not located on a river estuary. This saved it from the dangers of silting up and it also favoured the close anchorage of ships which were hauled ashore by elephants. Of course, the trade in these war horses was a lucrative one. Each stallion, Barbosa reported, cost 'from four to six hundred cruzados, and some specially chosen for his own [King's] use he buys for nine hundred or a thousand cruzados'. Prior to the Portuguese success in transferring this money-spinning trade to Goa by the second decade of the sixteenth century, Cannanore had been reaping the profit from the horse trade for some considerable time and had served as the main port where the Persian horses were disembarked for the Vijayanagara monarchs.

The importance of the horse trade in the prosperity of this port town is also conspicuous from another point of view. On the eve of the arrival of the Portuguese, pepper, the most important commodity of maritime trade—produced in the hinterland of Cannanore—was usually transported to the port of Calicut for export. The success of the Zamorins in attracting the pepper supply from the hinterland of Cannanore with the help of the wealthy West Asian Muslim traders settled in Calicut deprived the Cannanore the most profitable branch of Malabar maritime trade. Nevertheless, Cannanore maintained its importance probably because of its strategic importance as the supplier of horses to the Vijayanagara monarchs. This is a cogent explanation of why the Vijayanagara ruler responded sharply to the problems between the Mappilas and the Portuguese at Cannanore in 1505, which could have affected the ongoing horse trade at the port.

Beyond this imperial interest, the horse trade constituted one of the main sources of the income of the Kolathiris before the Portuguese takeover of the trade in the sixteenth century. It earned them the nickname of 'lords of the horses'. Each horse, which was disembarked at the Cannanore port, provided an income of 25 ducats in port tax to the Kolathiri. These horses were taken via the inland trading routes across the Ghats to Vijayanagara. Considering the weak resource base of the Kolathiris, who depended on the rather meagre incomes from their private estates and customary payments from their subjects, this additional income must have certainly strengthened their political legitimacy. It is not surprising that the attempts of the Portuguese Estado to divert the horse trade from Cannanore to Goa elicited a vigorous protest from the Kolathiris.

The expropriation of the income from the horse trade, which had directly enriched the Kolathiris' exchequer, may have had an impact on the existing power relations in Kolathunadu. It was precisely at this juncture, contemporary Portuguese travellers noticed the gradual emergence of local Muslim traders as an influential factor in regional politics and indeed Cannanore witnessed the emergence of a Mappila royal family, known as the 'Arackal Swarupam', by the middle of the sixteenth century. It is noteworthy that the increasing clout of the Arackal Swarupam in the political sphere of Cannanore ran in a reverse with the waning economic position of the Kolathiris.

The Arackal Ali Rajas

The reinvigoration of political and economic conditions in West Asia after the emergence of Islam in the ninth century AD triggered remarkable changes in the pattern of the Indian Ocean trade. The Islamic trade diaspora established at various port cities across the Indian Ocean world intensified the trade relations between West Asia and India. This gradually brought about the emergence of

Islamic trade settlements in different parts of the Indian Ocean regions. The presence of Muslim traders along the coast of northern Kerala can probably be traced back as far as the emergence of Islam in West Asia itself. Since Kerala had commercial contacts with West Asia long before Islam entered the stage, it is not at all surprising that the religion newly sprung in Arabia should gain an early foothold on the Malabar Coast. At an early date, the temporary marriages (mutua) entered into by these Arab traders with the local women and the 'conversion' of the lower strata of the Malabar society gave rise to an autochthonous Muslim community along the coast—the Mappilas. In due course, the growing Islamic commercial presence stimulated the proliferation of a number of new trading centres along the Malabar Coast. Indeed, on the eve of the Portuguese arrival in Malabar, they were so powerful that 'if the King of Portugal had not discovered India, Malabar would already have been in the hands of the Moors, and would have had a Moorish King'. Although the commercial power of these Muslim traders (who were mainly West Asian Muslims) had somewhat abated by the second half of the sixteenth century because of the Portuguese attempt to control the pepper trade in Malabar, the Mappila Muslims remained the driving force behind the commercial prosperity of Cannanore, even during the Dutch period. One of the most important developments in the history of the Muslim community in Kolathunadu during the seventeenth century was the solid establishment of the Arackal Swarupam as one of the prominent taravadus in the political economy of the region.

Some scholars trace the origins of the Arackal Swarupam back to an earlier period. However, the available evidence does not allow an origin earlier than the sixteenth century. Ibn Battutta, who visited Malabar during the fourteenth century, gives a detailed description of the kingdoms and Muslim settlements along the Malabar Coast, but does not refers to the Arackal family. Also Duarte Barbosa, who lived in Cannanore as a Portuguese official for a long period, keeps silent about it. The earliest indigenous source which provides information on the origin of the Ali Rajas is the Arabic text Tuhfat-ul-Mujahidin written by Sheikh Zain-ud-Din in 1583. Zain-ud-Din, describing the political incidents during the Portuguese period, says that:

> In the year 952 A.H. [1526-7], 8 Muharram, Farangis [Portuguese] killed Abu Bakr Ali and his nephew Kunji Supi who where the leaders of the Muslims in Cannanore. Abu Bakr Ali is the uncle of Ali Adiraja of Cannanore and Kunji Supi is the father of Ali Adiraja.

It may appear remarkable that in this source a Muslim chief is styled 'raja'. Although we can see similar attempts to attain royal dignity on the part of some other Muslim trading magnates in Calicut during the sixteenth century, they failed to establish their authority as they were unsuccessful in overriding the established political power in the region. Whereas they failed, the Arackal Ali Rajas succeeded in evolving as an independent power centre within the traditional political setup of Kolathunadu.

The authority in the Arackal Swarupam, as that of other taravadus, was organized along the matrilineal line in which the muppu was the criterion by which to ascend in the power hierarchy within the house and become the Ali Raja. The immediate second stanam or position in the hierarchy was that of the Karanavar. Similar to other swarupam polities, power was not concentrated in the hands of the Ali Rajas, but disseminated within the Arackal Swarupam and was shared by various 'men of prowess' in the Bazaar. The Karanavar, who was the immediate second to the Ali Raja in the line of succession in the Swarupam, also wielded considerable influence in the commercial and political life of Cannanore. The account of Alexander Hamilton incontrovertibly reveals that other influential Mappilas of the Bazaar shared power alongside the Ali Raja. This indicates the inner working of a 'bazaar government' run by various co-operating merchants.

However, in comparison with the other swarupams in Kerala, the distribution of authority within the Arackal Swarupam appears to have been less complex, pointing towards the comparatively recent origin of the house. One of the peculiar customs of this Swarupam which differentiated it from other taravadus was that women known as the 'Arackal Beebis' were not excluded from muppumura making them free to attain the highest position in the hierarchy. Unlike other taravadus, the Arackal Swarupam attained its legitimacy in the regional power system not through its control of landed properties, but through maritime trade.

Nevertheless, its limited control over the land does not seem to have adversely affected the legitimacy of the Arackal Swarupam in asserting its status in Kolathunadu, as controlling 'land' did not necessarily imply the possession of sakti. It was the control over people which counted more in this regard. The Arackal Swarupam successfully exercised control, albeit of varying intensity, over a large number of people who were associated with the maritime enterprise of the house in Malabar. The surplus accumulated through trade undoubtedly helped the Swarupam to expand its influence over people, who subsequently became integrated into the extensive redistribution system functioning under the Ali Rajas.

Consonant with the postulated state of flux in the region, which can be associated with the waxing and waning of sakti, the dependent groups were constituted of fluctuating circles at different levels. While the Swarupam effectuated its direct, that is, more stable sway over an inner circle consisting mainly of the Cannanore Bazaar, its influence became more dissipated towards outer circles. Obviously such control was essentially fragile and inconsistent. It entirely depended on the success or failure of the Swarupam in maintaining its control over the regional maritime trade and hinterland trade networks. The political strategies adopted by the Arackal Swarupam in its dealings with both the European companies and local elites in Cannanore during the pre-colonial period have to be analysed from this perspective.

Moreover, the significant role of the Ali Rajas in the coastal rice trade gave rise to a 'community of subsistence' under the Arackal Swarupam. Given the failure of the region to produce surplus rice to support its entire population, the rice trade with Canara was crucial to the day-to-day life of Kolathunadu. The nearly complete dependence of the Cannanore Bazaar and its vicinity on this supply significantly strengthened the legitimacy of the Arackal Swarupam. It seems that the Arackal House worked along the same line as the wet-land controlling taravadus in Kolathunadu which were supposed to provide subsistence for the dependent communities of labourers and service classes. Succinctly, the Arackal Swarupam replicated the regional political taravadus in all aspects. It evolved into the embodiment of sakti exercising control over a significant resource base and a widespread community of dependents across the region. This formed the essence of the political legitimacy of the Arackal Swarupam in Kolathunadu. The folk traditions of the region also locate the political status of the said Swarupam within the cultural matrix of Kolathunadu, in which the Arackal Swarupam is depicted as a nodal point of sakti within the regional cosmic order.

Legitimacy and Sakti

As in the case of other political families of Kerala, the origin of the Arackal House is entangled in various 'myths' and 'legends'. As there were with the history of the Kolaswarupam, there were attempts to rationalize the influential political status attained by the Arackal House from both Brahmanical and regional perspectives. Here we find various traditions linking the Arackal House either to the Kolaswarupam or to the legendary Cheraman Perumal depending on the viewpoint of the narrator. While some of these 'legends' explain the origin of this family as an offshoot of the Kolaswarupam, thereby pointing its right to share the political dignity of the latter, the Arackal Swarupam itself traced its origin directly to Cheraman Perumal. However, the first legend seems to have been more popular than the latter in the seventeenth-eighteenth centuries. This is conspicuous from the reports sent by VOC officials concerning the Ali Rajas.

They [the Ali Rajas] have their origin from a princess of Kolathiri who was made pregnant by a prominent Moor or Arab and who in due course was reconciled with the King, and had the honorary title of Crau or prince bestowed on him and with the power over the Muslim bazaar [of Cannanore], the Lakkadive Islands and many other good lands.

With a little deviation, in his Memoir the Dutch chief Adriaan Moens also refers to this story: He is of Kolathiri extraction. A certain princess of this dynasty, on account of having to do with a person of lower standing, had lost her caste or nobility, and in order to cover up the disgrace, she was given in wedlock to a rich Arabian Moor on whom was conferred the title of prince and the general name of Ady Ragia, in that country indicating that he was the head of the Moors of that kingdom.

Whatever the authenticity of this story may be, the permeation of it in the society indicates that it attained a sort of historicity among at least a segment of the people, allowing them to come to terms with the powerful presence of the Ali Raja in the political economy of Kolathunadu. In spite of such a strong articulation of the legend in the society, there is no evidence to show that the Ali Raja depended on it to legitimize his political power in Kolathunadu. The available correspondence of the Kolaswarupam and the Ali Rajas with the Dutch Company in Kerala does not refer to this relationship between the two swarupams. This indicates that the actual power relations in Kolathunadu were not articulated essentially through such 'legitimacy' claims, but through sakti.

Interestingly, the Brahmin view articulated though the Keralolpathi legend tried to delineate the Ali Rajas as pure traders without any political and nuptial relations with the Kolaswarupam.

This could be considered a deliberate ideological move on the part of the Brahmins to explain the powerful presence of the Arackal family in Kolathunadu within the varna order, in which the Ali Rajas were attributed the status of a Vaishya. Whatever the ideological overtones of such a story, the very appearance of the Ali Rajas in this Brahmanical narrative itself proves the incontrovertible position attained by the former in the power structure of Kolathunadu.

Theoretically, the Ali Raja derived authority from the Kolathiri. In practice, at least by the seventeenth century, the claim of the Kolathiris to political superiority over the Ali Rajas did not have any actual relevance in determining the power status of the Ali Rajas in Kolathunadu. The endeavours of the Dutch Company to grasp the inner workings of the power relations in Cannanore often met with difficulties and its officials had a hard time comprehending the dynamics of the local society. Van Reede, who showed a special interest in understanding the Kerala body politic, did discern the peculiarity of the regal status enjoyed by the Arackal family. In his attempt to interpret the political status of the Ali Rajas in Kolathunadu, he was confronted with the task of explaining the title 'raja' attached to them. He observed that the title 'Ali Raja' does not mean that 'he wields a regal or sovereign authority over the other Muslims, as it was meant [by the Dutch] in the beginning' of their establishment in Cannanore. Van Reede qualifies this title only as an honorary epithet bestowed on the Ali Raja by the 'real' raja—the Kolathiris. He felt it a mistake on the part of the Company to make its earliest commercial dealings in Cannanore with the Ali Raja after adopting the misconception that was he 'an independent lord of the Muslims'.

Nevertheless, undeniably this new realization of the 'actual' political status of the Ali Rajas had to do more with the recognition of the Ali Raja as the main commercial competitor of the Company in Cannanore, whose power was completely dependent on trade and shipping. In spite of this, Van Reede's remarkable observation made clear the limited scope of 'rajaship' in Kerala—at least in the case of the Ali Rajas. The Arackal Swarupam, as did the other swarupams of Kerala, did not exercise any sort of territorial sovereignty over a well-defined 'kingdom'. Its political status and consequently its authority were characterized by a network of personal relations transgressing spatial limits. The Arackal

Swarupam maintained control over a group of dependents, operating as a part of a commercial network which blurred regional concepts and social identities. The nucleus of this maritime kingdom was in Cannanore from where the control mechanism was operated. In brief, the Arackal Swarupam was a 'house by the sea', which attained its regal status through maritime trade.

Many of the foreign travellers who visited Kerala during the sixteenth and the seventeenth century did not fail to observe the contradiction between power and status. This indicates the inherent tension within the socio-political setup of Kerala. At the beginning of the sixteenth century, Tome Pires commented; 'There are great kaimals in this country, some of whom are greater than many of these kings, though they have not the title of king'. His concept of 'greatness' was concomitant with military power. Barbosa also mentioned the great lords of Malabar 'who wish to be called kings, which they are not'. In his interpretation, kingship in Malabar was something expressed through special privileges from which others were barred, such as minting coins and roofing houses with tiles. Nevertheless, he was not blind to the fact that these prerogatives could have been achieved by force. Barbosa attributes kingship to only three political powers in Kerala, such as 'Venattadikal' (the king of Travancore); Kolathiri; and the Zamorin of Calicut. The subtle differences between a 'king' and a 'lord' emerge more explicitly in the narrative of Pyrard of Laval. He noticed the existence of 'petty kings of petty territories' enjoying sovereign power in their own lands, albeit vaguely subordinated to a greater king. He makes only a subtle difference between these little lords and 'great king'—a difference in power.

The narrowing difference in the resource base of the old royal houses and the newly emerging power centres is visible in these foreign observations. The subtle differences among the various lords of Malabar who were striving to develop new resource bases, especially through maritime trade, created a complex socio-political situation in which incessant conflicts and ever-changing power relations became a common feature. This development was apparent in Kolathunadu, where the Kolaswarupam was gradually losing its political claims to newly emerging power groups. In this context, it is noteworthy that the rise of the Arackal family to the position of a royal lineage was not merely attributable to its 'ritual' relationship with the Kolaswarupam. The political status of the

Arackal family in Kolathunadu was elevated by its success in achieving power or sakti, which ineluctably legitimized its position within the traditional power concept of Kolathunadu. This is conspicuously apparent in the account of Pyrard of Laval who visited this region in the first decade of the seventeenth century.

The people of the country [Cannanore] have told me that it is not long since the Malabars [Muslims] of Cannanore were in like condition with the rest of their race, and obeyed that

Nair King [Kolathiri], but that they became so strong that they made a king for themselves, and no longer recognised the Nair king nor paid him any tribute: he resides far in the interior, and is often at war with the king of Cannanore.

By the end of the sixteenth century, the control exercised by the Ali Rajas over the Laccadive and the Maldive Islands made them the unassailable merchant magnates of Cannanore. It is interesting to note that although the relationship between the Muslim traders of Cannanore and Calicut was very cordial throughout the sixteenth and seventeenth centuries, in particular in their mutual struggle against the Portuguese, in 1599 the Ali Raja held himself aloof from the final struggle of Kunjali Marakkar IV against the Portuguese-Zamorin alliance. In fact, it appears that he was on the most amicable terms with the Portuguese at Cannanore. Here the Ali Raja's conduct was first of all that of a pragmatic commercial leader rather than that of an Islamic leader, which bought him political success. In spite of its close contact with the Islamic world around the Indian Ocean rim, the Arackal Swarupam did not introduce a new concept of kingship into Malabar or perhaps it was not able to do so in the existing economic-cultural environment of Kolathunadu. Its power was deep-rooted in the traditional socio-cultural milieu of Kolathunadu. The Arackal House was only a facsimile of the existing Malabar kingship—a swarupam kingship brought about and nourished by the traditional ideology of power in Kolathunadu.

Conclusion

Pre-colonial Kolathunadu presents the picture of a political system in which power was disseminated in numerous socio-political components or taravadus. The Kolaswarupam claimed a primus inter pares status among these power groups, which it justified by its superior control over the resources derived from landed properties and maritime trade. This obviously helped the Kolathiris to maintain a larger dependent populace within the bounds of their distributive system.

However, the gradual hiving off of the Kolaswarupam in the course of time into various lineages naturally resulted in the segmentation of the resource base of the Swarupam, which undermined its superior claims in the social hierarchy. Over and beyond this, new nodes of power began to emerge by successfully appropriating a chunk of the limited resource base of the region. The emergence of the Arackal Swarupam by the middle of the sixteenth century effectively closed off the possibility for the Kolaswarupam to extract fiscal surplus from the Indian Ocean trade. The only possibility open to it to extract fiscal surplus was through agricultural expansion. This was its Achilles' heel as

Kolathunadu is a narrow strip of land lying between the Western Ghats and the Arabian Sea and could not provide sufficient space for the development of an extensive agricultural sector. The unfavourable demographic concentration also adversely affected the agricultural expansion in the region. The limited scope in the economic sphere prevented the Kolaswarupam from developing into a centralized political system with a strong resource base. Instead, by the seventeenth century, it had faded into a weak symbol of authority, deprived of any actual power.

In the peculiar socio-economic atmosphere of the region, the locally entrenched concept of sakti seems to be more relevant than the Brahmanical conceptualisation of kingship. Power, manifested through such signs as material wealth, political momentum, charisma, and the ability to sustain a dependent community under control, was well suited to encompassing various emerging power groups within its frame. There seems a good case to argue that the acceptance of the Arackal Swarupam as an intrinsic part of the local socio-cultural system was made possible by the open, ideological premise of sakti. By the seventeenth century, the Arackal Swarupam successfully emerged as a power centre in the regional cosmos through the accumulation of wealth from oceanic trade by the seventeenth century. Control over a trade network and the resultant formation of a dependent community facilitated the Arackal Swarupam in entrenching its political status in Kolathunadu. This decisive importance of maritime commerce in determining the socio-political status of the Mappilas in general and the Ali Rajas in particular in Kolathunadu call for an analysis of the emergence and expansion of a maritime trade network under the Ali Rajas in a long-term perspective.

Balija

Balija is a sub caste of the Kapu or Naidu caste of Andhra Pradesh. They are an Agrarian/Merchant/Warrior community spread out in the Indian states of Andhra Pradesh (concentrated in the Rayalaseema region), Tamil Nadu, Karnataka and Kerala. They are also referred to by their caste title Naidu and Naicker. Kapus constitute about 25% of the total population of Andhra Pradesh. The Balija Sub-Caste is Classified as an O.C (Forward Caste) by the Government of Andhra Pradesh.

Origin:

- Kapus were the inhabitants of the Andhra region, people who migrated from the north, cleared forests for agriculture and built settlements.
- Kapu are the descendants of the Kaampu tribe, an Indo-Aryan tribe, which migrated from Kampilya, Mithila and Ayodhya, ancient cities situated in the Gangetic Plains of North India.
- This migrant tribe initially settled down along the banks of the Godavari river, cleared forests and built Settlements and Towns. To this day, a heavy concentration of Munnuru Kapus and Telagas are found on the banks of the Godavari in the North Telangana districts of Adilabad, Nizamabad, Karimnagar, Warangal, Khammam and the coastal districts of East Godavari and West Godavari, in which lies the Godavari delta and the Krishna Delta (Krishna & Guntur Dt).
- The settlement slowly spread among the geographical area of the three Shaiva Lingams of Draksharamam (East Godavari district), Srisailam (Kurnool district) and Srikalahasti (Chittor district).
- This Settlement& Geographical Area was referred to as Tri-linga Desam in the Ancient Texts and the people who were settled in this region were called Telaga and the language spoken by them was called Telugu.

- This settlement of Telagas started referring to themselves as Balija when the Balijas became quite prominent in the medieval period (around about 1000 CE) with their political and economic contributions by primarily the Setty Sub-Division of Balija.
- The Kapus were primarily a military/agrarian community who took up military service and were into cultivation during peace time. Consequently the Kapu subcastes also evolved based on occupation.
- Kapu subcastes dedicated to military service included Telaga, Munnuru Kapu and Ontaris (who served as special forces). Munnuru Kapu's were a detachment of the Telagas who migrated to the current Telangana Districts and served under the Kakatiyas and Nizams.
- Kapus engaged in trade were referred to as Balija. Balijas who took up military service and protected trading caravans were called Balija Nayakulu or Balija Naidu.
- A significant number of Kapus have today diversified into industry, arts and academia. However, a substantial segment of the population are still farmers.

Sub Castes

The other geographical names of Balija are:

- Kapu (In Andhra, people refer themselves as Kapu without mentioning the sub-caste).
- Balija (Rayalaseema region and Nellore district of Andhra Pradesh, Tamil Nadu and Karnataka regions).
- Telaga (Coastal Andhra and Telangana Regions)
- Munnuru Kapu (Telangana Region of Andhra Pradesh and erstwhile Hyderabad Region)
- Ontari (Coastal districts like East Godavari, West Godavari and Visakhapatnam)
- Turpu Kapu (Northern costal region of Andhra Pradesh).

The Balija Sub-Caste of Andhra Pradesh & Tamil Nadu are classified as an O.C (Forward Caste) but they are sometimes confused to be a B.C. (Backward Caste) since a lot of other Castes also carry the Suffix Balija in their Caste Names.

Note Perika Balija, Krishna Balija/Dasari, Surya Balija, Voda Balija (Fishermen), Vada Balija (Boya), Ediga Balija/Goud (Toddy Tappers), Chettu Balija/Goud (Toddy Tappers) of Coastal Andhra, Ontari-Mudiraj Ayyaraka Patrulu, Venna Kapu, Kapu Savara, Konda Kapu and Reddy Subcastes (Dommari Kapu. Godugulanati Kapu, Kodithi Kapu, Kuruva Kapu, Musugu Kapu, Nallevelama Kapu, Pakanati Kapu, Paala Kapu, Palle Kapu, Panta Kapu, Pedakanti Kapu, Pokanati Kapu, Sajjana Kapu, Velama Kapu, Yerlam Kapu) are not part of the Kapu/Balija Caste.

Etymology of Balija:

- It is believed that when Kapus organised themselves into their own trading guilds, such as 'veera balanja', then the Sanskrit term vanijya became balanja and balija, just as it became it became baniya in other places.
- Thurston and Rangachari describe the Telugu trading classes as fire-born merchant and artisan castes: Balijas (with their offshoots Kavarais and Janappans) believe they originated when their God Chamundeshwari threw rice into the sacrificial fire from which a host of warriors sprang out.
- Bali in Sanskrit means tax. The Balijas also served as tax-collectors during medieval times in Andhra and Karnataka.
- The word 'balija' has not been found in old inscriptions. According to the book "Symbols of substance, court and state in Nayaka period Tamilnadu":
- The balijas of Karnataka claim to have derived their term as descendents of a king named Ballaja of Hoysala or Kadama dynasty. However, there is no evidence to the same.
- Primarily agriculturists, traders or warriors by occupation they seem to have been formed by a small social change that seem to have occurred among some sections of the Kapu community according to some historians. The original Balijas seem to have migrated from the Balijipeta of Srikakulam District.
- The Balija trace their mythological origins to Himavanta (father of Parvati) when he sacrificed a bull to Lord Brahma and from the fire emerged a person who brought forth

combs, bangles, perfumes, sandals, powder, beads, and coloured half-leaf rolls for the ear for Parvati (Government Of Madras Staff, P. 105 Gazetteer of the Nellore District: brought up to 1938).

- Veera Balaingyas were mentioned in Chalukyas of Badami, Kakatiya dynasty inscriptions as powerful and wealthy merchants who were known as "Five Hundred Lords of Ayyavolu" (or modern Aihole in Bagalkote District of Karnataka State). They were highly respected in the Chalukyan and Kakatiya society. The Setty Balijas were primarily tax collectors and merchants.
- Balijas shared the same history with Kunbi and Kurmis. Kunbhee in Hindustani is known as Kapu in Telugu.
- According to David West Rudner in 'Religious Gifting and Inland Commerce in Seventeenth-Century South India' (The Journal of Asian Studies, Vol. 46, No. 2 (May, 1987), page 361): "Balija Chettis are a caste that fissioned off from Balija Nayaks ("warrior") caste as recent as the 19th century. Accordingly they have closer kinship ties to these Nayak warriors than to Chetti merchants".
- According to the 1891 census data, the merchant groups of Agrawal, Khatri, Balija, Barnwal together constituted just 5% of the population. However, in the census of 1981, Balija formed 22.5% of the total population of Andhra Pradesh. It may be hypothesised that the Balija grouping received members from other castes during this time as a generic term for 'trader'. This may be so expected since the ties of kin and caste did play an important but unexplored role in South Indian commerce.

Note Most of the Western Historians who based their research from Madras often used to collate other castes like Perika, Voda, Surya Balija, Ediga Balija with the Balija Naidus without tracing their origin to the Mother caste Kapu.

Balija Branches

- Balija Naidu
- Gajula Balija/Sugavansi (pure) Balija. Myth is that Siva's wife Parvati did a severe penance in order to look beautiful for Shiva. A man sprung from the sacrificial fire and this

person was the ancestor of the Gajula Balija. The Gajulu Balija are known as Kavarai in Tamil Nadu.

- Kota Balijas or Kaacha Balijas
- Rajamahendravaram Balija or Musukama Balija, traders named after a special ear ornament worn by women. They are named after the Rajamahendram town of Rajahmundry.
- Kavarai (Kavara Balija Naidu or Gavara Balija Naidu).
- functioned as taluka headmen)
- Anamala
- Gandavallu (or Gundapodi Vandlu, supposed to have been originally Komatis. They sold turmeric, kumkum (colour powder), dye powder, beads, combs, cosmetics, etc.
- Linga (Lingayat bâlijas)
- Ralla (a sub-sect of Kurubas, traded in precious stones, sub-sect Muktyala or Mutyala traded in Pearls)
- Pagadala (traded in Corals, also a sub-sect of Ralla)
- Pusa (traded in Beads, also supposedly a sub-division of the Yerukulas that is also called as Korvanji)
- Ravuth (Ravuthan or Rowthan, title of Kannadiyan)
- Gonuguntla (Desayi Chettis named after a village Gonuguntla)
- Gandavarapu (Gonuguntla balijas who migrated to Cuddapah)
- Gopati (Gopita or Gopa balija, also a title)
- Mulaka (sold roots, village vaidhyas, also name of a tribe)
- Miriyala (pepper traders)
- Nemilli (peacock)
- Pakanati
- Poludasu
- Oppanakkaran (Trader).

Balija Historical Dynasties

The Balijas were well-known in the several kingdoms as traders/merchants who were appointed as tax-collectors for various vassal states. Their involvement in the formation of several rich and powerful trading guilds wielded considerable power in the social structure.

One such trading guild was the Ayinavol trading guild in Prakasam District. Balija Naidus rose to power during the 1300-1700 AD with the advent of the Vijayanagar Empire when they were appointed as poligars and nayakas.

The Vijayanagar rulers had a policy of consolidating power by granting the Palegars/Poligars, Palaiyakkarar local Administrative rights.

And they in turn relied on the bands of soldiers that these Paleggallu/Palegars put at the disposal of the Vijayanagar rulers in times of war. While not being restricted to controlling small princely states as Palegars/Poligars, some the Balijas eventually commanded some of the biggest kingdoms in the form of Madurai Nayaks, Thanjavur Nayaks and Kandi Nayaks (Ceylon/Srilanka).

They ruled in Tamil Nadu with 13 lines of Kings for about 300 years. Some of the famous kings were:

Madurai Dynasty

- Garikepati (Kotikam) Nagama Nayaka
- Kotikam Nayakas [Viswantha Nayaka, Kumara Krishnappa Nayaka, Muthu Krishnappa Nayaka, Tirumala Nayaka, Muthu Alakadri Nayaka, Chokkanadha Nayaka, Ranga krishna Muthu Veerappa Nayaka, [Rani Mangamma belongs to Raja Kambala Naicker, Tuluva Nayaka (pronounced Tholuva in Tamil) belongs to Tuluvas Community Originated from Tulu Nadu in Coastal Karnataka and spread in Rayalaseema during the Tuluva dynasty rule in Vijayanagara], Vijaya Ranga Chokkanatha Nayaka and Rani Meenakshi].

Thanjavur Dynasty

- Alluru Nayakas and [Sevappa Nayaka, Achutappa Nayaka, Raghunadha Nayaka, Vijayaraghava Nayaka].
- Chenji/Gingee Dynasty
- Tupakula Krishnappa Nayaka and [Chennappa Nayaka, Gangama Nayaka, Venkata Krishnappa Nayaka, Venkata Rama Bhupaala Nayaka, Thriyambamka Krishnappa Nayaka, Varadappa Nayaka, Ramalinga Nayani Vaaru, Venkata Perumal Naidu, Periya Ramabhadra Naidu].

Channapatna Dynasty

- Rana Jagadeva Raya and his family ruled the territory of Baramahal along with a large strip of the Mysore plateau stretching to the Western Ghats. They ruled from Channapatna as the capital City in the present Karnataka State. Rana Peda Jagadeva Raya, Rana Immadi Jagadeva Raya, Rana Ankusa Raya, Rana Kumara Jagadeva Raya, Rana Immadi Ankusa Raya were some notable members in this line.

Some prominent kings left a legacy worth its mention in every Indian history book in the form of several temples and forts built in Tamil Nadu during this period, like the Tirumala Nayaka Mahal and commissioning the re-building of the Madurai Meenakshi Temple.

The following were the Kingdoms of Balija Naidus.

- Madurai Nayaks
- Tanjavur Nayaks
- Chandragiri Nayaks who ruled Chandragiri
- Kandy Nayaks who ruled Sri Lanka
- Gingee Nayaks/Chenchi Nayaks, Thundeera
- Channapatna Rayas who ruled Baramahal area.

Apart from these there were several small kingdoms and principalities which formed the power structure on which the Vijayanagar Kingdom flourished.

- Kattabomman Veerapandiya Kattabomman belonged to Raja Kambala Naicker branch of Balija Naidu caste (Kavarai) whose ancestors migrated to Tamil areas from parts of Andhra and erstwhile areas of Andhra Pradesh such as Bellari in the present day Karnataka. They attained the name Raja Kambala as they being Royal Kavarai (Balija) Naickers used to perform ceremonies placing the worshipping articles on a carpet (Kambali).
- Salaraju Tirumala Nayak of Madurai is Kapu.
- Penukonda After Krishna Deva Raya, Venkatapathi Rayalu, the Emperor of Vijayanagar, took over. He made Raya Dalavayi Koneti Naidu (son of Kasturi Naidu, grandson of Akkappa Naidu, great-grandson of Kanaka Naidu of

Chandragiri), as the governor of Penukonda and conferred him the title with Maha-raja-raja-sri and celebrated Koneti Naidu's marriage to Swarna. Koneti Naidu hailed from the Vasarasi family of Balija caste. Koneti Naidu ruled Penukonda, Rayadurga and Kundurpi Forts for about 17 years (1635-1652AD). After the ruling of Koneti Nayudu his discendants Raya Dalavayi Sri Venkatapathi Nayudu, Peda Timmappa Nayudu, Venkatapathi Nayudu, Koneti Nayudu, Venkatapathi Nayudu, Rajagopala Nayudu, Timmappa Nayudu ruled this Penukonda country.

For a brief period after the Battle of Tallikota in 1565, Penukonda became capital of Vijayanagara kingdom.

- Ananthapur, Bukkarayapatnam, Dharmavaram [Linga Balijas of Hande Family. Hande Hanumappa Nayudu (1569–1582), Immadi Hampanaidu (1583–1595), Malakappa Naidu(1595–1619), His 4th Son Hampa Naidu (1619–1631), Siddappa Naidu (1631–1659), Pavadappa Naidu(1659–1671), Ramakka (1671–1690), Siddappa Naidu (1690–1696), Prasannappa Naidu (1696–1719), Pavadappa Naidu (1719–1737), Siddappa Naidu (1737–1740), Ramappa Naidu (1740–1745)]
- Tadipatri and Poddatur. Hande Malakappa Naidu's (1595–1619), 1st Son Devappa Naidu and his descendents.
- Bellari, Kurgodu and Surrounding Districts. Hande Malakappa Naidu's (1595–1619), 2nd Son Chinna Ramappa Naidu and his descendents.
- Konderpi and Kanakal: Hande Malakappa Naidu's (1595–1619), 3rd Son Lingappa Naidu and his descendents.
- Raya Durgam
- Kotakonda family Koneti Naidu
- Ramagiri
- Kalyanadurgam (of Butna family).
- Chandragiri
- Udayagiri
- Ramabhadra Nayak
- Poligars, land owners and tax collectors of Tamil Nadu where of Balija origin.

Sources, including the books, Social Changes among Balijas and Balijakula Charithra mention that the Madurai, Thanjavur, Khandi (Kandy), Thundeera (Gingee/Chenchi), Krishnadeva Raya and the Araveeti kings of Vijayanagar empire were interrelated and from the Balija/Kapu community.

A. Vijaya Kumari and Sepuri Bhaskar in their book 'Social Change Among Balijas' recorded (page 3) that the "Balija kings of Madurai and Tanjore claim to be Kshatriyas of Kasyapa gotra, while the Vijayanagar Rais say they are lineal descendents of sage Bharadwaja. Others trace their ancestry to the Kauravas of the Mahabharata. These Kshatriya descendents are an offshoot of the Kammas or Kapus, or they are a mixed community recruited from these and other Telugu castes".

Description of Sub-sects

- Balija Naidu: seem to have formed during the Kakatiya dynasty primarily to protect the Balija/Setty trading caravans from being attacked by bandits.
- Shetty Balija: These were rich and powerful traders and merchants of the Kakatiya Dynasty. There was mention of some very old trading guilds concentrated in Bellary in Karnataka. In fact historians suggest this was the first branch in Balijas.
- As per Thurston of "Castes and Tribes of Southern India", Kavarai is the name for Balijas (Telugu trading caste), who have settled in the Tamil country. Kavarais call themselves Balijas (Born from fire). They use the titles Naidu, Nayakkan, Chetti or Setti and Nayak. Kavarai or Gavarai is said to be a corrupt form of Kauravar or Gauravar, as descendants of Kuru of Mahabharata as Kauravas.
- According to Jogendranath Bhattacharya in "Hindu Castes and Sects" though Kavarais were originally devoted entirely to agriculture in the capacity of land owners, and their lands were cultivated by inferior castes, they were also involved in the other professions such as trading, sailing etc. Gajula Balija is the largest sub-division of Kavarais. The equivalent name for Gajula Balija in Tamil is Valaiyal Chetti. Gajula Balijas attained this name as they were involved in manufacturing and selling bangles. The other branch of the Kavarais was Kambalattars (Thottiyars/

Thottiyans). Kambalattars were originally Telugu speaking cultivators that migrated from Telugu and Karnataka lands to Western parts of Madura Country in sixteenth century during the reign of Madurai Nayaks. They had found employment in Madurai Balija Nayak dynasty and also got promoted as Poligars. The famous chieftain Veerapandiya Kattabomman Naicker belonged to this branch of Balija caste (Rajakambala Balija). Kambalattars primarily practiced Vaishnavism. They were known to be energetic and industrious people.

- Kota Balija: Few dynasties of Vijayanagara Empire, Madurai Nayaks, Thanjavur Nayaks, Gingee Nayaks and Nayaks of Kandy Kingdom dynasties were from this line. There are multiple references available divulging the interrelationship of Madurai, Thanjavur and Vijayanagar kings of Balija caste. Apart from historians such as Thurston, Rangachari and R.V.Russel there are others that attest to the Balija affiliation of the kingdoms of Thanjavur, Madurai and Vijayanagar.

According to the "Gazetteer of the Nellore district: Brought up to 1938" by the Government of Madras staff, the Desa section of Balija caste comprises the descendents of the Nayak kings of Madura, Tanjore and Vijayanagar. As per G.S.Ghurye in "Caste and Race in India", the Nayak kings of Madura and Thanjavur were Balijas. According to "Questioning Ramayana: A South Asian Tradition" by Paula Richman, the Thanjavur king Raghunatha Nayudu belonged to Balija caste. King Sevappa Naidu, the founder of Thanjavur dynasty and the predecessor of king Raghunatha Naidu had married the sister-in-law of Vijayanagar emperor Achyutha Deva Raya (half-brother of the emperor Sri Krishnadevaraya).

Racha, Rachu or Rachevar, is a title found in Balija, Dora, Golla, Kapu, Konda, Koya, Majjulu, Mutracha and Velama. The sect Ranagere were military and the sect Sarige were gold-lace (zari) makers.

Contribution to Literature

Balija kings encouraged many poets and contributed to literature themselves. The following is the list of Balja Naidus that made their contribution to Telugu and Sanskrit languages.

- Raghunatha Naidu (Thanjavur king): Sangeetha Sudha, Ramayana Katha Sangrahamu, Bharatha Katha, Sangrahamu, Ramayanam, Parijathapaharanam, Nalabhyudayamu, Achyuthabhyudayamu, Valmiki Charithram.
- Vijaya Raghava Naidu (Thanjavur king, son of Raghunatha Naidu): Raghunatha Nayakabhyudayamu, Yakshaganas and composition of poems.
- Pasupuleti Rangajamma (One of the queens of Vijaya Raghava Naidu): Mannarudasa Vilasam.
- Queen Ganga Devi (wife of Vijaya Nagar prince Kumara Kampana): Madhura Vijayam.
- Samukham Venkata Krishnappa Naidu (Poet in the court and Army chief of Vijaya Ranga Chokkanatha Naidu of Madura dynasty): Jaimini Bharatham, Ahalya Sankradana Vilasam, Radhika Santhwanam, Saarangadhara Charithra.
- Thupakula Anantha Bhoopaludu (Poet and Dalavai of Vijaya Ranga Chokkanatha Naidu of Madura): Vishnupuranam, Bhagavatham, Ramayanam, Bharatham, Garalapuri Mahathmyam, Bhagavadgeetha.
- Nanne Choda Prabhuvu (Telugu Choda prince, son of Chodaballi of Pakanadu, and Poet): Kumara Sambhavam.
- Gudaru Venkatadasa Kavi (Poet's surname is Gudaru and Gothram is Paidipala) : Balarama Charithram.
- Konidena Nagaya Kavi (Born in Yellammapeta in Kadapa district): Vedavedantha Sarasagraham, Ashtottara Sathakam, Brahmanarada Samvadam.
- Chekuri Siddha Kavi (Born in Yellammapeta, Kadapa district): Sreerama Karnamrutham, Dwadasa Manjareesthavam, Chathurdasa Manjareestavam, Venugopala Sathakam, Vishnupuranam, Sreeranga Mahathmyam, Haribhakthamrutha Saaramu.
- Macha Venkataraya Kavi (Born in Jalumuru, Visakhapattanam district): Vydarbhee Parinayam, Haribhajana Keerthana Kruthi, Chennakesava Ramayana Sangraham, Chaya Putra Sathakam, Mukhalingeswaro-daharanamu, Rukmini Natakam, Droupadi Vasthrapaharanam, Mayuradhwajopakhyanamu, Suddhandhra Nirvachana Niroshtya Kusa Charithram.

- Thumu Ramadasa Kavi (Born in Warangal): Rukmini Kalyanam, Gopika Vilasam, Mitravindo Dwaham, Kalidasu Natakam, Andhrapada Nidhanamu.
- Tripurana Venkata Surya Prasada Rao Dora Garu (Sri Dontihundamulku Darlu, Andhra Kalidasa, Kavibhushana, Bhirudankitulu, Sri Jayapura Samsthana Gaurava Asthana Kavulu, Born in Siddhantham in Visakhapattanam district): Nirvachana Kumara Sambhavamu, Raghu Vamsamu, Kiratharjuneeyamu, Uttararama Charithramu, Raghudayamu, Indumati Mandaramu, Rati Vilapamu, Pathala Khandamu, Moilu Rayabharamu, Sree Bhagavadgeethamruthamu.
- Erra Venkata swami: Vasthuguna Deepika.
- Erra Ayyanna: Telugu Kavaathu.
- Matla Anantharaju (Kadapa district, Telugu Chola descendent): Kakustha Vijayamu (Poems).
- Katta Varada Raju (decent from Karikala Chola, tanjore): Wrote a Ramayana.

7

Mughal Administration

Before following the fate of the Mughal empire under Aurangzeb's successors in the eighteenth century, it will be useful to outline the main features of administration under the four great emperors. The most prominent features of the administrations of the different rulers have already been noted, but a general view is necessary in order to understand the Mughal contribution.

The Central Government

First of all, it should be recognized that the Mughals drew heavily on the past, for the organization of their government was on essentially the same lines as that of the sultanate. The principal officers of the central government were four: 1) *diwan*; 2) *Mir Bakhshi*; 3) *Mir Saman*; and 4) *sadr*. The first of these dignitaries, the diwan, often called the wazir (the chief minister), was mainly concerned with revenue and finance, but as he had a say in all matters where any expenditure was involved, the work of other departments also came under his control. All the imperial orders were first recorded in his office before being issued, and the provincial governors, district *faujdars*, and leaders of expeditions came to him for instructions before assuming their duties. All the earning departments were under his direct control, and could spend only what was allotted to them by the diwan.

The Mir Bakhshi performed those duties which had been the responsibility of the *ariz-i-mamalik* during the earlier period. Owing to the organization of the civil services on military lines, his power extended far beyond the war office, and some foreign travellers called him the lieutenant-general or the captain-general of the realm. The main departure from the sultanate was in respect to work relating to state karkhanas, stores, ordinance, and communications, now so important that the dignitary dealing with it, called the Mir Saman, ranked as an important minister often senior in rank to the sadr. The sadr (or, more fully, sadr-i-jahan) was, as in the earlier period, director of the religious matters, charities, and endowments.

Occasionally a higher dignitary, superior to the wazir and other ministers was also appointed. He was called the *vakil*, and functioned like the *naib* (deputy) of the sultanate period. This appointment, as under the sultanate, was sporadic, depending on the wish of the monarch and the requirements of the situation. During the reigns of Akbar, Jahangir, and Shah Jahan, a period of ninety-seven years (1560–1657), there were ten vakils whose terms of service totalled about thirty-nine years. Ibn Hasan, the author of the Central Structure of the Mughal Empire, argues that the post was primarily for show and honour, with the vakil as the head of the nobility but not of the administration. To a large extent this is true, and normally the vakil was less effective than the wazir, who controlled the purse, but theoretically the vakil was the king's deputy and even the wazir referred to him whatever was "beyond his own ability." Abul Fazl calls him "the emperor's lieutenant in all matters connected with the realm and the household," adding that "although the financial offices are not under his immediate superintendence, yet he receives the returns from heads of all financial offices and wisely keeps abstracts of their return."

The splendour and stability of the Mughal rule was due to a succession of very capable rulers who attempted to build up an efficient administrative system, choosing their principal officers on the basis of merit. The most famous diwan under Akbar was Raja Todar Mal, who for a time acted as the chief minister of the realm, but the contribution of Khwaja Mansur and Mir Fathulla Shirazi to the building up of Akbar's revenue administration was perhaps equally great. Under Jahangir, Itimad-ud-Daula, the father of Nur Jahan, who was a diwan even before his daughter married the emperor, remained the chief wazir and diwan until his death. He was succeeded by his son, Asaf Khan, who became the vakil just before the death of Jahangir. Itimad-ud-Daula and Asaf Khan were able, efficient officers. Asaf Khan maintained his position until his death, but his successors were selected on the basis of their scholarship and technical efficiency. Allami Afzal Khan remained Shah Jahan's diwan for ten years, and the office was held from the nineteenth to the thirtieth years of Shah Jahan's reign by the celebrated Saadulla Khan who, like his predecessor, had won his post because of his learning, wisdom, and resourcefulness.

The diwan, who can perhaps be called the finance minister, had under him two principal officers, called *diwan-i-tan* and *Diwan-i-Khalsa*, who were in charge of salaries and state lands respectively. It is interesting that all the assistants of the Diwan-i-Khalsa under Shah Jahan's reign were Hindus, and five out of the seven under the diwan-i-tan belonged to the same community. Raja Raghunath Rai, who had been Diwan-i-Khalsa for some years, became sole diwan in the thirty-first year of Shah Jahan's reign, and maintained this position until his death, during the reign of Aurangzeb. Aurangzeb's principal wazir, who held office for thirty-one years, was Asad Khan, originally his Mir Bakhshi. Next to him, the most famous Mir Bakhshi of the Mughal period was Shaikh Farid, who played a decisive role in the enthronement of Jahangir.

The organization of public services was perfected during Akbar's reign, and was based on the mansabdari system, borrowed originally from Persia. Every important officer of state held a mansab or an official appointment of rank and emoluments, and, as members of an imperial cadre, were liable for service anywhere in the empire. In 1573–74 Akbar classified the office holders in thirty-three grades, ranging from commanders of ten to commanders of ten thousand. The principal categories of Mughal mansabdars, however, were three: those in command of ten to four hundred were commonly styled *mansabdars* (officers); those in command of five hundred to twenty-five hundred were *amirs* (nobles); and those in higher ranks belonged to the category of *umara-i-kabir* or *umara-i-azim* (grandees). The highest amir in the third category was honored with the title of *amir-ul-umara*. In the eighteenth century this title was usually given to the Mir Bakhshi. Until the middle of Akbar's reign, the highest rank which any ordinary officer could hold was that of a commander of five thousand; the more exalted grades between commanders of seven thousand and ten thousand were reserved for princes of royal blood. Toward the end of his reign and under his successors these limits were relaxed.

Originally each grade carried a definite rate of pay, out of which the holders were required to maintain a quota of horses, elephants, beasts of burden, and carts. But even in Akbar's days and in spite of safeguards introduced by him, the number of men actually supplied by the mansabdars rarely corresponded to the number indicated by his rank, and under Akbar's successors greater latitude was allowed.

The mansabdars were paid either in cash or by temporary grant of jagirs. Theoretically, the mansabdars received enormous salaries, which appear all the more excessive when it is realized that they did not normally maintain all the troops expected of them.

It was probably an awareness of this that led Shah Jahan to introduce the practice of paying salaries to the mansabdars for only four months of the year instead of twelve, the implication being that the actual income for part of the year was equivalent to what the emperor had originally intended for the whole year. Even with this reduction, the mansabdars lived extravagantly. The tendency to luxurious expenditure was undoubtedly heightened by the mansabdar's knowledge that on his death, his whole property would be taken over by the state, pending satisfaction of any outstanding claims by the treasury. But while there may have been little incentive to save within the system, the high scale of salaries enabled the state to attract the ablest and most ambitious individuals from almost the whole of southern and western Asia.

Appointment to the ranks of mansabdars was made by the emperor, usually on the recommendation of military leaders, provincial governors, or court officials. In addition to the mansabdars, there was a class known as *ahadis*, who though holding no official rank, were employed in posts in the palace. They were usually young men of good families, who were not fortunate enough to secure a mansab on their first application. Given an opportunity to show their worth, they could then be promoted to the ranks of mansabdars. These mansabdars have been compared to the Civil Service during British rule in that they formed an all-India cadre of officials, liable to transfer anywhere in the empire and providing the personnel for all major offices. The existence of a single imperial cadre undoubtedly gave a cohesion and unity to the Mughal empire that was lacking during the sultanate.

Provincial Administration

Provincial administration was greatly improved under Akbar, and in this respect the Mughal period differs substantially from the sultanate. The boundaries of the provincial units were more definitely fixed; and a uniform administrative pattern, with minor modifications to suit local conditions, was developed for all parts of the empire. Further, drawing upon the experiments introduced by Sher Shah, the provincial administration was strengthened, and each province was provided with a set of officials representing all branches of state activity. By the introduction of a cadre of mansabdars, liable to be transferred anywhere at the behest of the central government and by the introduction of other checks, the control over the provinces was made more effective.

The principal officer was the governor, called *sipah salar* under Akbar and *nazim* under his successors, but popularly known as *subahdar* and later only as subah. Next to him in official rank, but not in any way under his control, was the provincial diwan, who was in independent charge of the revenues of the province. He was usually a mansabdar of much lower status than the governor, but he was independent of the governor's control and was directly under the imperial diwan.

The next provincial functionary was the *Bakhshi*, or the paymaster. He performed a number of duties, including, occasionally, the functions of the provincial newswriter. The *diwan-i-buyutat* was the provincial representative of the Khan-i-Saman, and looked after roads and government buildings, supervised imperial stores, and ran state workshops. The sadr and the Qazi were entrusted with religious, educational, and judicial duties.

The *faujdar* and the *kotwal* were the two other important provincial officials. The faujdar, who was the administrative head of the sarkar (district), was appointed by the emperor but was under the supervision and guidance of the governor. The kotwals were not provincial officers, but were appointed by the central government in the provincial capitals and other important cities, and performed a number of executive and ministerial duties similar to the Police Commissioners during British rule in Bombay, Calcutta, and Madras. The ports were in charge of the *Mir Bahr*, corresponding to the modern Port Commissioner, but with powers over customs also.

The Mughals interfered very little with the local life of the village communities, for they had no resident functionary of their own in the villages. The Muqaddam was normally the sarpanch (head of the village panchayat, or council) and these panchayats continued to deal with local disputes, arrange for watch and ward, and perform many functions now entrusted to the local bodies.

Finances

The tax structure of the Mughal empire was relatively simple in its theoretical formulation, however much it was complicated by changing needs and local circumstances. Both revenue and expenditure were divided between the central and the provincial government. The central government reserved for itself land revenue, customs, profits from the mints, inheritance rights, and monopolies. Land revenue was the most important source of income, as it has been throughout Indian history, and more than doubled in value between the reigns of Akbar and Shah Jahan. The principal items of expenditure for the central government were defence, the general civil administration of the empire (including the religious organizations), maintenance of the court and the royal palace, and the cost of buildings and other public works. The provincial sources of income were the assignments of land revenue granted to the provincial governor and his officials as a remuneration for their services, a variety of local taxes and cesses, transit dues and duties, and fines and presents.

The Mughal revenue system was based on the division of the empire into subas or governorships, sarkars or districts, and parganas, consisting of number of villages which were sometimes styled mahals. (These were replaced during British rule by the somewhat large tehsils or talukas.) The revenue staff had also to perform miscellaneous administrative duties, including the keeping of the public peace, and recruitment of the military forces. The suba was modelled after the central imperial structure. The sarkar was in the charge of the faujdar, or military commander, who combined the functions of the modern district magistrate and superintendent of police. The revenue work in the sarkar was looked after by the amalguzar, who would correspond to the modern afsar-i-mal (revenue officer).

The levy of land revenue was based on survey settlements calculated after a detailed measurement and classification of the cultivated areas. The nature of the crops grown and the mean prevailing market prices were also taken into consideration in fixing the final assessment. This assessment system, evolved after many experiments, became the basis of the survey settlement of the British period. Akbar's revenue system in most areas was raiyatwari, the revenue being collected directly as far as possible from the individual cultivator, and was payable in cash. Akbar introduced the system in the greater part of northern India, and during the viceroyalty of Aurangzeb, it was extended to the Deccan. The revenue system as evolved under Akbar was thoroughly sound, but the government demand was heavy and amounted to one-third of the produce. Abul Fazl tried to justify it by referring to the abolition of many miscellaneous cesses and taxes, but it is not certain whether all the cesses abolished by royal order were given up by subordinate officials. In the settlement of the Deccan during Aurangzeb's viceroyalty, the state share was reduced to one-fourth.

Mughal emperors, particularly Akbar and Aurangzeb, continued to make cautious experiments and improvements in the land-revenue system. The basic data was collected by detailed measurement of land and assessment of the yield and estimates of productivity of each pargana or assessment area. When sufficient data had been collected the system of group assessment was introduced, with the alternatives of measurement and sharing being held in reserve.

That the Mughal rulers wanted the revenue system to operate fairly is evident from the guidance to collectors of revenue given in the *Ain-i-Akbari*. "The Collector was directed to be the friend of the agriculturist; to give remissions in order to stimulate cultivation ... to grant every facility to the raiyat, and never to charge him on more than the actual area under tillage; to receive the assessment direct from the cultivator and so avoid intermediaries; to recover arrears without undue force; and to submit a monthly statement describing the condition of the people, the state of public security, the range of market prices and rents, the conditions of the poor and all other contingencies."

The specifications were high—at least on paper, but anyone who studies the procedure for giving relief to the raiyats in case of hardships, the general instructions to the collectors, and the details of the assessment system and mode of recovery is bound to be struck by the professional competence of men like Todar Mal, Shah Mansur, and Amir Fathullah Shirazi, as well as the statesmanlike benevolence motivating the state's basic policy. The British paid special attention to revenue administration, and introduced many significant improvements, but it can be said without injustice that on certain points the Mughal system compared favourably with the one that evolved over a long period in British India. As an example, one may take the assessment of lands newly brought under cultivation or reclaimed after having fallen out of cultivation. A variety of scales of assessment was applied to such lands, such as a low initial rate, rising to the full amount after five years. The collector was also able to vary the revenue demands to encourage wasteland being cultivated. Regulations under the British were neither so liberal nor so flexible for this particular kind of cultivation.

Another important difference between the British and the Mughal systems was the position of the village accountant, or Patwari. Throughout the Mughal period the Patwari, who was responsible for the maintenance of the financial records, was an employee of the village, not of the revenue administration. Under the British system, however, he became an employee of the government. This altered his relationship to the people, because previously he had been an agent for the people, but now he became an instrument of government. This was one factor that led to the weakening of village autonomy.

The Mughal theory and practice of revenue administration must be seen as the essential elements underlying the later administrative structure of India. The great memorial to Mughal rule is not so much the great architectural monuments that fill the subcontinent, but the governments of the great successor states, India and Pakistan, which following the model of the period of British rule, have maintained an administrative pattern that derives from the Mughals. "The District system with the district officer as head of the public services and general factotum or Poo Bah, the erection of an administrative hierarchy upon the basis of land revenue collection, and the development of an involute maze of office procedure, these features of Mughal rule were all accepted as the foundation of British rule; and, indeed, to an astonishing degree, in India and Pakistan today local administration is Mughal in spirit."

Military Organization

The weakest part of Mughal administration was the military organization, precisely the area where one might have expected the most efficient centralized control. But instead of a large standing army, the emperors depended upon four different classes of troops for the maintenance of order and the defence of the empire's borders. There were, first of all, the soldiers supplied by the mansabdars; the number a mansabdar was expected to provide upon the demand of the emperor were specified in his warrant of appointment or were indicated by his rank. Another class of troops under the command of a mansabdar was known as dakhili, whose services were paid for by the state. A third class were the ahadis, or "gentlemen troopers," drawing higher pay than those in the ordinary service; according to the *Ain-i-Akbari*, they might get as much as five hundred rupees a month, in contrast to the seven or eight rupees of the regular troopers. Finally, the chiefs who had been permitted to retain a degree of autonomy were required to provide contingents under their own command.

The artillery was paid wholly out of the imperial treasury. Recognizing its importance, Akbar had given it his special attention, but his efforts to secure from the Portuguese some of their better pieces were unsuccessful. European gunners were employed later on in appreciable numbers, but no permanent improvement was effected. During the eighteenth century the Mughal army shared in the decline of the other imperial institutions, and little advantage was taken of technical improvements in weaponry. When Nadir Shah invaded India in 1739 the jazair or swivel guns employed by his troops were superior to anything the Mughals could bring against them.

There are no existing statistical records of the strength of the Mughal army. The best estimate is probably that of Sir Jadunath Sarkar, who concluded from evidence from the reign of Shah Jahan that in 1648 the army consisted of 440,000 infantry, musketeers, and artillery men, and 185,000 cavalry commanded by princes and nobles. The army could still count on the personal valor of the commander of an individual contingent, but pitted against disciplined European soldiers, or hardy, resourceful Maratha horsemen, it did not prove effective. The loose organization of the army, the paucity of officers, the failure to build up a well-knit and active pyramidical organization, reduced the efficiency of the army. There were no uniforms, and discipline was poor, particularly in lower ranks. The cavalry was the only branch which was considered respectable and fit for a gentleman to join, while the ordinary "Indian foot soldier was little more than a night watchman and guardian over baggage." The Mughal practice of taking along a great number of camp followers, including occasionally the families of the soldiers and the royal harem, made the army a very cumbersome, slow-moving organization.

Descendants of a people who knew nothing of the sea, the Mughals had little success in creating a navy. They had no large fighting vessels, and the ships that they maintained were primarily for the furtherance of the commercial operations of the state. After the conquest of Gujarat, the Mughal army reached the shores of the Indian Ocean, but Akbar failed to build a navy.

He tacitly acquiesced in the Portuguese supremacy by making no effort to challenge their authority, and by taking out licenses from them for the ships which he sent to the Red Sea. To deal with the pirates in the Bay of Bengal, and also for the purpose of communication over the vast river system of Bengal, a river flotilla was maintained at Dacca. Under Akbar it consisted of 768 small armed vessels and boats, estimated to cost about 29,000 rupees a month. It was not effective against the Magh and Portuguese pirates, but it was reorganized under the efficient administration of Mir Jumla and Shayista Khan, and in 1664 the latter was able to inflict a decisive blow against the pirates.

A few years later Aurangzeb had an opportunity to make at least tentative arrangements for the defence of the seas along the west coast of India. A coastal chieftain known as the Sidi of Janjira had provided protection for the ships and ports of the sultan of Bijapur. When the Sidi's territories were attacked by Shivaji, however, the sultan did not come to his assistance, and in 1670 the Sidi offered his services to Aurangzeb. Since Aurangzeb needed all the help he could get in the Deccan, he took the Sidi into his service, placing him under the Mughal governor of Surat, and subsidizing his fleet. The Sidi was assisted by another fleet based on Surat, and in every way treated as an official of the empire, but the Mughal command of the sea was too slight to make supervision of so independent a force possible. In course of time his descendants established themselves as the rulers of the state of Janjira south of Bombay.

The Judiciary

The judicial system of the Mughals was very similar to that of the sultanate. It became more systematic, particularly under Aurangzeb, but as compared with the judicial structure of British India, it was very simple, being based on a different approach to many categories of disputes. Normally no lawyers were allowed to appear. The disputes were speedily settled, often on the basis of equity and natural justice, though of course in the case of Muslims the injunctions and precedents of Islamic law applied where they existed. Many crimes—including murder—were treated as individual grievances rather than crimes against society. The complaints in such cases were initiated by the individuals aggrieved, rather than by the police, and could be compounded on payment of compensation. The aim of the judicial system was primarily to settle individual complaints and disputes rather than to enforce a legal code, as is indicated by the fact that the criminal court was normally known as the *diwan-i-mazalim*, the court of complaints.

All foreign travellers have commented on the speedy justice of the Mughal courts and the comparatively few cases coming before them. The latter was partly due to the general prejudice against litigation, but even more to the fact that a large number of disputes, particularly those affecting the Hindus, were settled by the village and caste panchayats, and did not come before the official courts. The Hindus were not debarred from taking cases before the Qazi or the governor—and frequently did so where other arrangements did not prove effective—but normally they had their own arrangements for settling their disputes. Badauni has recorded that according to Akbar's orders the cases of Hindus were to be decided by the Hindu judges and not by the qazis. The Jesuit Father Monserrate says that "Brachmane (Brahmans) governed liberally through a senate and a council of the common people" —referring presumably to the administration of justice by these agencies. Local usage and custom ruled in most rural areas, and, according to one estimate, perhaps not one person out of a hundred in the Punjab, for example, was governed by the provisions of either the classic Hindu or Muslim law.

The judicial courts provided by the Mughals were principally of two types—secular and ecclesiastical. Except during the reign of Aurangzeb, the principal courts for settlement of disputes were presided over by the emperor, the governors, and other executive officers. Akbar used to spend several hours of the day disposing of judicial cases, and governors followed the same procedure in the provinces. In the *Ain-i-Akbari* we find the instructions issued to a governor detailing the judicial procedure he should follow.

Apart from the secular courts and the panchayats, the principal agency for the settlement of disputes was the qazis' court. The Qazi, being the repository of Muslim law, attended the hearing of cases by the executive authority, whether governor, faujdar or kotwal, and assisted the latter in arriving at a decision consonant with Quaranic precepts. Presumably the civil disputes of Muslims were, as a rule, left to the qazis to be settled according to the canon law. When both parties in a dispute were Hindus, the point at issue was referred to Hindu pandits for an opinion. This principle was supported by the *Fatawa-i-Alamgiri*, the authoritative digest of Islamic law, where it is held that "Dhimmis ... do not subject themselves to the laws of Islam either with respect to things which are merely of religious nature, such as fasting or prayer, or with respect to such temporal acts, as though contrary to [Islam], may be legal by their own, such as sale of wine or of swine's flesh, because we [Muslim jurists] have been commanded to leave them at liberty in all things, which may be deemed by them to be proper according to the precepts of their own religion." These provisions presumably related to religious matters. In the case of Muslims, the secular types of criminal suits went to the kotwal, while the religious and civil cases, such as concerning inheritance, marriage, divorce, and civil disputes went to the qazis' courts.

The death penalty normally had to be confirmed by the emperor, but there seem to have been departures from the rule. A Dutch resident of India states that fines represented the normal mode of settling all disputes in Mughal India. Capital punishments and mutilations were frequent, and there are records of impaling, dismemberment, and other cruel punishments. They were, however, limited in their incidence and were inflicted only under the royal orders. Furthermore, they were confined to those cases where an example was to be made of the individual concerned. Imprisonment was not a method of punishment that appealed to the Mughals. It was seldom used as a sentence in private cases, though it was sometimes resorted to for preventive purposes. Whipping was commonly used. The Muslim punishment of parading the offender in an ignominious condition seems to have been frequently used, as it coincided with the Hindu tradition as well.

The assessments made by two acute British observers on Mughal government as they saw it in a period of decline may serve as summary of the Mughal achievement as administrators. Luke Scrafton, who was resident for the East India Company at the capital of Bengal in 1758, declared that until the invasion of Nadir Shah in 1739 "there was scarce a better administered government in the world. The manufactures, commerce, and agriculture flourished exceedingly; and none felt the hand of the oppression but those who were dangerous by their wealth or power." Mughal government was despotic, and official corruption increased from the reign of Jahangir, but on the whole, the judgment of the English historian, Sidney Owen seems just: "Whatever its defects, it was ... a grandly conceived, well-adjusted, and beneficent structure of government. ... Taxation was light; and its most productive source, the land revenue, was moderately assessed, and equitably adjusted. Foreign commerce was protected and favoured; and the English East India Company throve, and multiplied its factories, under the shadow of the Imperial authority. The judicial system, though what we should consider crude and capricious, as well as too often corruptly exercised, was not liable like our own to the tedious delays which have been its reproach, and which have so much tended to obstruct, and even defeat, the course of justice. And the right of appealing to the Emperor from inferior tribunals, though too generally a futile privilege, was sometimes really remedial, and probably was a standing check to judicial iniquity. Much the same may be said as to the provincial Governors."

8

Economic and Social Developments under the Mughals

IT WAS the normal policy of the Timurid rulers, both in their original Central Asian homelands and in India, to encourage trade. As in much else, Sher Shah Suri during his brief reign (1538–1545) set a pattern that was followed by the later Mughals, especially Akbar, when he encouraged trade by linking together various parts of the country through an efficient system of roads and abolishing many inland tolls and duties. The Mughals maintained this general policy, but their rule was distinguished by the importance which foreign trade attained by the end of the sixteenth century. This was partly the result of the discovery of the new sea-route to India; but even so, progress would have been limited if conditions within the country had not been favourable.

Trade and Industry

Both Akbar and Jahangir interested themselves in the foreign seaborne trade, and Akbar himself took part in commercial activities for a time. The Mughals welcomed the foreign trader, provided ample protection and security for his transactions, and levied a very low custom duty (usually no more than 2½ percent ad valorem). Furthermore, the expansion of local handicrafts and industry resulted in a reservoir of exportable goods. Indian exports consisted mainly of manufactured articles, with cotton cloth in great demand in Europe and elsewhere. Indigo, saltpeter, spices, opium, sugar, woolen and silk cloth of various kinds, yarn, asafoetida, salt, beads, borax, turmeric, lac, sealing wax, and drugs of various kinds, were also exported. The principal imports were bullion, horses, and a certain quantity of luxury goods for the upper classes, like raw silk, coral, amber, precious stones, superior textiles (silk, velvet, brocade, broadcloth), perfumes, drugs, china goods, and European wines. By and large, however, in return for their goods Indian merchants insisted on payment in gold or silver. Naturally this was not popular in England and the rest of Europe, and writers on economic affairs in the seventeenth century frequently complained, as did Sir Thomas Roe, that "Europe bleedeth to enrich Asia." The demand for articles supplied by India was so great, however, and her requirements of European goods so limited, that Europe was obliged to trade on India's own terms until the eighteenth century, when special measures were taken in England and elsewhere to discourage the demand for Indian goods.

The manufacture of cotton goods had assumed such extensive proportions that in addition to satisfying her own needs, India sent cloth to almost half the world: the east coast of Africa, Arabia, Egypt, Southeast Asia, as well as Europe. The textile industry, well established in Akbar's day, continued to flourish under his successors, and soon the operations of Dutch and English traders brought India into direct touch with Western markets. This resulted in great demand for Indian cotton goods from Europe, which naturally increased production at home. Even the silk industry—especially in Bengal—was in flourishing condition. Bernier wrote: "There is in Bengal such a quantity of cotton and silk, that the kingdom may be called the common storehouse for these two kinds of merchandise, not of Hindoustan or the Empire of the Great Mogul only, but of all the neighbouring kingdoms, and even of Europe."

Apart from silk and cotton textiles, other industries were shawl and carpet weaving, woollen goods, pottery, leather goods, and articles made of wood. Owing to its proximity to sources of suitable timbers, Chittagong specialized in shipbuilding, and at one time supplied ships to distant Istanbul. The commercial side of the industry was in the hands of middlemen, but the Mughal government, like the earlier sultans, made its own contribution. The emperor controlled a large number of royal workshops, busily turning out articles for his own use, for his household, for the court, and for the imperial army. Akbar took a special interest in the development of indigenous industry. He was directly responsible for the expansion of silk weaving at Lahore, Agra, Fathpur-Sikri, and in Gujarat. He opened a large number of factories at important centers, importing master weavers from Persia, Kashmir, and Turkistan. Akbar frequently visited the workshops near the palace to watch the artisans at work, which encouraged the craftsmen and raised their status. It is said that he took such an interest in the industry that to foster demand he "ordered people of certain ranks to wear particular kinds of locally woven coverings ... an order which resulted in the establishment of a large number of shawl manufactories in Lahore; and inducements were offered to foreign carpet-weavers to settle in Agra, Fathepur Sikri, and Lahore, and manufacture carpets to compete with those imported from Persia." In the course of time, the foreign traders established close contracts with important markets in India, and new articles which were more in demand in Western Europe began to be produced in increasing quantities. Among the foreign inventions that excited Akbar's interest was an organ, "one of the wonders of creation," that had been brought from Europe.

Urban Life

All foreign travellers speak of the wealth and prosperity of Mughal cities and large towns. Monserrate stated that Lahore in 1581 was "not second to any city in Europe or Asia." Finch, who travelled in the early days of Jahangir, found both Agra and Lahore to be much larger than London, and his testimony is supported by others. Other cities like Surat ("A city of good quantity, with many fair merchants and houses therein"), Ahmadabad, Allahabad, Benares, and Patna similarly excited the admiration of visitors. The new port towns of Bombay, Calcutta, Madras, and Karachi developed under British rule, but they had their predecessors in Satgaon, Surat, Cambay, Lari Bunder, and other ports.

The efficient system of city government under the Mughals encouraged trade. The pivot of urban administration was the kotwal, the city governor. In addition to his executive and judicial powers, it was his duty to prevent and detect crime, to perform many of the functions now assigned to the municipal boards, to regulate prices, and in general, to be responsible for the peace and prosperity of the city. The efficient discharge of these duties depended on the personality of the individual city governor, but the Mughals tried to ensure high standards by making the kotwal personally responsible for the property and the security of the citizens. Akbar had decreed (probably following Sher Shah Suri's example of fixing the responsibility on village chiefs for highway robberies in their territory) that the kotwal was to either recover stolen goods or be held responsible for their loss. That this was not only a pious hope is borne out by the testimony of several foreign travellers who state that the kotwal was personally liable to make good the value of any stolen property which he was unable to recover. The kotwals often found pretexts to evade the ultimate responsibility, but in general they took elaborate measures to prevent thefts.

Most of this flourishing commerce was in the hands of the traditional Hindu merchant classes, whose business acumen was proverbial. Their caste guilds added to the skills in trade and commerce that they had learned through the centuries. Not only were their disputes settled by their panchayats, but they would frequently impose pressure on the government by organized action. Foreign visitors record that the governors and kotwals were very sensitive to this, and in spite of hardships inseparable from a despotic system of administration, the business communities had their own means of obtaining redress.

Bernier, writing during Aurangzeb's time, declared that the Hindus possessed "almost exclusively the trade and wealth of the country." If Muslims enjoyed advantages in higher administrative posts and in the army, Hindu merchants maintained the monopoly in trade and finance that they had during the sultanate. A Dutch traveller in the early seventeenth century was struck by the fact that few Muslims engaged in handicraft industries, and that even when a Muslim merchant did have a large business, he employed Hindu bookkeepers and agents. Banking was almost exclusively in Hindu hands.

In the years of the decline of the Mughals, a rich Hindu banker would finance his favourite rival claimant for the throne. The role of Jagat Seth of Murshidabad in the history of Bengal is well known. Even the "war of succession" out of which Aurangzeb emerged victorious was financed by a loan of five and a half lakhs of rupees from the Jain bankers of Ahmadabad. Here one sees a contrast with British rule, when the British not only monopolized the higher civil service posts but also controlled most of the major industries as well as the great banks and trading agencies.

Rural Conditions

Conditions in the rural areas during the Mughal period were much the same as at present, with one important difference—the Muslim rulers had scarcely disturbed the old organization of the villages. The panchayats continued to settle most disputes, with the state impinging very little on village life, except for the collection of land revenue, and even this was very often done on a village basis rather than through individuals, with the age-old arrangements being preserved. The incidence of land revenue was substantially higher under the Mughals and in Hindu states like Vijayanagar than in British India, but the administration was more flexible, both in theory and in practice, in its assessment and collection. Apart from the remission of land revenue when crops failed, there was reduction in government demand even when bumper crops caused prices to fall. For example, between 1585 and 1590 very large sums had to be written off because a series of exceptionally good harvests had resulted in a surplus, and peasants could not sell their crops. The state also advanced loans to the cultivators, and occasionally provided seed as well as implements for digging wells. Loans advanced to the cultivators for seeds, implements, bullocks, or digging of wells were called *taqavi*—an expression which has continued in modern land revenue administration.

Health and Medical Facilities

A feature noticed by many foreign travellers was the good health of the local inhabitants. Fryer, writing of the mortality among the English at Bombay and the adjacent parts, says that "the country people lived to a good old age, supposed to be the reward of their temperance." Bernier also speaks of "general habits of sobriety among the people," though this did not apply to a few cases among the upper classes or the royal family. The European travellers found "less vigour among the people than in the colder climates, but greater enjoyment of health." From their accounts, even the climate would appear to have been healthy. "Gout, stone complaints in the kidneys, catarrh ... are nearly unknown; and persons who arrive in the country afflicted with any of these disorders soon experience a complete cure." The Mughal emphasis on physical fitness and encouragement of out-of-door manly games also raised the general standard of health. The ideal was that everyone was to be trained to be a soldier, a good rider, a keen shikari, and able to distinguish himself in games. Ovington found that the English at Surat were "much less vigorous and athletic in their bodies than Indians." It is possible that the drinking habits of the Europeans made them an easy prey to ill-health in the tropics.

Public hospitals had been provided in Muslim India, at least since the days of Firuz Tughluq (1351–1388), and though it would be ridiculous to compare them with the arrangements introduced by the British, the system seems to have been extended during the Mughal period. Jahangir states in his autobiography that on his accession to the throne he ordered the establishment, at government expense, of hospitals in large cities. That this order was actually made effective is shown by the records of salaries paid by the government and of grants for the distribution of medicine.

The supply of local physicians was not plentiful; and judged by the demand for European doctors, particularly surgeons, they were apparently not equal to all demands. The general health of the inhabitants suggests, however, that the medical services were not completely inadequate, and the local physicians were able to deal with normal problems. As early as 1616 they knew the important characteristics of the bubonic plague and suggested suitable preventive measures. According to an account in *Iqbal Nama*, which was written in Jahangir's reign: "When the disease was about to break out, a mouse would rush out of its hole, as if mad, and striking itself against the door and the walls of the house, would expire. If immediately after this signal the occupants left the house and went away to the jungle, their lives were safe. If otherwise, the inhabitants of the village would be spirited away by the hands of death." As modern scholars have pointed out, this observation includes two facts about the plague whose significance has been corroborated by modern science: the association of the death of rodents with the disease, and the necessity of evacuating the infected quarter.

A crude form of vaccination against smallpox seems to have been employed by Eastern doctors, for it was vaguely realized that the introduction of a mild form of cowpox prevented the virulent form of smallpox. An article in the Asiatic Register of London for 1804 contained a translation of a memorandum by Nawab Mirza Mehdi Ali Khan describing from personal observations the method adopted by a Hindu medical practitioner of Benares. A thread drenched in "the matter of a pustule on the cow" was placed on the arms of a child to cause an easy irruption, thus avoiding a virulent attack of smallpox.

In ancient times, the use of medicines had been well developed among the Hindus, but dissection was considered to be irreligious. The Muslims, who did not have this restriction, performed a number of operations. As Elphinstone pointed out: "Their surgery is as remarkable as their medicine especially when we recollect their ignorance of anatomy. They cut for the stone, couched for the cataract, and extracted the feotus from the womb, and in their early works enunciate no less than one hundred and twenty-seven surgical works." According to Manucci, Muslim surgeons could provide artificial limbs.

Social Customs

The marriage customs of Hindus and Muslims had many similarities. Early marriages were much in vogue amongst the Hindus, with seven considered the proper age for a girl to be married. To leave a daughter unmarried beyond twelve years of age was to risk the displeasure of one's caste. The Muslims also betrothed their children between the ages of six and eight, but the marriage was generally not solemnized before they had attained the age of puberty.

Among the wealthier classes polygamy and divorce are said to have been very common. The custom of secluding women, known as purdah, was very strictly observed. Marriage negotiations were undertaken by the professional broker or the friends of either party. The marriage ceremonies were more or less the same as they are at present, and the character of the average Indian or Pakistani home and the socio-ethical ideas which influence it have not undergone any fundamental change. The son's duty to his parents and the wife's duty to her husband were viewed almost as religious obligations. "Superstitions played a prominent part in the daily life of the people. Charms were used not merely to ensnare a restive husband but also to secure such other ends as the birth of a son or cure of a disease. The fear of the evil eye was ever present ... and the young child was considered particularly susceptible. ... People believed in all sorts of omens." Astrologers were very much in demand, even at the Mughal court.

The Muslim aristocrats lived in great houses decorated with rich hangings and carpets. Their clothing was made of finest cotton or silk, decorated with gold; and they carried beautiful scimitars. There was a considerable element of ostentatious display involved in this, however, for their domestic arrangements did not match the outward splendour of their dress and equipment. Manucci, a keen observer, refers to Pathans who came to court "well-clad and well-armed, caracolling on fine horses richly caparisoned and followed by several servants," but when they reached home, divested themselves of "all this finery, and tying a scanty cloth around their loins and wrapping a rag around their head, they take their seat on a mat, and live on ... rice and lentils or badly cooked cow's flesh of low quality, which is very abundant in the Mogul country and very cheap."

The courtly manners and the elaborate etiquette of the Muslim upper classes impressed foreign visitors. In social gatherings they spoke "in a very low voice with much order, moderation, gravity, and sweetness. ... Betel and betelnut were presented to the visitors and they were escorted with much civility at the time of departure. Rigid forms were observed at meals. ... Dice was their favourite indoor game. Polo or chaugan—for which there was a special playground at Dacca—elephant-fights, hunting, excursions and picnics, were also very popular." The grandees rode in palkis, preceded by uniformed mounted servants. Many "drove in fine two-wheeled carts, carved with gilt and gold, covered in silk, and drawn by two little bulls which could race with the fastest horses."

The Position of the Hindus

The Hindu upper classes undoubtedly shared in the material culture of the Mughals, for, as already noted, they had a virtual monopoly of trade and finance. Furthermore, they had long held many high posts in the government. The contrast between the position of Hindus under the Mughals and of Indians in general under the British was often made by Indian historians during the period of the nationalist movement. Thus a Hindu historian writing in 1940 could argue that "under Shah Jahan Hindus occupied a higher status in the government than that occupied by the Indians today."

The vitality of the Hindus was shown in more than their ability to maintain footholds within administrative and commercial life. Widespread religious movements, having, as we have seen, their roots partly in the vivifying contacts of Hinduism with Islam, had produced a religious enthusiasm among the masses that was transforming the older Brahmanical religion.

Although Muslim historians ignore this religious revival among the Hindus, there is enough evidence to indicate its importance during Mughal rule. The new regional literature of Bengal and Maharashtra, which owed much to the new movement, is a clear mirror of what was taking place in Hindu society. In Bengal, there was not only the rise of a new literature, but numerous temples were built during the late seventeenth century. The significance of this phenomenon becomes clear if it is remembered that practically throughout the second half of the seventeenth century, Aurangzeb was on the throne. His alleged ceaseless campaign of temple destruction obviously could have been neither thoroughgoing nor universal.

The developments in intellectual life were even more marked. The rise of Navadipa as a great center of Sanskritic learning, and the vogue of navyanyaya (new logic) belong to this period.

In relation to Islam, Hinduism exhibited a new vigor, greater self-confidence, and even a spirit of defiance. Hinduism is not generally thought of as a missionary religion, and it is often assumed that during Muslim rule conversions were only from Hinduism to Islam. This is, however, not true. Hinduism by now was very much on the offensive and was absorbing a number of Muslims. When Shah Jahan returned from Kashmir, in the sixth year of his reign, he discovered that Hindus of Bhadauri and Bhimbar were forcibly marrying Muslim girls and converting them to the Hindu faith. At death these women were cremated according to the Hindu rites. Jahangir had tried to stop this practice but with no success, and Shah Jahan also issued orders declaring such marriages unlawful. Four thousand such conversions are said to have been discovered. Many cases were also found in Gujarat and in parts of the Punjab. Partly to deal with such cases, and partly to conform to his early notions of an orthodox Muslim king, Shah Jahan established a special department to deal with conversions. After the tenth year of his reign, he seems to have ceased trying to prevent the proselytizing activities of the Hindus. There are several later cases of the conversion of Muslims, not recorded by the court historians. A number of Muslims—including at least two Muslim nobles, Mirza Salih and Mirza Haider—were converted to Hinduism by the vairagis, the wandering ascetics of the Chaitanya movement, which had become a powerful religious force in Bengal. There were also cases of conversions from Islam to Sikhism. When Guru Hargovind took up his residence at Kiratpur in the Punjab some time before 1645, he is said to have succeeded in converting a large number of Muslims. It was reported that not a Muslim was left between the hills near Kiratpur and the frontiers of Tibet and Khotan. His predecessor, Guru Arjan, had proselytized so actively that he incurred Jahangir's anger, and, as Jahangir mentions in his autobiography, the Hindu shrines of Kangra and Mathura attracted a number of Muslim pilgrims.

The Hindu position was so strong that in some places Aurangzeb's order for the collection of jizya was defied. On January 29, 1693, the officials in Malwa sent a soldier to collect jizya from a zamindar called Devi Singh. When he reached the place, Devi Singh's men fell upon him, pulled his beard and hair, and sent him back empty-handed. The emperor thereupon ordered a reduction in the jagir of Devi Singh. Earlier, another official had fared much worse. He himself proceeded to the jagir to collect the tax, but was killed by the Hindu mansabdar. Orders to destroy newly built temples met with similar opposition. A Muslim officer who was sent in 1671 to destroy temples at the ancient pilgrimage city of Ujjain was killed in a riot that broke out as he tried to carry out his orders.

Muslim historians, in order to show the extreme orthodoxy of Aurangzeb, have recorded many reports of temple destruction. On a closer scrutiny, however, there seem to be good grounds for believing that all the reports were not correct, and that quite often no action was taken on imperial orders. We read, for example, about the destruction of a certain temple at Somnath during the reign of Shah Jahan and again under Aurangzeb. It is likely that in this and in many similar cases, the temple was not destroyed on the first order. According to accounts by English merchants, Aurangzeb's officers would leave the temples standing on payment of large sums of money by the priests. However, new temples whose construction had not been authorized were often closed.

If the situation is closely examined, it appears that the complaint of Shaikh Ahmad that under Muslim rule as it existed in India, Islam was in need of greater protection than other religions does not appear to have been completely unfounded. Aurangzeb tried, of course, to reverse this trend, and some other rulers also had occasional spells of Islamic zeal, either from political or religious causes. But by and large, it is perhaps fair to say that during Muslim rule, Islam suffered from handicaps which almost outweighed the advantages it enjoyed as the religion of the ruling dynasty. This paradox becomes understandable if the basic Muslim political theory is kept in mind, under which the non-Muslim communities, so long as they paid certain taxes, were left to manage their own affairs. This local and communal autonomy severely circumscribed the sovereignty of the Muslim state, and in most matters the caste guilds and the village panchayats exercised real sovereignty, which they naturally utilized to safeguard their creed and way of life. It was this power which enabled them to evade, or even defy, unwelcome orders from the capital. A curious light on the situation is thrown by the penalties and economic losses which a Hindu had to suffer on the adoption of Islam. Practically until the end of Muslim rule, a Hindu who became a Muslim automatically lost all claim to ancestral property.

This extraordinary position was a natural result of the application of Hindu law, which, according to the Muslim legal system, governed Hindu society even under Muslim government, and under which apostacy resulted in disinheritance. Shah Jahan, who began as an orthodox Muslim, tried to redress the balance by issuing orders that "family pressure should not prevent a Hindu from being admitted to Islam," and laid down that a convert should not be disinherited. Whether these orders could overcome the subtle but solid pressure of the joint family system and the power of the caste panchayats must remain a matter of speculation. The question, however, of handicaps or advantages of one community against another is not of fundamental significance. The important fact is that during normal times conditions of tolerance prevailed. This was of special interest to European visitors, almost all of whom commented on the concessions enjoyed by non-Muslims under Muslim rule. The Jesuits were critical of this policy of tolerance, declaring the destruction of Hindu temples by Muslims "a praiseworthy action," but noting their "carelessness" in allowing public performance of Hindu sacrifices and religious practices. When Akbar granted the followers of the Raushaniya sect the freedom to follow their religion, Monserrate sadly commented that "He cared little that in allowing everyone to follow his own religion he was in reality violating all religions."

Even in Aurangzeb's reign a cow could not be slaughtered in important places like Surat, and attempts made by some English merchants to obtain beef led to riots. According to one account: "In Surat the Hindus paid a fixed sum to the Mohammadans in return for sparing the cows. In 1608 a riot was caused at Surat by a drunken sailor Tom Tucker who killed a calf. Similar occurrences at Karwar and Honavar led to outbreaks, in one of which the whole factory was murdered." But nothing brings out the Mughal administration's respect for the susceptibilities of the Hindus as well as the experience of the Portuguese missionary traveller, Manrique. "In a village where he stopped for the night, one of his followers, a Musalman, killed two peacocks, birds sacred in the eyes of Hindus, and did his best to conceal the traces of his deed by burying their feathers. The sacrilege was, however, detected, the whole party arrested, and the offender sentenced to have a hand amputated, though this punishment was eventually commuted to a whipping by the local official, who explained that the emperor had taken an oath that he and his successors would let the Hindus live under their own laws and customs and tolerate no breach of them."

Although the Mughals interfered little with Hindu customs, there was one ancient practice which they sought to stop. This was sati, or the custom of widows, particularly those of the higher classes, burning themselves on their husbands' funeral pyres. Akbar had issued general orders prohibiting sati, and in one noteworthy case, personally intervened to save a Rajput princess from immolating herself on the bier of her husband. Similar efforts continued to be made in the succeeding reigns. According to the European traveller Pelsaert, governors did their best to dissuade widows from immolating themselves, but by Jahangir's orders were not allowed to withhold their sanction if the woman persisted. Tavernier, writing in the reign of Shah Jahan, observed that widows with children were not allowed in any circumstances to burn, and that in other cases governors did not readily give permission, but could be bribed to do so. Aurangzeb was most forthright in his efforts to stop sati. According to Manucci, on his return from Kashmir in December, 1663, he "issued an order that in all lands under Mughal control, never again should the officials allow a woman to be burnt." Manucci adds that "This order endures to this day." This order, though not mentioned in the formal histories, is recorded in the official guidebooks of the reign. Although the possibility of an evasion of government orders through payment of bribes existed, later European travellers record that sati was not much practiced by the end of Aurangzeb's reign. As Ovington says in his Voyage to Surat: "Since the Mahometans became Masters of the Indies, this execrable custom is much abated, and almost laid aside, by the orders which nabobs receive for suppressing and extinguishing it in all their provinces. And now it is very rare, except it be some Rajah's wives, that the Indian women burn at all."

Any generalization about Indian history is dangerous, but the impression one gains from looking at social conditions during the Mughal period is of a society moving towards an integration of its manifold political regions, social systems, and cultural inheritances. The greatness of the Mughals consisted in part at least in the fact that the influence of their court and government permeated society, giving it a new measure of harmony. The common people suffered from poverty, disease, and the oppression of the powerful; court life was marked by intrigue and cruelty as well as by refinement of taste and elegant manners. Yet the rulers and their officials had moral standards which gave coherence to the administration and which they shared to some extent with most of their subjects. Undeniably, there were ugly scars on the face of Mughal society, but the sixteenth and seventeenth centuries had a quality of life that lent them a peculiar charm. The clearest reflection of this is seen in the creative arts of the period.

9

Jagirdari System Crisis in Mughal Period

The Mughal Empire held sway over a large part of India for nearly three centuries, but acrostic decline in its power and prestige came about by the first half of the eighteenth century. Not only did the political boundaries of the Empire shrink, the decline also saw the collapse of the administrative structure so assiduously built by rulers like Akbar and Shah Jahan. In the wake of the collapse of the Mughal power a number of Independent principalities emerged in all parts of the Empire.

However, the processes of the decline and the emergence of regional polities have been intensely debated among historians. It has also been a subject on which scholarly opinion is more sharply divided than on any other aspect of Mughal history.

The historiographical perspective on the Mughal decline can be divided into two broad sections. First, the Mughal-centric approach, i.e., historians attempt to identify the causes of the decline within the structure and functioning of the Empire itself.

Secondly, the region-centric approach where the perspective goes out of the precincts of the Empire into the regions to look for the causes of turmoil or instability in different parts of the Empire.

Empire-Centric Approach

The Empire-centric approach for explaining Mughal decline has progressed through different stages. Initially, theories focused on the individual learned their policies. William Irvine and

Jadunath Sarkar wrote the first detailed histories of this period (W. Irvine, The Later Moghuls, reprint, New Delhi, 1971; Jadunath Sarkar, The Fall of Mughal Empire, I. Calcutta, 1938; History of Aurangzeb, I-V, Calcutta 1912, 1916, 1919 and 1924). They attributed the decline to a deterioration in the characters of the Emperon and their nobles. Sarkar had analysed the developments of this period in the context of law and order. According to Sarkar, Aurangzeb was a religious fanatic. He discriminated against sections of the,nobles and officials on the basis of religion. This led to widescale resentment among the nobility. He argued that Aurangzeb's successors and their nobles were mere shadows of their predecessors and were thus unable to set right the evils of Aurangeb's legacy.

Jagirdari Crisis

In 1959 the publication of Satish Chandra's Parties and Politics at the Mughal Court. 170740 (Delbi, 1982, 3rd edition) marked the first serious attempt to study the structure of the Mughal Empire. Both its functioning and its plans were examined to understand the nature of the Empire and the masons for its subsequent decline. Satish Chandra studied the working of certain key institutions of the Empire. The two institutions he scrutinised were mansabdari and the jagirdari.

The nobles in the Mughal Empire were the core state officials. They were given ranks corresponding to their status in the Mughal official hierarchy. These ranks were called Mansab. Each holder of a Mansab, called mansabdar, was paid in assignments of land revenue (Jagir). Among the various obligations, the mansabdar had to maintain a requisite contingent of troopers.' These troopers were paid and maintained out of the revenue of the Jagir. They formed the base of the mansabdar's power, and assisted him in the collection of land revenue. Availability of the revenues to be assigned and the ability of the Mughals to collect them thus became two crucial pre-requisites for an effective working of the system. According to Chandra, Mughal decline has to be seen in the Mughal failure, towards the end of Aurangzeb's reign, to maintain the system of the mansabdar-jagirdar. As this system went into disarray, the Empire was bound to collapse.

Athar Ali's work on nobility and their politics in the late seventeenth century appeared in 1966 (M. Athar Ali, The Mughal

Nobility under Aurangzeb, Bombay, 1966 reprint, 1970). In this work the problems attending the annexation of the Deccan states, the absorption of the Marathas and Deccanis into the Mughal nobility, and the subsequent shortage of Jagir have been emphasized. The sudden increase in the number of nobles, caused due to the expansion of the Empire into the Deccan and Maratha territory, created a crisis in the functioning of the Jagir system. According to Athar Ali, the nobks competed for better jagh, which were increasingly beconsng rare due to the influx of nobles from the south. The logical consequence was the erosion in the political structure which was based on jaglrdari to a large extent.

In an important paper publishe& in 1969, S. Nurul Hassan puts forward the argument that the agtsrian nations as they developed during the Mughal rule gave rise to an authority structure which worked like a pyramid. In this form the rights of various kinds came to be superimposed upon each other. As a result bulk at the revenue demand of the state was transferred on to the cultivators. In the eighteenth century, with the decline of the Mughal authority, and with pressure on Jagirs agricultural economy began to face a crisis.

The zemindars as a class, were quite loyal to the state. But in the kind of agrarian situation that obtained in the Mughal empire, conflict between them and the state as also among themselves could not be checked. This often resulted in law and order problems and decimated the authority of the state. After the death of Aurangzeb and weakening of the imperial authority this equilibrium got distrirbed. The zemindars in this situation could be contained only by a group which would he independent of the support of the zemindars. Since such a class had not emerged by this time, the pattern of agrarian relations could not be changed. The cripple of the system became inevitable.

Agrarian Crisis

After the pioneering" work of Satish Chandra, historians continued to address themselves to various aspect of the functioning, of the Empire in order to identify the reason for its political collapse. The focus had evidently shifted from personalities and policies of individual rulers to larger and broader developments that were weakening the very structure on which the Mugbal edifice had been built. Irfan Habib attempted an in-depth analysis of the collapse of the Empire in his seminal work. (The Agrarian System of Mughal India, New Delhi 1963.) According to Habib, the mechanism of collection of revenue that the Mughals had evolved was inherently flawed. The imperial policy was to set the revenue at the bighesr rate possible to secure the greatest militery strength for the Empire, the nobles.

On the other band, tended to squeeze the maximum from their Jagirs, even if it ruined the peasantry and destroyed the revenue paying capacity of the area. Since, the nobles' Jagirs were liable to be transferred frequently, they did not find it necessary to follow a far-sighted policy of agricultural development. As the burden on the peasantry increased, they were often deprived of their very means of survival. In reaction to this excessive exploitation of the peasantry, the latter had no option but to protest. The forms of rural protest in Medieval India were varied in nature. In many areas the peasants took to flight. Entire villages were left deserted due to the large scale migration of peasants to the towns or other villages. Very often the peasants protested against the state by refusing to pay the revenue and were up in arms against the Mugbals. Habib argued that these peasant protests weakened the political and social fabric of the Empire.

Re-examination of 'Crisis'

J.F. Richards, M.N. Pearson and P. Hardy also give a pivotal position to the Mugbal involvement in the Deccan and the affairs of the Marathas in their explanation of the decline of the Empire. (Journal of Asian Studies, Vol. XXXV No.2, Feb, 1976, pp. 221-63. However, they differ from the Aligarb historians in their understanding of the nature of the Empire. For instance, according to Pealson, Mughal rule was indirect. It was not state control but local ties and norms which governed the lives of people. It was only foot the nobles that the concept of the Mughal Empire outweighed other "primordial attachments". The nobles were bound to the Empire only by patronage, which depended on the "constant military success" of the Emperor. Pearson emphasizes the absence of an impersonalised bureaucracy, and its not too optimistic consequences for the Mughal state. Once Mughal patronage slackened due to the lack of any further military expansion, and, a shortage of fertile areas to be allotted as Jagirs arose, the "personalised bureaucracy" of the Mugbal Empire showed signs of distress. This indeed sounded the death-knell for the Mughal system.

He made use of newly discovered archival sources to make a clear distinction between the crisis in Jagirdar. In his opinion, the crisis of the Jagir system did not occur because of the growth in the size of the ruling class and the corresponding decline in the revenues earmarked to be assigned in Jagir. In fact, Jagir system was in crisis because of non-functionality. According to Satish Chandra, it is important to understand the structure of the Medieval Indian society before one can talk about the background of the non-functionality of Jagirdari.

This of course was based on his ability to muster enough revenue and resources from his jagir in order to maintain the requisite contingent of troopers. Any factor which could disturb this neat balancing of jagirdar-zamlndar-peasant parameter would ultimately cause the decline of the Empire. Satish Chandra argues that in the 17th century the social conflicts which the Mughals were unable to resolve within the %road framework of the class alliance forged by them, were reflected in financial crisis and in the crisis of the jagir system, the two being interrelated. The crisis of the jagir system had made its appearance fairly early in the history of the Empire. The problem re-surfaced under Jahangir and Shah Jahan when the Eipire had expanded to fringe arms beyond the fertile tracts of the Ganga-Yamuna doab. Towards the end of Shah Jahan reign, the difference between jama in jagir lands became too glaring. A mansabdar was lucky if the realisation from his jar was more than five-monthly (i.e., revenue equivalent to five months' revenue only in a year). The number of sawars he maintained had to be reduced proportionally. In Deccan, the realisation was even less—about three-monthly, and the power and influence of the jagirdar proportionally lower. Once the military power of the Jagirdar was eroded, the tripler relationship which sustained the Empire fell apart.

According to Satish Chandra, perhaps the only manner in which the crisis of the jagirdari system could have been deferred for a longer period was a rapid development of the economy, both in agricultural and non-agricultural sectors. Trade was a supplementary source of income for rulers and nobles. Indeed what we need to know is whether the money saved by the nobles was used for investment in trade on a regular basis, or was trade made to yield money for the ostentatious living of the nobles? Some regional studies of traders and politics in Mughal India suggest that as a class, on an all India basis, the merchants were not rich or powerful enough to claim a share in state power. Trade and politics, by and large, remained segregated in Mughal India.

Developments in the agricultural sector were no less different. For a number of reasons, the state polides were aimed at preserving the small peasant economy. Thus, the khud-kasht (the rich peasants) were not allowed to cultivate their lands with the help of hired labour, or to extend their cultivation at the expense of the land held by pahis (middle level peasants who did not own land and moved with their implements of production from village to village). Some of the rich peasants used their wealth to lend money on interest, or mortgaged the lands of the poor peasants, reducing them to the position of share croppers. Thus, the only lines on which they could grow was to become intermediary zamindars or mahajans (grain dealers-cum-money-lenders). This perhaps explains the slow development of the agricultural economy, and its inability to avoid a precipitation of the jagirdari crisis. Satish Chandra further argues that the fundamental basis for the Jagirdari crisis was the medieval social system which limited agricultural growth. The administrative system was nared on this structure, the two acting and reacting on each other. All the other factors like the growth in the size of the ruling class, the growing ostentatious life style of the nobles which limited the surplus available for expanding production and resulted in slow economic growth were contributory factors to the growth of the crisis.

(Satish Chandra, Medieval India: Society, the Jagirdari Crisis and the Village. Delhi, 1982).

The Mughal decline has also been explained in terms of participation in the eighteenth century politics of groups conventionally regarded as non-political. Karen Leonard argues that "indigenous banking firms were indispensable allies of the Mugbal State", and that the great nobles "were more than likely to be directly dependent upon these firms". When in the period 1650-1750 thew banking firms began "the redirection of their economic and political support" towards regional politics and rulers, including the English East-India Company in Bengal, this led to bankruptcy, a series of political crises and the down fall of the Empire (Karen Leonard, 'The "Great Firm Theory of the Decline of the Mughal Empire', Compamtive Studies in Society and History, Vol. 21 No. 2, April, 1979, pp. 161-7).

The assumptions of Leonard conclusions do not get adequate support from the existing studies of Mughal polity and economy. Philip Calkins and M.N. Peanon, researching on Bengal and Gujarat respectively, give some evidence of merchants, participation in poritics (Philip C Calkins, 'The Formation of a Regionally Oriented Ruling Group in Bengal', Journal of Asian Studies. Vol. XXM No. 4, Aug, 1970; M. N. Pearson, Merchants and Rulers in Gujarat, California, 1976). However, Pearson refrains from suggesting that the Mughal finance system was dependent on merchants' credit. Calkins also limits his generalisation to the period and the region he examines. Leonard's source material is the same as that used by Calkins and Pearson. However, Leonard's conclusions remain unconvincing because no fresh evidence has been adduced.

Muzaffar Alam and Chetan Singh have used in their works region-centric approach to explain Mughal decline (M. Alam, The Crisis of Empire in Mughal North India, Awdh and the Pudab, 1707-1748, New Delhi, 1986; Chetan Singh, Region and Empire. Pudab in the Seventeenth Century, New Delhi, 1991). While Muzaffar Alam has made co-oparative study of the developments in the Mughal Subes of Awadh and Punjab, Chetsh Singh has made an in-depth study of the regional history of the 17th century Punjab.

Their studies are significant in that they throw new light on both the nature of the Mughal Empire as well as the process of its.weakening and eventual decline in the-17th and early 18th century.

Viewing the Mughal State from the perspective of the regional literature of the Mughal suba of Awadh, Alam suggests that the Mughal Empire signified a grdinating agency between conflicting communities and the various indigenous, socio-political systems at different levels. The basis of the Empire in a measure had been negative; its strength lay in the inability of the local communities and their systems to mobilize beyond relatively narrow bounds. Political integration in Mughal India was, up to a point, inherently flawed. It was to a large extent conditional on the co-ordination of the interests and the political activities of the various social groups led by local magnates.

This, in turn,.was dependent on the latter realizing that they could not amass fortunes by themselves. For it was very evident that the nobles were dependent for their position and power directly on the Emperor who appointed them. They had no hereditaty estates to consolidate or bequeath to their descendants. Their resources were scrutinized and regulated by the Empire. They were in a way representatives of the Mughal Emperor. Yet the nobility also had its tensions.

The policy of jagir transfer, by checking the noble's ambition to build a personal base, was meant to strengthen the imperial organisation. But it inconvenienced the nobles who opposed and resisted its implementation.

In many regions of the Mughal Empire it was left unimplemented in the 17th century. Alongside the local elites (zamindars) and the nobles, the village and qasba based madad-i maash holders (men of learning, who were given revenue free grants of land by the Mughal Emperors) and a very large numbers of lower level officials drawn from various regional and local communities, were all integrated intimately into the frameworks of the Empire.

The madad-i maash holdings were scattered in the zamindaris. They were meant to establish pockets of influence for the Empire in the far flung regions of the countryside. The emperors were of the view that the madad-i maash grantees would keep in check the power of the recalcitrant zamindars and thereby aid in balancing the social and political groups that constituted the base of the Empire.

According to Alam, the Mughal decline in the early 18th century has to be seen in the inability of the state to maintain its policy of checks and balances between the zamindars, Jagirdars, madad-i maash holders and the local indigenous elements; like the shaikhzada in Awadh.

In the early 18th century, there was a thrust 'of the nobles towards independent political alignments with the zamindars in order to carve out their own fortunes. Alongside there was an attempt between the various co-sharers of Mughal power (the zamindars, madad-i maash holders, etc.) to encroach on each other's rights and territorial jurisdictions. These developments were not entirel) incompatible with what happened earlier. But in the hey-day of the Empire these tensions had been contained. This was achieved at times by the use of military force and at other times by balancing out the power of one social group by settling another in the vicinity (e.g., the distribution of the madad-i-maash grantees in and around the zamindaris of Awadh).

Alam's major concern is to analyse what triggered of the imbalancing of the social and political equilibrium in the early 18th century. In other words, what caused the Mughal edifice to collapse in the early 18th century?

He is of the view that the late 17th and early 18th century, at least in the Awadh and Punjab regions, registered unmistakable economic growth. This is 'in sharp contrast to the more generalised argument about the early 18th century being in the throes of a financial crisis was postulated by Satish Chandra and others.

Social groups that had hitherto shared Mughal power and contributed to the political stability of the Empire, now began to take advantage of the economic boom in their regions. Many of them amassed wealth which helped them to increase their power to encroach on, the rights and privileges of others. The political edifice of the Empire was bound to suffer in the face of these developments.

Muzaffar Alam concludes that the decline of the Mughal ares manifested both in Awadh and the Punjab in a kind of political transformation and in the emergence and configuration of the elements of a new subadari.

The genesis for the emergence of independent regional units was present in both the provinces. But in Punjab it ended in chaos, while Awadh witnessed a stable dynastic rule. Muzaffar Alam's plea to understand the complexities of Mughal decline by looking at regional development in the early 18th century India has been followed up by Chetan Singh. His book Region and Empire takes a new lock at the regional history of the Mughal North India. The history of the Mughal suba of Punjab is reconstructed in the context of both the Mughal politics as well as the wider political changes that swept through the contemporary West Asian world. He argues that the Mughal administrative infrastructure no doubt linked the region to the Mughal administrative core. Yet, this conventional form of integration had its limitations. For local society and polity were subjected to a variety of stresses and the administrative system responded by transgressing the formal administrative divisions and sub-divisions of the Mughal governmental system.

This was true both of the general administration where pragmatic considerations led to flexibility in the creation of local offices and the kind of function they performed, as well as of revenue administration. In the revenue administration, with the passage of time, certain norms and conventions evolved which along with formal rules and* regulations contributed to the stability of the Mughal Empire.

However, by the late 17th century the silting of the river Indus had adversely affected the riverine traffic of Punjab. Its most serious implication was the gradual erosion of the highly commercialised Punjab economy.

The political upheavals in contemporary Turkey, fall of Qandahar to the Shah of Iran and the Mughal attempt to recover it virtually brought overland traffic to a standstill. This development coincided with the Yusufzai uprising (1667) in North-West Punjab and the Afridi rebellion in 1678. Singh argues that these political disturbances had grave social and economic consequences for Punjab: they disrupted trade and thereby gradually eroded the economy which was based on a commercialised agrarian sector. The loosening of Punjab's socio-economic structure led to social unrest in Punjab.

However, Singh contends that since the benefits of trade and commerce had been unequally distributed in the region, the discomforts caused by the decline of trade varied in different areas of the Punjab. Thus the areas most closely associated with the Sikh rebellion were those that were also.among the most commercialised and therefore most easily affected by economic regression. Thus, he concludes, the social unrest which eventually led to the dissociation of Punjab from the Empire was the product of long term processes. These processes had silently and steadily been at work in the region even before the political weakening of Empire had gained momentum in the 18th century.

It is here that Singh's study adds a new adimension to the already mooted question of the 'crisis of Empire'. For contrary to

Muzaffar Alam's study of Mughal Awadh and Punjab, which traces the dissociation of these regions from the Mughal Empire from the early 18th century, Singh sees the process at work in the hey day of the Empire. Thus, looking at the disintegration of the Empire from the point of view of the regional history of Punjab different picture emerges. Not only did different subae of the Empire dissociate from it for different reasons, but very often the dissociations were caused by political, social and economic developments beyond the purview of the Mughal Empire.

It is difficult to find a single explanation commonly applicable to the problems of the Mughal Empire in all its regions and provinces. For similar reasons it is difficult to accept a view of Mughal decline which applies uniformly to all parts of the Mughal Empire. The Mughal Empire at best represented a consensus of both the centre and the peripheries. In the early 18th century, it was this consensus which was disturbed. Different peripheries that had constituted the Empire followed their own different paths of developments. The eighteenth century regional histories thus indicate the endeavour to make use of the possibilities for growth within existing social structures.

Evidently the regional history perspective on Mughal decline negates the application of one general theory to explain Mughal collapse all over India. For the Mughal Empire, at best, represented a consensus between the centre and the peripheries. The peripheries were integrated to the Mughal core not merely administratively. For there was an economic and cultural assimilation between the conqueror and the vanquished. It was on certain shared economic and cultural spaces that the Mughal state structure rested.

Regions, held together by these heterogenous linkages to the Mughal core, were bound to be vulnerable to the kinds of social, economic and cultural changes that swept through 17th century Mughal India.

Different regions were affected in different ways. While in some regions links with the Mughal core were severed, in others they were retained. It was logical that the different regions followed different paths of dissociation from the Mughal Empire. Mughal decline was thus much more complex than what the historians subscribing to the Mughal-Centric approach would have us believe.

The decline of the Mughal Empire, it was initially believed, was the consequence of an administrative maladjustment due to which erupted a crisis in the jagir system, which ultimately led to the emergence of regional powers. Subsequently, the enquiries pertaining to the economic infrastructure of the Mughal empire point towards an agrarian crisis at the close of the seventeenth century, giving rise to rebellions by the Jats, Satnamis and Sikhs. To accept, however, one single explanation for the Mughal declining explanation that will cover all regions and provinces of the Empire-is a difficult proposition. In the early eighteenth century, probably the delicate equilibrium that had so long sustained the edifice of the Mughal system got disturbed. What followed then was a process of readjustment of all the diverse constituents of this system, the result being a dislocation of the Empire and the emergence of regional powers.

10

Economic Conditions during Muslim Rule

These people [the Bengalis] owe all their tranquility and prosperity to themselves, for its source lies in their devotion to agriculture, whereby a land originally covered with jungle has been reclaimed by their unremitting toil in tilling and planting.

The Political Economy of the Sultanate

The advent of Indo-Turkish rule fundamentally altered Bengal's physical and social landscape. In the mid fourteenth century, for example, the visiting Chinese merchant Wang Ta-yuan noted that the agrarian frontier had pushed far into the delta's hinterland, transforming formerly forested areas into fields of rice paddy (see chapter epigraph above). It was under Muslim rule, too, that Bengal's economy first became thoroughly monetized.

Now it is true that kings of the Chandra dynasty (ca. 825–1035) had minted silver coins, and that from the ninth or tenth century at least the delta's southeastern corner had been integrated into a wider Indian Ocean economy. But in Pala or Sena times, the major part of the delta is not known to have used metal coinage at all. By contrast, from the thirteenth century to the seventeenth, the Muslim rulers' silver coin, the *tanka*, circulated uninterrupted throughout the region.

In fact, the sequence of local conquests and bulges in the money supply suggests that Indo-Turkish rulers were driven into Bengal's hinterland, at least in part, by their thirst for uncoined silver. Each new conquest on Bengal's southern, eastern, or northern frontiers was followed by an expansion in the volume of silver coinage in circulation, the victors minting *tankas* from the accumulated silver stocks of defeated Hindu kingdoms. Sultan Rukn al-Din Kaikaus's conquest of southeastern Bengal in 1291 was followed by a substantial inflow of bullion, for example, which was quickly converted to coinage.

The conquest of the Sonargaon region in eastern Bengal by Sultan Fakhr al-Din Mubarak Shah (r. 1338–49) was also followed by increases in the silver supply. The same was true of Sultan Sikandar's 1358 conquests in Kamrup, or northern Bengal. The supply of coined silver levelled off during the late fourteenth century, but in 1420, when Sultan Jalal al-Din Muhammad reconquered much of eastern Bengal after an unsuccessful rebellion there, stocks of silver coinage again soared. So did they in 1494 when Sultan 'Ala al-Din Husain Shah reconquered Kamrup in northern Bengal.

In addition to silver coined from the booty of defeated kingdoms in the region, substantial quantities of treasure were imported in exchange for goods locally manufactured for export. As early as 1415 we hear of Chinese trade missions bringing gold and silver into the delta, in addition to satins, silks, and porcelain.

A decade later another Chinese visitor remarked that long-distance merchants in Bengal settled their accounts with *tankas*. The pattern continued throughout the next century. "Silver and Gold," wrote the Venetian traveller Cesare Federici in 1569, "from Pegu [Burma] they carrie to Bengala, and no other kind of Merchandize."

The monetization of Bengal's economy and its integration with markets throughout the Indian Ocean greatly stimulated the region's export-manufacturing sector. Although textiles were already prominent among locally manufactured goods at the dawn of the Muslim encounter in the tenth century, the volume and variety of textiles produced and exported increased dramatically after the conquest.

In the late thirteenth century, Marco Polo noted the commercial importance of Bengali cotton, and in 1345 Ibn Battutah admired the fine muslin cloth he found there. Between 1415 and 1432 Chinese diplomats wrote of Bengal's production of fine cotton cloths (muslins), rugs, veils of various colours, gauzes (Pers., *shana-baf*), material for turbans, embroidered silk, and brocaded taffetas.

A century later Ludovico di Varthema, who was in Gaur between 1503 and 1508, noted: "Fifty ships are laden every year in this place with cotton and silk stuffs.

These same stuffs go through all Turkey, through Syria, through Persia, through Arabia Felix, through Ethiopia, and through all India." A few years later Tome Pires described the export of Bengali textiles to ports in the eastern half of the Indian Ocean. Clearly, Bengal had become a major centre of Asian trade and manufacture.

Ashraf and Non-Ashraf Society

Bengal's Muslim society from the thirteenth century through the sixteenth was overwhelmingly urban, concentrated in the sultanate's successive capital cities—Lakhnauti from 1204, Pandua from about 1342, and Gaur from about 1432—and in the provincial towns of Satgaon, Sonargaon, and Chittagong.

Although new garrison towns regularly sprang up in the interior, as the numismatic and epigraphic evidence shows, the preeminence of the capital cities was assured, since members of the provincial nobility, regardless of where their land assignments were located, had to maintain residences there.

Gaur, especially, was by all accounts a splendid city (see figs. 1 and 2). "One of the best that I had hitherto seen," wrote Ludovico di Varthema in the early sixteenth century, when it had attained a population of forty thousand. In 1521 a visiting Portuguese described the city as very big, stretching for four leagues along the river and, it is said, extending so far inland that houses are still found beyond six leagues....The town is situated on a large plain which is flat like the whole of the surrounding area.

The streets and lanes are paved with brick like the Lisbon New Street. The market is everywhere and everything—food and other goods alike—is in plentiful supply and very cheap. The streets and cross-lanes are so full of people that [it] is impossible to move and it has reached the point where the high noblemen have taken to being preceded along the road to the palace by men carrying bamboo sticks to push people out of the way.

Foreigners were much impressed by the wealth of long-distance merchants residing in the sultanate's capitals. In 1415 a Chinese envoy wrote of men in Pandua who "wear a white cotton turban and a long white cotton shirt. On their feet they wear low sheepskin shoes with gold thread. The smarter ones think it the correct thing to have designs on them. Everyone of them is engaged in business, the value of which may be ten thousand pieces of gold." Around 1508, Varthema found in Gaur "the richest merchants I have ever met with." Ten years later, Duarte Barbosa also described wealthy Arabs, Iranians, Abyssinians, and "Indians" of Gaur. "The respectable Moors," he wrote, walk about clad in white cotton smocks, very thin, which come down to their ankles, and beneath these they have girdles of cloth, and over them silk scarves; they carry in their girdles daggers garnished with silver and gold, according to the rank of the person who carries them....They are luxurious, eat well and spend freely, and have many other extravagancies as well. They bathe often in great tanks which they have in their houses. Every one has three or four wives or as many as he can maintain.

The nobles and merchants described above formed part of the Muslim elite, or *ashraf*, which also included urban Sufis, religious officials (*'ulama*), and foreign-born soldiers and administrators. In fact, foreign origin, even if only of one's ancestors, formed an important, if not defining, element of *ashraf* identity. Writing around 1495, the poet Vipra Das referred to the Muslim preachers (*mullas*) and judges (*qazis*) of Satgaon as "Saiyids," "Mughals," and "Pathans"—that is, men claiming an Arab, Central Asian, or Afghan origin. About a century later the poet Mukundaram (fl. 1590), like Vipra Das a native of the southwestern delta, described urban Muslims as men who had immigrated from points west of Bengal. Religious sentiment also inclined *ashraf* Muslims to look westward. In 1505 the patron of a mosque in Sonargaon proudly counted himself as one "who has made a pilgrimage to Macca and Madina, and has visited the two foot-prints of the Prophet." Similarly, a 1567 inscription on the congregational mosque in Old Malda compared it with the holy shrine in Mecca, referring to Malda's house of worship as the "second Ka'aba" (*thanî ka'aba*). For the devout, phrases such as these served to mitigate the great distance separating Bengal from Islam's holiest shrines in Arabia, tenuously linked to the delta by a long and dangerous sea voyage.

Prominent among the *ashraf* were judges, or *qazîs*, who possessed sufficient expertise in Islamic Law to arbitrate disputes involving fellow Muslims. Below them in status were the *mullas*, the ubiquitous ordinary preachers and the least-educated members of the Muslim establishment. An inscription on the congregational mosque at Satgaon, dated 1529, hints at how these two members of the *ashraf* interrelated:

> *Because the body of* mullas *and landholders (*arbal*) will be cursed by God if they defraud public endowments, it is binding and necessary that governors and* qazîs *prevent such frauds, so that on the Day of Judgment they will not be seized for their oppressions.*

This suggests that the court relied on the *qazîs*, together with governors, to curb what it considered the *mullas'* fraudulent ways—in this case, a tendency to defraud public endowments. *Qazîs* were also the most visible representatives of royal authority vis-a-vis non-Muslims, since they were charged with maintaining public order generally. In the early sixteenth century, for example, when the devotees of a Hindu cult caused a public disturbance with their ecstatic singing in the West Bengal town of Nadia, local Muslims complained to the town's *qazî*. Although the judge excused that particular violation of public order, he warned that he would punish future infractions by confiscating the property of violators.

Socially distinct from the *ashraf* were Muslim urban artisans who formed part of Bengal's growing industrial proletariat. Their organization into separate, endogamous communities (*jati*) with distinctive occupations paralleled the organization of Hindu society in the southwestern delta, and suggests their origins in that society. Mukundaram mentions fifteen Muslim *jatis* in a list of communities inhabiting an idealized Bengali city of his day—weavers (*jola*), livestock herders (*mukeri*), cake sellers (*pithari*), fishmongers (*kabari*), converts from the local population (*garasal*), loom makers (*sanakar*), circumcisers (*hajam*), bow makers (*tirakar*), papermakers (*kagajî*), wandering holy men (*kalandar*), tailors (*darji*), weavers of thick cord (*benata*), dyers (*rangrej*), users of hoes (*halan*), and beef sellers (*kasai*). So thoroughly were these groups integrated with Bengali society that by the late sixteenth century, when Mukundaram was writing, it was impossible to conceive of a city that did not have, alongside a long list of Hindu *jatis*, a full complement of Muslim artisan groups.

Moreover, these groups constituted the earliest-known class of Bengali Muslims. Fully five of them—the weavers, loom makers, tailors, weavers of thick ribbon, and dyers, were linked to the growing textile industry, and were probably recruited from amongst existing Hindu castes already engaged in these trades, or from amongst former agriculturalists or unskilled labourers responding to labour demands created by the expanding industry. Government demand appears to have brought into existence still other groups of Muslim artisans. The bow makers, for example, provided weaponry for the kingdom's armed forces, while papermakers would have met both the bureaucracy's appetite for files and the Muslim religious elite's demand for books. In fact, nearly half of the Muslim *jatis* listed by Mukundaram bore Perso-Arabic names, suggesting that they had come into being only after the Turkish conquest.

Upper Classes and Luxurious Life

> *'All the surplus produce' was swept into the coffers of the Mughal nobility and pampered them in a degree of luxury not dreamt of even by kings in Persia and Central Asia.' —Jadunath Sarkar.*

Nobles and courtiers, army commanders and provincial governors, in fact all high officials of the Muslim government formed the upper classes. In 'civilian' upper classes could be counted the Ulama and the Mashaikh, scholars and historians, and some very rich Muslim merchants. A study of the high classes under two major categories-nobles, and Ulama and Mashaikh-would suffice to give a general idea of the life of Muslim upper classes, their composition, their corruption, their licence, their hopes and fears, and their high style of living.

The Nobles

The nobles constituted the ruling bureaucracy. In the early years of Muslim rule (1206-1399) foreign adventurers and warriors monopolised appointments to high offices. In the beginning the Turks formed the bulk of the ruling elite. Besides, Persians, Abyssinians, Egyptians, Afghans and converted Mongols also continued to obtain high positions. Under the Lodi Sultans (1451-1526), Afghan adventurers of various tribes and clans flocked to India like 'ants and locusts'. Even in the Mughal times (1526-1707-1857) the imperial service remained predominantly foreign with Iranis and Turanis forming the core of the cadre. The Turanis hailed from Central Asia where the Turkish language was spoken.

Iranis comprised the Persian speaking people and belonged to the region presently extending from Iraq and Iran to Afghanistan.

The Mughal nobles were also known as Mansabdars. The *Mansabdars* were not only government officers, but also the richest class in the empire. They formed a closed aristocracy; entrance into this class was not usually possible for the common people, whatever their merits. Naturally, therefore, the most important factor which was taken into account when nobles were appointed was heredity. The *Khanazads,* the scions of royalty and sons and descendants of *Mansabdars,* had the best claim to such appointments.

The Indian Muslim nobles, who were local converts, also rose to be officers in the upper cadres, but foreigners were always preferred. The fourteenth century Persian chronicler Ziyauddin Barani, who was born in India but traced his ancestry to a Turki Noble, credits the foreigner Turks with all possible virtues and the Indian Muslims with all kinds of imperfections. The invectives he hurls on the converted Sultan Nasiruddin Khusrau Shah (C.E. 1320), are too well known to need repetition. Muhammad Tughlaq always preferred foreign Muslims to Indians for appointment as officers. The rebellion of Ain-ul-mulk Multani (1339) during his reign was a symptom of the resentment felt by the India-born nobles against this policy of prejudice. In turn Khan-i-Jahan, a Telingana Brahmin convert, dominated the court of Sultan Firoz Tughlaq. The career of Mahmud Gawan, the minister of the Bahmani Sultan Muhammad III (1463-1482), illustrates both the reasons for which preference was given to foreigners and the jealousy it engendered. Foreign nobles looked down upon Indian Muslim nobles, and considered them as 'lowborn', although not all foreign Muslims were of high lineage.

Right through the Muslim rule, low origin foreigners used to come as individuals and in groups to seek employment in India. Writing about the foreign element in the Mughal nobility in seventeenth century Bernier says that 'the Omarahs mostly consist of adventurers from different nations who entice one another to the court; and are generally persons of low descent, some having been originally slaves, and the majority being destitute of education. The Mogol raises them to dignities, or degrades them to obscurity; according to his own pleasure and caprice.' W.H.

Moreland, however, does not consider all foreign immigrants as of low descent. He says that in Mughal India 'there were huge prizes to be won' and one need not wonder that the service should have attracted to the court the ablest and most enterprising men from a large portion of Western Asia.' High and low, foreign and Indian, the Muslim nobles after all belonged to one and the same cadre, and they tried to come closer together. On the one hand, foreign Muslims used to become locals after the lapse of a few generations. Bernier writes that 'the children of the third and fourth generation (of Uzbegs, Persians, Arabs and Turks)' are held in much less respect than the new corners.' On the other hand, the low-born Indian Muslim became elitist with rise in economic status. There was a saying: 'Last year I was a *julaha*, this year a *sheikh*; and the next year, if the harvest be good, I shall be a *saiyyad*.' 'Belonging to Islam' was a great cementing force, and, whatever the colour of the skin, all Muslim nobles tried to feel as one, as belonging to the ruling elite, as searching for exotic roots. It was aristocratic on the part of the orthodox Muslim to feel that he was in India, but not of it. He durst not strike his roots deep into the native soil. He must import traditions, language and culture. His civil and criminal law must be derived from the writings of jurists and the decisions of judges in Baghdad and Cairo. The Muslim in India was an intellectual exotic; he considered it *infra dig* to adapt himself to his environment.

Besides the competition between Indian and foreign Muslim nobles, there was also constant contest between Muslim and Hindu nobles. With the permanent establishment of Muslim rule, the policy of the sultans was generally to keep the Hindus excluded and appoint only Muslims. But the Hindus possessed native intelligence and experience, sons of the soil as they were, and many of the best Hindus had to be employed, especially during the Mughal period. The Hindus in a way were 'indispensable'. To them belonged, according to Badaoni, 'half the army and half the land. Neither the Hindustanis (Indian Muslims) nor the Mughals can point to such grand lords as the Hindus have among themselves.' Bernier too did not fail to notice this.

These nobles were in attendance on the king in the capital or in camp, and in outstations held civil and military assignments, as governors of provinces or commanders of the army. Indeed they were expected to cultivate versatility, there being no distinction between civil and military appointments and duties. Raja Birbal, after many years as court wit, met his death fighting Yusafzais as commander of troops on the frontier while Abul Fazl, the most eminent literary figure of the time, distinguished himself in military operations in the Deccan.

The nobles were called Umara and were graded as Khans, Maliks, Amirs and Sipehsalars in the Sultanate period, and as Mansabdars under the Mughals. According to Barani a Sarkhail commanded ten horsemen; a Sipehsalar ten Sarkhails; an Amir ten Sipahsalars; a Malik ten Amirs; and a Khan, ten Maliks. According to the author of *Masalik-ul-Absar*, a Khan commanded more or less 100,000 troops, an Amir 10,000, a Malik a thousand, and so on. The term Amir was normally used in a generic sense to denote a high officer. In Akbar's time and after, all the great men of the Mughal Empire were graded and appointed to a *mansab* (rank) in the imperial service. From the lowest rank, that of the commander of ten, upto the rank of 400 an officer was known as Mansabdar. From 500 onwards a noble was known as Amir, or Khan, or Khan-i-Azam. They were all generally spoken of as Umara.

The Umara were highly paid. Their remuneration was paid sometimes in the form of a cash salary, at others by the grant of a revenue assignment or *iqta*. 'The *iqta* was basically a salary collected at source.' According to the chroniclers of the Sultanate period every Khan received two lakh *tankahs*, every Malik from 50 to 60 thousand *tankahs*, every Amir from 40 to 50 thousand *tankahs*, and so on. The salaries during the Mughal period were equally high. It has been computed by expert opinion that a commander of 5000 could count on at least Rs.18,000 a month under Akbar and his successor.

He could even improve upon this amount if he practised judicious economy in his military expenditure and had the good fortune of securing a profitable *jagir*. A commander of 1000 could similarly count on receiving Rs.5000 a month (equal to from rupees 25,000 to 30,000 in 1914), while a commander of 500 would have received the equivalent of Rs.5000 to 6000 at the same rate. 'While therefore the precise figures are uncertain, it appears to be reasonable to conclude that the higher ranks of the Imperial Service were remunerated on a scale far more liberal than that which now prevails in India (C. 1914), or for that matter in any portion of the world.'

Luxurious Life

Their high salaries and emoluments introduced into the lives of the Umara all the uses and abuses of luxury. They lived with such ostentation that it was not to be seen elsewhere in the world, and 'the most sumptuous of European courts cannot compare in richness and magnificence with the lustre beheld in Indian courts.' Their splendid life-style may be studied in its two aspects-private inside the harem and public outside of it. They lived in magnificent mansions some costing four to six thousand gold *tankahs (dinars)* and provided with all amenities. By the seventeenth century the Mahals of the nobles had gained in architectural excellence and constructional designs. At Agra, on the banks of the Jumna, 'many persons have erected buildings of three or four storeys,' writes emperor Jahangir. Asaf Khan's palace had a fair Diwan Khana which was flanked by 'diverse lodgings for his women neatly contrived with galleries and walks.' Asaf Khan's palace was exceedingly handsome and costly, but the others were equally elegant. The basic pattern of the mansions of the nobles was the same. One portion of the building was the Diwan Khana or the men's quarters but 'the greater portion was occupied by their ladies and was called Zenan Khana.'

'In the houses of the nobles the women's apartments are in the centre, and it is generally necessary to traverse two or three large courts and a garden or two before reaching there.' Bernier's observations about the houses of nobles of Delhi are similar to those of Pelsaert at Agra. They were spacious and along with 'courtyards, gardens, trees, basins of water, small *jets deau* in the hall or at the entrance, and handsome subterraneous apartments which are furnished with large fans.' While encamping, their tents were made equally magnificient. 'All the arcades and galleries were covered from top to bottom with brocade, and (even) the pavement with rich carpets.'

The nobles' ladies were numerous and spendthrift. Pelsaert says that 'as a rule they have three or four wives'. All live together 'surrounded by high walls' called the *mahal,* having tanks and gardens inside. Each wife has separate apartments for herself and her slaves, of whom there may be 10, or 20, or 100, according to her fortune. Each has a monthly allowance for her (expenditure). Jewels and clothes are provided by the husband according to the extent of his affection'. Their Mahals were adorned with 'superfluous pomp and ornamental dainties.' The ladies made extensive use of gold and silver, for ornaments and jewellery, as well for their utensils and table service. Even their bedsteads were 'lavishly ornamented with gold and silver.' During the earlier period, there is also mention of gold bath-tubs and gold horse-shoes.

For the security and supervision of these hundreds of ladies, dozens and dozens of maids and eunuchs were required. The harem paraphernalia cost tons of money. Furthermore, it was a fashion for the Umara to visit the houses of dancing girls, take them or call them to their own mansions and pay them handsomely. Throughout the medieval times the nobility indulged in the expensive hobbies of women, wine, song and drugs. Chess and *chausar* they played at home; big game shooting, taming and flying birds, playing chaugan and practising with swords were their outdoor recreations. Dozens of falconers, pigeon-boys and attendants were employed to keep their birds and horses in trim. The nobles, their ladies, and even their slave-girls dressed in the best of cotton fineries and richest embroidered silks. Their food was rich and full of delicacies. Their boon companions partook of it freely.

Most of the nobles 'were soaked in wine and sunk in debauch' but they were also patrons of art and poetry. Since I have made a comprehensive study of the luxurious life of the medieval Muslim nobility in my monograph entitled *The Mughal Harem,* I shall refrain from repeating here what I have already stated therein in detail except reproducing one paragraph from the book. 'The large establishment of wives and servants rendered the nobles immobile. No Indian scholars, engineers or travellers went abroad to learn the skills the Europeans were developing in their countries. While people from Europe were frequently coming to Hindustan, no Indian nobleman could go to the West because he could not live without his harem and he could not take with him his cumbersome harem to countries situated so far away. Europe at this time was forging ahead in science and technology through its Industrial Revolution, but the Mughal elites kept themselves insulated from this great stride because of inertia. Consequently, the country was pulled back from marching with progress, a deficiency which has not been able to be made up until now.'

Outside their mansions the Umara were extra ostentatious. Since they attained to highest honours 'at court, in the provinces, and in the armies; and who are, as they call themselves, the Pillars of the Empire, they maintain the splendour of the court, and are never seen out-of-doors but in the most superb apparel; mounted sometimes on an elephant, sometimes on horseback, and not unfrequently in a *paleky* attended by many of their cavalry, and by a large body of servants on foot- not only to clear the way, but to flap the flies and brush off the dust with tails of peacocks; to carry the spitoon, water to allay the Omrah's thirst.'

Over and above the expenses on their 'large establishment of wives, servants, camels and horses,' the nobles were expected to present valuable gifts to the king on birthday anniversaries, Ids, Nauroz and other festivals, according to their pay and status. 'Some of them, indeed take that opportunity of presenting gifts of extraordinary magnificence, sometimes for the sake of ostentatious display, sometimes to divert the king from instituting an inquiry into their excessive exactions, and sometimes to gain the favour of the king, and by that means obtain an increase of salary. Some present fine pearls, diamonds, emeralds and rubies; others offer vessels of gold set with precious stones; others again give gold coins'. The king also gave some gift in exchange, but the presents of the nobles were much costlier and often extracted by the king.

During a festival of this kind Aurangzeb, having paid a visit to Jafar Khan, the Wazir made a present to the king of gold coins to the amount of one hundred thousand crowns, some handsome pearls and a ruby about the value of which prevailed great 'confusion among the principal jewellers, and it might have cost five hundred thousand crowns.' Thus the king sometimes took the initiative in contriving to extract costly presents and gathered huge amounts, for says Pelsaert, 'from the least to the greatest right up to the King himself everyone is infected with insatiable greed.' Money spent on bribes and presents often proved profitable investment, for, without presents the nobles could hardly expect timely response to his petition. Not only were gifts presented to the king, means had to be found for making valuable presents, every year, to a Wazir, an eunuch or a lady of the seraglio, or to any other person whose influence at court the nobleman considered indispensable.

Bribery and Corruption

Such high expenses of building spacious mansions, exchanging costly presents, maintaining a large harem of wives and concubines-in short, living in style at home and indulging in pompous display outside, could not be met by the aristocracy from their salaries alone. Therefore, the nobles augmented their income by other means. There were many sources from which extra amounts of money could come to their coffers, like enjoying a large military command, a profitable political appointment and a lucrative revenue assignment, and these were all inter-connected, all providing opportunities of corruption and exploitation.

Every nobleman or Mansabdar was alloted a quota of troops which he was expected to maintain. From the very beginning of Turkish rule the conquered land used to be distributed by the king among army officers, nobles, government officials and even soldiers as gifts, grants and rewards and also in lieu of personal salary, and for paying their soldiers. These grants were not hereditary, and were given as pay for military service. But in course of time the land-holders continued in possession of their land without rendering any military service. On inquiry it was found by Sultan Balban that about 2,000 cavalry officers had received villages in the Doab alone by way of pay during the time of Iltutmish, but for the next forty years or more many of the grantees had become old and infirm, or had died. But their sons and even slaves continued to live off the lands as if they were an inheritance. Many of them were clever enough to get the assignments recorded in their own names in the books of the Ariz-i-Mumalik obviously by bribing the officials'. According to their means by wine, goats, chicken, pigeon, butter and food-stuffs from their villages' to the Deputy Muster-Master and his officials.

Sultan Balban tried to improve matters and so did many other rulers but corruption remained entrenched.

The salary of the soldiers and expenditure on their horses usually formed part of the pay of the Umara or Mansabdars who were expected to spend it on them. But this system gave the nobleman an opportunity to retain some money from every man's pay and prepare false returns of the horses he was supposed to provide. 'Many of the lords who hold the rank of 5000 horses, do not keep even 1000 in their employ.' This practice was universal throughout the medieval period. It rendered the Amir's income very considerable, particularly when he was so fortunate as to have some good *jagirs* or suitable lands assigned to him. For some of the officers 'received double, and even more than that, in excess of the estimated value of their grants'.

There was thus the practice 'which prevails too much at all times' of purchasing governorships against hard cash. Sometimes the king assigned a governorship to the highest bidder. The governor or farmer of revenue so appointed had to compensate himself by mercilessly fleecing the merchants and peasants of the province. In this way many people without the smallest patrimony, some even originally wretched slaves, involved in debt, became great and opulent lords overnight. Bernier even complains that the Great Mogol did not select for his service 'gentlemen of opulent and ancient families; sons of his citizens, merchants and manufacturers' affectionately attached to their sovereign' and willing to maintain themselves' by means of their own patrimony' Instead he is surrounded' by parasites raised by the dregs of society.' That is how 'the misery of this ill-fated country is increased.'

For many an Umara just looted both the government and the people all at once. In this regard certain misconceptions may be removed at the outset. It is generally believed that corruption flourishes in a democracy or a soft state where no one can be punished until proved guilty, and that despotic rulers would not brook it. Another idea repeatedly put forward is that it is poverty and low salaries that breed corruption, and that it is bound to be reduced in proportion to the rise in emoluments and standard of living.

However, on a study of the records of medieval times, when autocracy was the order of the day, we find that corruption was quite well-grounded, and people and the government were unabashedly cheated. Cheating of the people and the government are almost synonymous. In the fourteenth century too, those who cheated the people could not rest at that, and they took every opportunity of defrauding the government whenever an opportunity presented itself. One such opportunity came when Muhammad bin Tughlaq introduced his famous token currency. Another, when he struck upon the novel (now commonly practised) idea of having large-scale farm cultivation. An area of about 45 miles square (30 *krohs*) was set aside for intensive farming in which not a patch was to be left uncultivated at any time by changing crops constantly. A hundred *shiqdars* were appointed to supervise the project. They promised to cultivate thousands of *bighas* of land and also to reclaim waste land. Each one of them received fifty thousand *tankahs* in cash as advance (*sondhar*) from the State. But they turned out to be greedy and dishonest persons. They cheated the government, squandered the money on personal needs and did not care to cultivate the allotted area. In this way the State lost not less then 70,00,000 *tankahs* in all. Of the advance not even a hundredth or a thousandth part could be recovered and the avaricious *shiqdars* embezzled the whole amount. And all this callousness was there about a measure which had been undertaken to ameliorate famine conditions.

A few more instances of corruption from the Sultanate period may be mentioned to appreciate the depth and extensivity of the malady. During the reign of Firoz Shah the profession of soldiers was made hereditary. Also old men were not retired on compassionate ground and efficiency of the army naturally suffered. Over and above this, corruption was galore in the Diwan-i-Arz. Horses of little value were brought to the Diwan and were passed as serviceable, obviously by greasing the palms of the clerks. In this reference a story narrated by Shams Siraj Afif is worth citing. Once the Sultan overheard a soldier complaining to a friend that because he did not have the necessary money to pay as bribe, he had not been able to get a fitness certificate for his horse at the Diwan-i-Arz. 'The Sultan inquired how much was needed, and the soldier said that if he had a gold *tankah* he could get a certificate for his horse. The Sultan ordered his purse-bearer to give a *tankah* to the soldier.' The trooper went to the Diwan-i-Arz with the *ashrafi* and paying it to the clerk concerned got the certificate. He then returned and thanked the Sultan. Encouragement to corruption from the head of the State was a matter of concern. But what else could Afif say but that Firoz Shah was a very kind-hearted and affectionate Sultan!

These cases of bribery, corruption and embezzlement concern government officials of not so high a status among the upper classes. But the highest nobles of the State indulged in them. The story of the deception of Kajar Shah, the Master of Mint, speaks for itself. It is so interesting that its incidents may be given in some detail. Firoz Tughlaq had issued several varieties of new coins and *shashgani* (or six-*jital*-piece) was one of them. As the coin went into circulation, it was reported to the Sultan by two courtiers that there was a deficiency of one grain of silver in the *shashgani,* and they prayed for an investigation. If what they had said was proved to be true, they pleaded, the officials responsible for debasement of the coin must take the consequences. The Sultan immediately directed the Wazir, Khan-i-Jahan Maqbul, to investigate the matter. Khan-i-Jahan was equally keen about the enquiry. Indeed he observed that 'the coinage of kings was like an unmarried daughter, whom no one would seek after, however beautiful and charming she might be, if any aspersion had, rightly or wrongly, been cast upon her character. So also was the case with the royal coins; if any one honestly or falsely alleged a debasement of the currency, the insinuation would spread, the coinage would earn a bad name, and no one would take it.'

The affair was as scandalous as it was unique. To hold an open inquest was ruled out because the bona fides of the government itself were in question. Therefore the Wazir decided on a secret investigation, and sent for Kajar Shah, the Master of Mint, and asked him if his officials had been covetous. Kajar Shah knew that his game was up and he thought it best to make a clean breast of it to the Wazir. Khan-i-Jahan could not displease the Sultan, who had insisted that the intrinsic value of the coin should be tested in his presence. But he also could not allow the government to get into disrepute, and now that he had known the truth, he thought it best to hush up the case. Therefore, he recommended to Kajar Shah to arrange the matter over with the goldsmiths that they so manage their performance before the king that the process of debasement of the *shashgani* may not be detected. The goldsmiths, charcoal dealers and stove (*angusht*) managers were all tutored and everything was given a foolproof finish. Firoz Shah was requested to watch the operation sitting in a private apartment with Khan-i-Jahan Maqbul. Kajar Shah and his accusers were called in. The goldsmiths were also brought in. The charcoal dealers brought the stoves and placed them before the goldsmiths. Several *shashgani* pieces were placed in the crucible, which the goldsmiths put upon the fire. The Sultan meanwhile entered into a conversation with his minister, and while he was so engaged, the workmen adroitly picked up the required pieces of silver and surreptitiously threw them into the melting pot. After a while the crucible was taken off the fire and the contents were weighed; the *shashgani* was proved to be of full standard value. Kajar Shah was presented with a robe of honour and other favours. He was seated on an elephant and taken round the city so that people might understand that the *shashgani* was of full value. The 'honest' accusers were thus proved false and banished.

Another instance. An important nobleman, Shamsuddin Abu Rija, the Auditor General (Mustaufi), had earned wide notoriety as a professional bribe-taker, embezzler and at that a tyrant. Shams Siraj Afif, historian contemporary of Firoz Shah, devotes thirty-five pages to record the crimes of Abu Rija. The three years during which he held the office of the Auditor General, his hand of greed extended to all officers, Zamindars and Amils. Those who gave him bribes, were permitted to go scot-free; others who did not, were implicated by him on one charge or another and punished. Nobody dared to raise a voice against his criminal breach of trust or his atrocities, because he was a hot favourite of the Sultan. Even before he was made the Mustaufi, he, as the deputy governor of Gujarat, had borrowed 90 thousand *tankahs* from the Provincial Treasury for his own use, but had not refunded the amount. To hide his improper gains he had built a new mansion in Delhi and had buried underground thousands of gold *Ashrafis*. At last the Sultan could not keep his eyes closed to Shamsuddin's black deeds because a number of nobles, including the Khan-i-Jahan, son of Khan-i-Jahan Maqbul, insisted that he should be brought to book. Shamsuddin's mansion was searched and his reserves of gold dug out. He was imprisoned and tortured so severely that he could never ride a horse again. Strangely enough when Firoz's son Muhammad ascended the throne, he recalled Shamsuddin Abu Rija and reinstated him with all honours.

But the one man who amassed probably the largest amount of wealth in the Sultanate period, escaped scot-free. This man was Bashir, a slave of Firoz Shah. He had originally come as a part of the dower of Firoz's mother. In course of time, and through the favour of Sultan Firoz, he rose into prominence and got the title of Imadul Mulk. His one passion was acquisition of wealth. Related to the sultan as he was, he soon accumulated crores of *tankahs*. Gunny bags required for storing the coin alone were estimated to cost 2,500 tankahs, the price of each bag being four *jitals*; but Imadul Mulk objected to this extravagant outlay for bags and directed that pits should be dug in the ground and the money placed therein like as corn is stored. He had amassed thirteen crore *tankahs* but he was greedy about acquiring more.

Just imagine thirteen crore *tankahs*. The total revenue of a year during Firoz's reign was six crore and seventy-five lac *tankahs*; and one individual slave of the Sultan (Bashir-i-Sultani) had acquired wealth amounting to two years' total revenue of the country. Could corruption go further? 'There were many rich Khans and Maliks in the time of Firoz Shah,' writes Afif, 'but no one was so rich as he; indeed there never had been one so rich in any reign or in any kingdom.' Still the officers of the Revenue Department could not call him to account; they were indeed afraid of him, for he was a favourite of the Sultan. To please the Sultan, Imadul Mulk once presented him with a crore of *tankahs*. But twelve crores still remained with him. At his death, the Sultan ordered nine crores to be deposited in the State exchequer on the plea that 'Bashir is my property (as his slave), and so his property is mine.' Three crores were left with Imadul Mulk's son Ishaq who also got the title of his father. Afif adds that Ishaq himself was an extremely rich man and did not stand in need of his father's wealth.

The chronicler philosophises by saying: 'These nobles accumulated so much wealth by lawful and unlawful means (*vajeh na vajeh*), and then leaving it undertook the last journey where they were to account for all this wealth.' But such ill-gotten gains at least created havoc in this world, because, according to Afif himself, 'much of the trouble that came about in the time of Sultan Muhammad (son of Firoz) was due to the accumulation of such wealth in the hands of a few nobles.'

Thus there was corruption in the army, in civil administration and in the royal mint. Hoarding, black-marketing and bribery were commonly practised. Even the judiciary was not free from corruption, and that too during the reign of a strong and stern monarch like Alauddin. Talking of Qazi Hamiduddin Multani, Ziyauddin Barani cryptically remarks, 'it would not be proper to write about his qualities in history.' He also says that not 'the godfearing and abstemious but corruptible, greedy and mundane' people were appointed as judges. His one complaint was that judges used to stretch the meaning of the Quranic texts to carry out the wishes of the Sultans.

The indictment by Maulana Shamsuddin Turk of the judiciary of the day is also worth citing. The Maulana who hailed from Egypt, addressed a letter to Alauddin saying that 'ill-fated wiseacres of black faces sat in mosques with abominable law books and made money by cheating both the accuser and the accused, and the Qazis' did not bring these facts to the notice of the king.' It is said that Shamsuddin Turk was opposed to Qazi Hamiduddin, and therefore wrote in such a way, but in *Mutla-i-Anwar*, Amir Khusrau also observes that the Qazis were ignorant of the principles of law. The appointment of Ibn Battutah, who did not know a word of law, as the Qazi of the capital by Muhammad bin Tughlaq, came to him as the greatest surprise.

Having studied some prominent cases of bribery, corruption and hoarding, of the nobles, and the rich upper class people in the Sultanate times, let us analyse their genesis and their prominent aspects. It is clear that corruption had nothing much to do with poverty or a low standard of living. During Balban's rule the nobility and armymen, who could not or would not perform their duties for which lands had been granted to them, were not poor. But they wanted their privileges to continue; about performing their duties they were not concerned. Fakhruddin, the Kotwal, who pleaded their case with the king was moved as much by compassion as by self-interest. He was himself old and in course of time stood to lose all privileges if the orders of Balban were not amended. The people who minted counterfeit coins found in the token currency of Muhammad bin Tughlaq a challenge to their intelligence and ingenuity, and took advantage of the golden opportunity provided by it to get rich. The officials of the Diwan-i-Arz who took a gold *tankah* for issuing the fitness certificate to the cavalryman in the days of Firoz were not poor; they were habitual bribe-takers. The *shiqdars* or officers who embezzled the money advanced to them for cultivation by Muhammad bin Tughlaq again, were not poor. The people who minted debased currency, the wholesalers and retailers who indulged in hoarding and black-marketing, men like Kajar Shah and Bashir-i-Sultani, did not do what they did because they were poor, but because they were greedy and opportunists. The object of the opportunists was to get rich, of the rich to get richer. Their luxurious life, their women and wine and their ambition to amass wealth, kept the torch of corruption burning.

Individual cases of corruption and embezzlement apart, the sure and perennial sources of extra income of the nobles were two-what they could save on their troops and what they could collect in addition to the nominal value of their assignments-and able and unscrupulous men made as much extra wealth as possible from both these. In the words of Shihabuddin Ahmad, 'The *khans, maliks, amirs,* and *isfah-salars* receive the revenues of the places assigned to them by the treasury 'Generally speaking they bring in much more than their estimated value' Some of the officers receive double, and even more than that, in excess of the estimated value of their grants.' What this practice meant to the poor peasant would be discussed later. The irony of the matter was that everyone knew about it, including the king himself. The king was even a party to the system for he allotted good lands to his favourite nobles. Even Sher Shah Suri, who is regarded as a friend of the agriculturists, changed his *amils* (revenue collectors) every year, or second year, and sent new ones, for he said that 'there is no such income and advantage in other employments as in the government of a district. Therefore I (Sher Shah) send my good old loyal experienced servants to take charge of districts, that the salaries, profits, and advantages, may accrue to them in preference to others; and after two years I change them, and send other servants like to them, that they also may prosper'.

In the Mughal period the same trends continued. Things might have improved under the able and shrewd Akbar, but only might. He too was part of the system. He too was surrounded by the same sort of people who were ready of speech and expert at intrigue. Corruption in the Mughal times was so widespread-in the army, in civil administration and even in judiciary-that narration of individual cases cannot just be done. Exceptions apart, the more important the Amir, the larger his expenses, and the greater his attempt at grabbing more and more wealth. 'The biographical notices collected by Blochmann' afford instances of the possibilities which Akbar's service offered. Hakim Ali, for instance, came from Persia to India poor and destitute, but won Akbar's favour, and being his personal servant rose to the rank of 2000. Peshrau Khan again was a slave who was given to Humayun as a present; a commander of 2000, he rendered service in many different capacities and died leaving a fortune of 15 lakhs' (equivalent to nearly a crore of rupees at modern values). No one was immune from this temptation. Sheikh Ibrahim Chishti of Jaunpur died at Fatehpur, bidding farwell 'to mountains of gold', 25 crores in cash taken into the treasury; 'the rest' in the words of Badaoni, 'fell to the share of his enemies-his sons and representatives.' Under Akbar's successor things were certainly bad. 'Jahangir believed in frequent transfers, and the certainty of a speedy change meant increased activity in exploitation'. Under Shahjahan and Aurangzeb the peasant was systematically fleeced.

'The exaction of official perquisites or gratuities' was the universal and admitted practice. Official corruption was, however, admitted in society to be immoral, and there were many officers above corruption.' But the receiving and even demanding of presents by men in power was the universal rule and publicly acknowledged. Nur Jahan's father, when prime minister under Jahangir, was shameless in demanding presents. So also was Jafar Khan, one of the early Wazirs of Aurangzeb. Jai Singh offered a purse of Rs.30,000 to the Wazir for inducing the emperor to retain him in the Deccan command. Bhimsen expresses his disgust at having to pay everybody at Court in order to get or retain a petty civil office. The qazis grew enormously rich by taking bribes, the most notorious of them being Abdul Wahab. So also did many *sadars*. Even the emperor was not exempt from it. Aurangzeb asked an aspirant to a title, 'Your father gave to Shahjahan one lakh of rupees for adding *alif* to his title and making him Amir Khan. How much will you pay me for the title I am giving you'? Qabil Khan in two-and-a-half years of 'personal attendance' on Aurangzeb amassed 12 lakhs of rupees in cash, besides articles of value and a new house for selling to suppliants his good offices. As Jadunath Sarkar says, 'this pressure was passed from the emperor downwards; each social grade trying to sqeeze out of the class below itself what it had to pay as present to the rank above it, the cultivator of the soil and the trader being the victims in the last resort'.

Escheat

In short, the upper classes in the employment of the state were, by and large, ever busy in amassing wealth from all possible sources and enjoying it to their hearts' content. But only during their life-time. At the death of a noble, all his property, movable and immovable, was reclaimed by the government. 'Immediately on the death of the lord,' writes Pelsaert, 'who has enjoyed the king's *jagir*, be he great or small, without any exception-even before the breath is out of his body-the king's officers are ready on the spot, and make an inventory of the entire estate, recording everything to the value of a single piece, even to the dresses and jewels of the ladies, provided they have not concealed them.' Concealing was very difficult. As a rule all the possessions of a noble, and his transactions were managed by his *diwan* and many other subordinates and accountants. Hence they could not be kept secret. When the noble died all his subordinates were detained, ordered to show all books and papers to the king's officers, and if there was any suspicion about their disclosure, they were tortured till they told the truth. 'The king takes back the whole estate' except in a case where the deceased has done good service in his lifetime, when the women and children are given enough to live on, but no more,' while most of the servants were left on the street 'with a tom coat and a pinched face.'

On the face of it, forfeiture of the property of a deceased noble looks unjust, but in reality it was not. Under the escheat system the king saved the corrupt Amir and himself the bother of instituting an enquiry and presenting a charge-sheet. He let the grandee undisturbed to enjoy his ill-gotten wealth as long as he lived, but after his death acquired it in full. In his discretion the king sometimes left part of the wealth as pension to the widow and heirs, but generally the sons of an Amir had to start life anew. It was a bull-dozer law, and applied to both the innocent and the guilty. But there were hardly any innocent grandees. They knew very well about the law, and therefore spent so lavishly while in office, that in addition to their great income, most of them took huge amounts as loan from the State Treasury and the king was justified in recovering the loan from their property.

And after all, as per the convention, the king was the heir of the Umara. The Mughal emperors seem to have followed the Delhi Sultans in making a claim upon their nobles as if they were their slaves. We have seen how a high officer of the title of Imadul Mulk, was declared by Firoz Tughlaq as 'Bashir is my property (as a slave) and so his property is mine'. The Mughal claim to such succession is not elaborated in the *Ain-i-Akbari*, but is noticed by a number of European travellers from the time of Akbar onwards. It was not declared in so many words but the Mughal nobles in status were not much better off than slaves. The grandees were prohibited from contracting marriage alliances without the emperor's permission.

The noble was obliged, whatever be his rank, to fall prostrate on the ground in obeisance to his master. Although 'the price paid in human dignity was terrible', yet he paid it as his position, his promotion, indeed his very existence depended on the pleasure of the king. Manucci, writing about the last years of Aurangzeb says: ' To get the *hazari* or pay of one thousand, it is necessary to wait a long time and work hard.' This is one side of the coin. The other is that whether foreign or Indian, the nobles maintained a measure of individual independence. The pleasure of enjoying oneself with vigour and liberty amidst the chances of war and of life; the delights of activity without degrading labour; and the taste of an adventurous career full of uncertainty, inequality and peril, instilled in them a passionate desire of personal independence. There was a degree of brutality and an apathy for the weak and the poor. Nevertheless, at the bottom of this mixture of brutality, materialism and selfishness, lay the love of independence. It drew its strength from the moral nature of man, from a desire to developed one's own personality which the upper class elites loved and cherished in medieval India as is found to be the case in all ages. Their status might have been that of a servant of the ruling power, but they themselves felt as mini-rulers in their own assignments, and carried their swords like whipping sticks. Pelsaert noticed that the houses of the nobles at Agra were 'hidden away in alleys and corners', and Bernier found that the dwellings of the Umara at Delhi were scattered in every direction. Manucci also observed that in Delhi many nobles 'are very pleased to have their dwellings far from the royal palace'. The reason was that these people enjoyed the pleasures of idleness and women's company away from mutual suspicion and court intrigues, and had it not been for official and court duties, the grandees would never have bothered to leave their houses at all, in order to enjoy uninterrupted intimacy of their female beauties.

The private and public life of the nobles, the system of seraglios, the widespread corruption, the custom of escheat, and so many other conventionalities of the upper classes, all left a legacy which is visible in many spheres of Muslim social life even now. Obviously, these cannot be discussed in any detail in a work of this size. A few observations, however, would indicate areas where such remnants of the legacy of Muslim rule could be found. For instance, because of escheat, writes Pelsaert, 'everything in the (Mughal) kingdom is uncertain. Wealth, position, love, friendship, confidence, everything hangs by a thread? The nobles build (mansions) with so many hundreds of thousands, and yet (because of escheat) keep them in repair only so long as the owners live? Once the builder is dead, no one will care for the buildings' one cannot contemplate without pity or distress' their ruined state.' Many old Muslim *havelis,* which have survived and are still inhabited bear out Pelsaert's statement.

Mughal corruption was of two kinds-polite custom, and outright bribery and embezzlement. In the first, a person did not meet his senior or superior empty-handed; he presented some gift. This practice was not harmful. But the high corruption, bribery embezzlement, widely prevalent under Muslim rule, as averred by contemporary chroniclers and foreign visitors has never left the Indian scene, and the roots of the present day corruption may be traced to earlier times. Similarly, the sophistication associated with the Mughal court etiquette and the luxurious life of the harem is still to be seen in the graceful and refined behaviour of upper class Muslims, especially of their women. In the words of Jadunath Sarkar, 'the general type of Muhammadan population' are more refined and accustomed to a costiler mode of life, while Hindus of the corresponding classes, even when rich, are grosser and less cultured. The lower classes of Hindus, however, are distinctly cleaner and more intellectual than Muslims of the same grade of life.' But let us here keep confined to upper classes.

Ulama and Mashaikh

Muslim scholars and Sufi Sheikhs, though not all rich, also belonged to the upper classes because of the respect they enjoyed in society. Most of them were patronised by kings and nobles, many were actually in their employ. Some of them were very well-off.

The Ulama

Ulama (plural of alim or learned) used to be well-versed in the Muslim law. As such they assisted Muslim monarchs in administering their dominions according to the Shariat. That way they also helped the Muslims in organizing their lives according to the Shariat which comprehends not only beliefs and practices, public and personal law, and rules of behaviour but even includes dress and personal appearance. Acquiring knowledge for the sake of earning money was looked down upon; hence tradition classified the Ulama into two categories, *Ulama-i-Akhirat* (the pious) and *Ulama-i-su* (the worldly). Knowledge was an extremely valuable ornament in an age when the educated were few and the Ulama were respected for their learning and ability.

Naturally, there was hardly any secular approach to education. Great emphasis was laid on theological education (*manqulat*). The most important subjects taught were Hadis, Fiqh (jurisprudence) and Tafsir (exegesis). The institutions of higher learning, called *madrasas*, were essentially schools of theology, with auxiliaries of grammar, literature and logic. 'These *madrasas* were the strongholds of orthodoxy and were subsidised by the state.' A high value is placed on Muslim orthodoxy everywhere, because it is claimed that it maintains the identity of the community as against other communities. In actual practice it has served as a force against an integrated living, even coexistence, with other communities.

In a word, the Ulama were an orthodox lot. Those who were denied the life of affluence usually took to teaching (as *mutawalli*) in some mosque or under the thatched roof of their own mud houses. Some other Ulama or *danishmands* became pious preachers and scholars. Very often they too had to work under indigent circumstances. Some outstanding scholars were appointed as teachers in *madrasas* established by the Sultans. It was the ambition of the Ulama to join government service. There were many offices which the establishment could offer to a scholar. In official hierarchy of such appointments the post of the Sadr-i-Jahan came at the top, then followed Qazis (judges), Muftis (interpreters of law) Muhtasibs (censors of public morals), Imams (who led prayers) and Khatibs (reciters of the Quran). The Sadr-i-Jahan was the chief of the judicial department. He served as the Qazi-i-Mumalik (chief judge) and recommended to the king about the appointment of junior Qazis. The Sheikh-ul-Islam was in charge of the ecclesiastical affairs of the empire. All those saints, *faqirs* and indigent scholars who enjoyed state patronage were looked after by him. Normally, only well-read scholars were appointed as Khatibs and Imams. So also was the case with Muftis and Muhtasibs. Muslim public opinion did not approve of the appointment of less qualified persons to these posts.

The Ulama received salaries pertaining to the offices they held. Most of the Ulama dabbled in politics. They wielded influence with the kings and nobles as interpreters of Muslim law. Their presence was indispensable to a ruler who was generally uneducated. During the protracted struggle between the crown and the nobility which raged throughout the Sultanate period, they aligned themselves with one or the other of political groups. They always remained on the right side of the regime and forgot the community whom they were expected to help in times of economic distress and political oppression. In this way they encouraged political oppression on the one hand and on the other they preached the necessity of obedience and submission by the people even to an oppressor, taking shelter under the Quranic injunction: 'Obey God and obey the Prophet, and those in authority among you.' Naturally, 'an unholy alliance with them smoothed the path of king's depotism'. They themselves did not lag behind in obsequiousness. Their collaboration with and integration into the state apparatus made them subservient to the regime, 'so much so that when Iltutmish nominated Raziya as his successor, there was not a single theologian in the Delhi Empire who could protest against this nomination on the grounds of Shariat.' The way they encouraged Sultans like Ruknuddin Firoz and Muizuddin Kaiqubad not to offer prayers or keep fasts during the month of Ramzan, and live licentious lives, shows how servile they had become and how they 'were wallowing in the dirty welters of politics.' Of course the Ulama were openly critical of one another and, for this they have been criticised by their contemporary writers like Amir Khusrau, Zia Barani, Abdul Haq Muhaddis and Abdul Qadir Badaoni. Kings like Iltutumish and Balban and prince Bughra Khan are also critical of them.

But in one thing they did not fail. They kept the rulers and the ruling class on the path of Islam and virtue by informing them 'correctly' about their duty towards the non-Muslims. Some modern secularist historians blame the Ulama for making Muslim rulers intolerant through their orthodox advice. Such writers fail to realise that it was not safe for the Ulama to cheat the Sultans by giving wrong interpretation of their holy scriptures vis-a-vis the treatment of non-Muslims. I have not come across any instance where the

Ulama deliberately gave a distorted version of their scriptures in this context. And why should they have done so' They were as much interested in seeing the Muslim state being run according to the Shariat as the Sultans. In short, they always interpreted their scriptures correctly and honestly when it came to the Hindus. So that a foreign visitor like Maulana Shamsuddin Turk, who is very critical of the Qazis of the day, condoned their faults for the reason that because of their right advice their king was prone to treating the Hindus terribly. The lifestyle of the Ulama did not come in the way of serving Islam. Like other Muslims of the higher classes, it was normal for the Ulama to keep harems, live luxuriously and drink wine.

Despite a few faults and a little criticism, therefore, the Ulama as a class were indispensable to the regime. They were advisers of the king and ran the establishment. It was from the Ulama class that the various officers of the government as well as religious institutions were chosen. It was through these people that the regime systematized the religious and social life of the Muslim community just as it organized the extension and administration of Muslim dominions in India through the nobility.

The Mashaikh

Equally influential, if not more, were the Sufi Mashaikh. In the early years of Muslim immigration, and more so with the establishment of Muslim rule in India, many Muslim *faqirs*, scholars and Sufi Mashaikh arrived in India. They entered Hindustan on their own or came with the invading armies. Later on, the disturbed conditions in Central Asia, consequent upon the Mongol upheaval also encouraged them to leave their homes in search of security. Many came to settle in India where peace and plenty and the protective arm of Muslim rule promised them all they wished.

Sufism may be defined as Islamic mysticism. In its early years in Central and West Asia, it was deeply influenced by Neo-Platonism, the monastic tradition of Buddhism and Christianity and the Vedantist and Yogic philosophy of Hinduism. All these were Islamized by the Sufis in such a way as to make them virtually unidentifiable. Nawbahar was a great Buddhist monastry in Balkh. The name of the city of Bokhara itself is derived from Vihar. Some Khurasan Sufis lived in caves like Buddhists. They were known as Shikafatiyah from the word Shikafat (cave). When

Hindu and Buddhist thinkers and saints converted to Islam in Central and West Asia during the eighth to eleventh centuries they carried their thought and philosophy to Sufism. Ibn-al-Arabi (1165-1241) wrote in his Diwan that idol-worship, Chritian ways and Kaaba were all acceptable to him as he believed in the religion of love.

The Sufism that came to India in the twelfth century with the Muslim Mashaikh did not, by and large, envisage direct communion with God without the intermedium of Islam. Just as the soul and body are one, in Islamic sufism *Tariqah* and *Shariah* are so interrelated. Some Sufis believed in the doctrine of Wahadat-ul-Wajud, or the Unity of Being which means 'There is nothing but God, nothing in existence other than He'. This theory, propounded by Sheikh Ibn al-Arabi and akin to Hindu Vedantism, was developed later on in order to harmonise the doctrine of mysticism with the teachings of orthodox Islam.

There were a number of Sufi orders or *silsila* as they are called. Abul Fazl mentions as many as fourteen. But four orders-Chishti, Suhrawardi, Qadiri and Naqshabandi-became prominent in India. Of these only the first two became more popular, for the latter two were extremely orthodox and 'legalistic in their strictness.' By the thirteenth century, northern India saw the flowering of two Sufi orders, Chishti and Suhrawardi, and we will concern ourselves with the Mashaikh of only these two orders. The founder of the Suhrawardi order was Sheikh Bahauddin Zakariya. He was born near Multan in Sind in 578 H. (1182-83 C.E.). He and his disciples played a leading part in the northwest and 'symbolically asked the Chishtis not to dispute possession (of the region) with them. Sheikh Bahauddin Zakariya (and his successors) mixed freely with the Sultans, took part in political affairs, amassed wealth and accepted government honours'.

The Chishtis established themselves at Ajmer in Rajasthan, some parts of the Punjab, Delhi, U.P. and Bihar and further east. They were probably the largest in number and represented what seems to be the most typical in the Sufi way of life. The first great Chishti Sheikh was Khwaja Muinuddin Chishti. He was born in Sijistan in eastern Persia in C.E. 1141. He came to India a little before or after the battle of Taraori or Tarain (1192) and settled down at Ajmer. There also he lies buried after his death in 1236. His mausoleum is a great centre of pilgrimage. He is known as

Gharib Nawaz or Friend of the Poor and Nabi-ul-Hind or Prophet of India. Sheikh Saiyyad Muhammad Gesu Daraz (he of the long locks) said that if people were unable to make the pilgrimage to Mecca, a visit once in their lives to the mausoleum of Muinuddin Chishti would convey the same merit.

Sheikh Muinuddin is very famous today. But he was not known as such to his contemporaries. The three contemporary chronicler-Hasan Nizami, Fakhr-i-Mudabbir and Minhaj do not refer to him at all. Early mystic records, the *Favaid-ul-Fuad* and *Khair-ul-Majalis* do not give any information about him. Barani makes no reference to him. Isami tells us only this much that Muhammad bin Tughlaq had once visited his grave. In all probability his fame spread from the time of emperor Akbar (1556-1605 C.E.) who held his memory in great reverence and often paid visit to his dargah in *Ajmer*. However, the legend and fame of Muinuddin rests, as of all other Sheikhs, on the magic-like miracles (*karamah*) he is supposed to have performed. It is difficult to say when the stories of the miracles of Sufis be and to be told but once this process had begun, it could not be stopped. It became a criterion by which Sufis were judged, and the common reason why people believed in them. They credited them with supernatural powers and feared and respected them. P.M. Currie quotes Mohammad Habib to say that most of the mystic records and Diwans are forgeries, 'but regard for public opinion has prevented them (Indian scholars) from making a public declaration that these are forgeries.' However, stories of miracles apart, 'he (Muinuddin Chishti) was Saiyid by descent. He did not depart in any way from Sunna, the Ulama could not fault him, and he performed the hajj.'

Sheikh Muinuddin Chishti had a number of disciples two of whom, Sheikh Hamid and Qutbuddin, had earned reverence of great and small. Sheikh Hamiduddin Nagauri lived with his wife as a villager. Sheikh Qutbuddin Bakhtiyar Kaki came to Delhi in the reign of Iltutmish and lived in a *khanqah* outside the city. He was very fond of *sama* (devotional music). Once he was so overtaken by *wajd* (ecstasy) that he collapsed and breathed his last. One of his principal disciples was Sheikh Fariduddin Ganj-i-Shakar (1175-1265) popularly called Sheikh Farid.

Sheikh Farid lived in extreme poverty bordering on starvation. He trained a large number of disciples, established many *khanqahs* and raised the prestige of the Chishti order. The greatest disciple of Sheikh Farid was Hazrat Nizamuddin Auliya (1236-1325). He was born at Badaun.

In 1258 he settled at Ghayaspur near Delhi where his shrine exists and a railway station is named after him. The Sheikh had a large circle of disciples who hailed from all sections of society, rich and poor, noble and plebian. In his life of almost a century, Nizamuddin Auliya witnessed the reigns of seven Sultans, but he did not attend the darbar of any one of them. He was popularly known as *Mahbub-i-Ilahi* (Beloved of God). His popularity was due to his saintly virtues and service to humanity. His disciples included Amir Khusrau, Ziyauddin Barani and the renowned Sheikh Nasiruddin Chiragh-i-Delhi whom he appointed as his successor (Khalifa). Professor Mohammad Habib rightly calls Nasiruddin the last great saint of the Chishti *Silsilah* to have enjoyed an all India status. This was the best period in India for Sufism in general and the Chishti *Silsilah* in particular. To this famous line of Sufis belongs Sheikh Salim Chishti, a contemporary of emperor Akbar, for whom the latter built a mausoleum in Fatehpur Sikri.

Many of the Sufi Mashaikh lived in poverty. Sheikh Hamiduddin (d. 1276 C.E.) lived in a small mud house in the city of Nagaur in Rajasthan. He eked out his meagre subsistence by cultivating a single *bigha* of land. His wife spent her time in cooking and spinning like a peasant woman. He was a strict vegetarian. He refused to accept government gift of land and money from the muqta of Nagaur and Sultan of Delhi.

'Sheikh Muinuddin and Sheikh Qutbuddin Bakhtiyar never owned houses of their own. Sheikh Farid Ganj-i-Shakar built a small *kachcha* house only when his family had considerably increased'. For many years during his early life Sheikh Nizamuddin Auliya had to wander from one quarter of the city to another in search of a house'. Generally starvation conditions prevailed in the houses of the Chishti saints'. Very often these saints did not possess sufficient clothes to cover their bodies.'

This is one side of the coin. The other is that Sheikh Muinuddin's sons owned land, which may have been granted to them directly or accepted by the Sheikh for their sake. Sheikh Fariduddin was destitute to the end of his days, but gifts were received and distributed at his *khanqah*. The *khanqah* of Nizamuddin Auliya, probably after he received money from Sultan Nasiruddin Khusrau, 'became an institution in which money, food and goods circulated freely'. However, the Sheikhs who lived in affluence were deemed to possess no less merit than those who elected to remain destitute.

The Sufi Mashaikh are also reported to have shunned the company of the nobles and nearness to the court. But that too was not always so. On the contrary, the attractions of staying near the throne were compulsive. Sidi Maula was a disciple of Sheikh Farid at Ajodhan.' He aspired for name and fame and shifted to Delhi. Once in the capital, Sidi Maula hurled himself headlong in the politics of the court and, after many vicissitudes paid with his life. But Sidi was not alone in this pursuit. As K.A. Nizami has pointed out, 'Even Chisht the cradle-land of the *silsilah* looked to Delhi for guidance in spiritual matters.' The Mashaikh mostly lived in cities and towns where they were popular with kings and people and enjoyed the respectability of upper class elite. Sheikh Qutbuddin Bakhtiyar Kaki was much admired by the people of Delhi headed by Sultan Iltutmish himself. Muinuddin Chishti was very much liked by the Muslims of Ajmer but he was suspected of dabbling in politics which prompted Prithviraj III to ask Ramdeva to expel him from Ajmer. Sheikh Nizamuddin Auliya used to hold his own *darbar* which was often more awe-inspiring than even the court of kings. The Sheikh was so popular with the people that Sultan Alauddin Khalji began to entertain suspicions about his influence and authority in Muslim society. With a view to ascertain the real intentions of the Sheikh, and to find out to what extent he was interested in seeking political power, the Sultan sent him a note seeking his advice and guidance on certain political problems. The Sheikh immediately surmised Alauddin's motives in sending the letter, and replied that he had nothing to do with politics and so could render no advice on political matters: he kept busy with seeking God's grace for Muslim monarchs (*duagoee*). Only after this was the Sultan's mind set at rest. But to many he was popularly known as Sultan Nizamuddin and his resting place as Dargah Sultanji Saheb.

Alauddin greatly respected Nizamuddin Auliya for his supernatural powers and knack for correct predictions. But his son Sultan Qutbuddin Mubarak Khalji disliked him because of his political leanings. He even declared a reward of a thousand *tankahs* for one who would cut off Nizamuddin's head. Once when they chanced to meet, the Sultan refused to acknowledge the salutations of the saint and even called Sheikh Ruknuddin from Multan to eclipse Nizamuddin's popularity. After Qutbuddin's death, Sultan Nasiruddin Khusrau ascended the throne at Delhi, but his authority was challenged by Ghazi Tughlaq. Khusrau Shah, to gain the support of the Sheikhs sent two or three lakhs of *tankahs* to each of them and five lakh *tankahs* to Nizamuddin Auliya. When Ghazi Tughlaq ascended the throne as Sultan Ghiyasuddin Tughlaq (1320 C.E.) he asked Nizamuddin to render the account of the amount he had received. The latter sent a reply, 'seemingly insolent', that the money belonged to the *Bait-ul-mal* (Public Treasury) and therefore he had given it to the poor. The Sultan took umbrage at the Sheikh's answer. The relations between the two were sore also because of the Sultan's dislike of sama in which Nizamuddin freely indulged. In this scenario, Nizamuddin Auliya began to support Ghiyasuddin's son, Muhammad Tughlaq, who aspired for the throne. When Ghiyasuddin Tughlaq went on an expedition to Bengal, Nizamuddin Auliya prophesied that the Sultan would never come back from there. When the news of his return was received in Delhi, a worried Prince Muhammad rushed to Nizamuddin with the tiding at which the Sheikh uttered the famous words, 'Delhi is still far off (*hanuz Delhi dur ast*)'. Nizamuddin Auliya was thus immersed in Delhi court politics, at least towards the end of his life (1320-25). But he was a Sufi. He had many disciples who were regular visitors to his *khanqah*. Such an one was Amir Khusrau.

Abul Hasan, popularly known as Amir Khusrau, was the most favoured disciple of Nizamuddin Auliya. He was a historian, a musician, a poet, a literaturer, a Sufi Sheikh, and a full-fledged protege of Delhi Sultans. His first patron was Prince Muhammad, son of Sultan Ghiyasuddin Balban. Thereafter for about forty years (1285-1325) he served a continuous succession of monarchs-Muizuddin Kaiqubad, Jalaluddin Khalji, Alauddin Khalji and Mubarak Shah Khalji-and his shrewdness was successful in keeping them all pleased. 'The Sultan (Kaiqubad) flattered him by calling him 'the seal of authors' and promised to give him a big reward which would free him from all worldly cares ever afterwards. His genius, if not character, helped him spend 'the whole of his life in spinning yarn' (or writing many untruths). Soon after, when Kaiqubad was murdered by Jalaluddin Khalji, he composed a new *masnavi, Miftah-ul-Futuh* in praise of his new patron. Six years later

Jalauddin was murdered by his nephew and son-in-law Alauddin Khalji who marched into Delhi with the late king's head held aloft on the point of a spear and, writes Dr. Wahid Mirza, our poet Khusrau 'was one of the first to offer his congratulations to the murderer whose hands were still red with the blood of his king, his uncle and his benefactor? The poet changed with changing time and turned with shifting wind.' No wonder, even Ghiyasuddin Tughlaq, who was hostile to Khusrau's *pir-o-murshid*, Nizamuddin Auliya, receives fulsome praise in Khusrau's *Tughlaq Nama.*

Amir Khusrau was very shrewd. When he found the reign of Qutbuddin Mubarak Khalji nothing to boast about, he wrote *Nuh Sipehr*, praising all things Indian, including the beauty of Indian women. In *Nuh Sipehr* he also wrote: 'They have four books in that language (Sanskrit), which they are constantly in the habit of repeating. Their name is *Bed* (Vedas). They contain stories of their gods, but little advantage can be derived from their perusal.' This betrays the one-track mind of Muslim elite in general. This weakness was shared by almost all Sufi Mashaikh, debunking the belief that Sufi Mashaikh treated Hindus and Muslims on terms of equality or helped bring the two communities nearer to one another. They were keen on maintaining only orthodox Muslim rule and showed a general disregard for others. Since it was believed that Muhammad bin Tughlaq was not orthodox, Sheikh Nasiruddin Chiragh obtained a promise from Firoz Tughlaq before supporting the latter's claim to the throne, to the effect that he would rule according to the Shariat. In 1409, when Raja Ganesh (Kans of Muslim chroniclers) obtained the throne of Bengal and sought to establish his authority by keeping the prominent Ulama and Sufis under control, Sheikh Nurul Haqq (Qutbul Alam) wrote to Sultan Ibrahim Sharqi of Jaunpur to come and save the Muslims of Bengal. Sultan Ibrabim responded to the call and Raja Ganesh, finding himself too weak to meet the challenge, came to the Sheikh and begged for his intercession, promising to agree to any conditions. Sheikh Nurul Haqq said he would intercede for him if he accepted Islam. The Raja retired in favour of his son Jadu, who ascended the throne as Sultan Jalaluddin Shah. Sheikh Nurul Haqq induced Sultan Ibrahim, much against his will, to withdraw his armies. Sheikh Abdul Quddus combined spirituality with dogmatism. 'His letters to Sultan Sikandar Lodi and Babur (1526-30) show that he was as anxious to maintain Muslim rule as any wordly Muslim, that he had no scruples in using the language of a courtier in asking the rulers' to establish the Shariah' 'Akbar's attempt at secularizing the state' had exasperated the divines, and Mulla Shah Ahmad and Sheikh Farid Bukhari exhorted court dignitaries to alter the state of things in the very beginning of Jahangir's reign, 'otherwise it would be difficult to accomplish anything later on.' There are many other such instance. It is understandable if disgruntled nobles and courtiers invited foreigners to 'rescue Islam,' but the Sufi Mashaikh by such actions compromised their image as 'Indians first' and respecters of all people as equals. They were as opposed to 'national integration' as any orthodox Muslim.

Similarly, many modern scholars have shown that some Sufi Mashaikh too resorted to aggressive and violent means in fighting infidelity. Even Sheikh Muinuddin Chishti's 'picture of tolerance is replaced by a portrait of him as a warrior for Islam.' Since I have studied this problem in detail elsewhere, I would not like to repeat the cases of aggressive proselytization of Sufi Mashaikh mentioned therein. However, one shocking instance of forcible conversion not mentioned in my book referred to above, may be given here. Saiyyad Jalaluddin Bukhari Makhdum-i-Jahanian of Sind (d.1384) fell very seriously ill. Nawahun, the *darogha* of Uchch, called on him to enquire about his health. As a matter of courtesy and to raise his sinking spirits, Nahawun said: 'May God restore your health' your holiness is the last of the saints as the Prophet Muhammad was the last of the prophets.' Sayyid Jalaluddin Bukhari even on death-bed construed it as an expression of faith in Islam and demanded a formal declaration of conversion from him. Nawahun firmly declined to make any such declaration. Thereupon he was charged with apostasy. He fled to the court of Firoz Shah Tughlaq in search of asylum and redress. When Sayyid Jalaluddin Bukhari expired, his younger brother Sadruddin Raju Qattal, rushed to Delhi in order to persuade Firoz Shah to execute Nawahun. Though some scholars of the capital did not agree with the viewpoint of Raju Qattal, the latter prevailed upon Firoz Shah in obtaining his permission for Nawahun's execution as a renegade.

Poor or rich, the Sufi Mashaikh lived as householders. Except Nizamuddin Auliya and Nasiruddin Chiragh, all Sufi Sheikhs married, and had large families. Since the word saint is associated with celibacy in people's minds of most religions, it would be pertinent to state that 'marriage is enjoined on every Muslim, and celibacy is frequently condemned by Muhammad. 'It is related in the Traditions that Muhammad said: When the servant of God marries, he perfects half his religion'? Consequently in Islam, even the ascetic orders are rather married than single.'

Sheikh Muinuddin Chishti took two wives-Ummatullah and Asmatullah, and had three sons and one daughter. He had married in his old age 'only to realize that his spiritual powers had greatly suffered on that account.' Sheikh Qutbuddin Bakhtiyar Kaki Ushi also married twice, late in life. He divorced one of his wives, soon after marriage, as her presence upset his programme of prayers. He had four sons. Sheikh Farid had a number of wives and a large family. Sheikh Nasiruddin Chiragh is reported to have stated that Sheikh Farid had a number of wives (*harem bisyar bud*). He had at least four wives and eight children. Sheikh Hamiduddin had led a very voluptuous life in his early years, but when he joined the circle of Sheikh Muinuddin Chishti, he adopted the life of a mystic in all sincerity. He had a number of children. Sheikh Qutbuddin Husain Kirmani, uncle of the author of *Siyar-ul-Auliya*, used to put on the garments of the finest Chinese silks and Kamkhawab and always used to have pan in his mouth. Sheikh Nizamuddin Auliya also relished betel.

All this was normal life and all these were normal pleasures. But Sufi Mashaikh, known by many names like Wali, Shah, Qalandar, Murshid, Marabout, Sheikh, Faqir and Darwesh, indulged in all kinds of pleasures and luxuries. The case of Sidi Maula was exceptional. He had ready at hand brand new *tankahs* under every coverlet to spend. So many people dined at his *khanqah* that, if Barani is to be believed, 'two thousand *man* of flour (*maida*), two to three hundred *man* of sugar and a hundred to two hundred man of vegetables used to be consumed in his kitchen every day.' But others were equally non-poor and generous. 'We know that Sheikh Farid was destitute to the end of his days, but we also know that gifts were received and distributed. It could be said generally of every *khanqah* that even in the bad days a person' was sure to get some sort of a meal and, with luck, a share of money' in every *khanqah* ideals of austerity fought against satisfaction of physical needs,' so that there was no dearth of money and parasites because of the well-to-do admirers of the Sheikh.

Sama or devotional music was a common feature of the *khanqah*. During *sama*, the Sheikhs and Qalandars placed strong insistence on the practice of *Nazar-ilal murd* or gazing at good looking boys. One reason why Ghiyasuddin Tughlaq could not see eye to eye with Nizamuddin Auliya was the latter's fondness for *sama* and his ecstatic fits. The Sultan was free from unnatural lust (*lawatat*) and did not allow 'handsome beardless boys' from coming near him. In the *khanqahs* were also used drugs of the hashish family, and even drinking was common. Love affairs of sufis were of common occurrence. Ahmad Yadgar mentions the case of a *faqir* who fell for the newly wed bride of the son of Tatar Khan. He relates another story about the love of a *darwesh* and a woman. Love between a Hindu girl and a *darwesh* created flutter and tension.

The Sheikhs used to marry in high families and possessed a clout which sometimes became a problem for Sultans. A sixteenth century Suhrawardi writer says that Sheikh Sadruddin Arif had married a divorced wife of Prince Muhammad, the eldest son of Balban. The circumstances of this marriage are given as follows: The prince divorced his wife, whom he passionately loved, in a fit of fury. When he recovered his normal state of mind, he felt deeply pained for what he had done. Legally he could not take her back into his *harem* unless she was married to someone else and then divorced by him. A man of genuine piety was searched to restore the broken relationship. Sheikh Arif, the most outstanding saint of the town, promised to marry the princess and divorce her the next day. But, after the marriage, he refused to divorce her on the ground that the princess herself was not prepared to be divorced. This incident led to bitterness between the saint and the prince. The latter even thought of taking action against the Sheikh, but a Mongol invasion cut short the thread of his life. Sheikh Salim Chishti had great influence with emperor Akbar, much more than Sadruddin Arif had in the time of Balban. And both Badaoni and Father Monserrate make unflattering comments about Sheikh Salim. The Sufi Mashaikh lived a full-fledged life, different from saints of other religions. But among Indian Muslims their memory has always been cherished with utmost reverence.

It is said that saint-worship among Muslims is a practice unique to India. *Dargahs* of Sufis, real or figurative, are found all over the country and Muslims flock to them in large numbers. It is a legacy of medieval times. One reason for this can be that most Indian Muslims are converted Hindus, who, when their places of worship were converted into (*khanqahs* and later) *dargahs*, did not give up visiting them. For instance, at the most holy *dargah* of Sheikh Muinuddin Chishti, the Sandal Khana mosque is believed to have been built on the site of a Dev temple. The other is that stories of miracles of saints give a hope and a chance to people to obtain fulfilment of their desires. Hence besides Muslims, a few Hindus also resort to such shrines.

Lower Classes and Unmitigated Exploitation

'The Muslims dominate the infidels, but the latter fortify themselves in mountains' rugged places, as well as in bamboo groves? Hence they cannot be subdued' —*Ibn Battutah*

Lower classes formed the bulk of the population. They were economically poor and socially degraded. They existed to provide food and apparel, services and comforts, to the higher classes, and resided in towns and villages. In urban areas these comprised all kinds of artisans from basket and rope makers to clothprinters, embroiders, carpet makers, silk-weavers, blacksmiths, tin workers, carpenters, oil-men, barbers, jugglers, mountebanks, street singers, brewers, tailors, betel leaf sellers, flower sellers, masons, stone-cutters, bullock-cart drivers, *doli*-carriers, water-carriers, domestic servants, *dhobis* and workers in a hundred other skilled and unskilled crafts.

In the villages there lived peasants and shepherds, besides a few artisans of the vocations enumerated above, although of inferior skill. The quality of work of the urban artisans and craftsmen used to be good. Let us take one example, that of stone-cutters and builders of edifices.

Timur or Tamerlane, who invaded Hindustan in 1398, was highly impressed with Indian craftsmen and builders and on his return home from India he took with him architects, artists and skilled mechanics to build in his mud-walled Samarqand, edifices like the Qutb Minar and the (old) Jama Masjid of Delhi constructed by Firoz Shah Tughlaq. Babur too was pleased with the performance of Indian workmen and described how thousands of stone-cutters and masons worked on his buildings in Agra, Sikri, Biana, Dholpur, Gwalior and Koil. 'In the same way there are numberless artisans of every sort in Hindustan.'

Despite this they were an exploited lot, and so were all others, tillers of the soil in the villages and workmen in towns. It is true that in the medieval times the concept of welfare state was not widely prevalent, although it was not entirely unknown, and many kings and nobles are known to have tried to promote the general wellbeing of the people. On a study of contemporary source materials, it appears that the condition of the people of India up to the fifteenth century was not deplorable. This is borne out by the evidence provided by Indian writers and foreign travellers from the eleventh to the fifteenth century. But thereafter there is hardly any foreign visitor to India in sixteenth-seventeenth century in particular, who was not struck by the extremely miserable existence of the lower class people. Such a situation prevailed in all parts of the country, north and south, east and west. We may attempt a study of the economic and social condition of these lower classes under two categories: (1) peasants and agriculturists, and (2) artisans and labourers, for better comprehension about their exploitation by the upper classes as well as the government of the day.

Peasants and Agriculturists

The condition of the peasantry in India, up to the fourteenth century, was not bad. Contemporary Indian writers and foreign travellers do not generally talk about poverty; on the contrary they give an impression of the wellbeing of the tillers of the soil. Alberuni (eleventh century) has said many things about the Hindus, but nowhere does he say that the people were living in suffering or want. Minhaj Siraj, Ibn Battutah, Shihabuddin Abbas Ahmad, the author of *Masalik-ul-Absar*, Al-Qalqashindi, the author of *Subh-ul-Asha*, Amir Khusrau and Shams Siraj Afif (thirteenth-fourteenth centuries), even talk of the prosperity of the people. Even Barani is impressed with their wealth and conveys this impression when he feels delighted at the action of contemporary Muslim rulers against rich landlords and cultivators. The decline of the political power of the Sultanate in the fifteenth century, saw a general recovery of people's strength and prosperity in good measure.

But by the sixteenth and seventeenth centuries conditions are quite different. They change to such an extent that almost all foreign and many Indian writers are struck by the crushing poverty of the Indian peasant and do not fail to write about it. Athanasius

Nikitin, Varthema, Barbosa, Paes, Nuniz, Linschoten, Salbank, Hawkins, Jourdain, Sir Thomas Roe, Terry and a host of others, all talk of the grinding poverty of the Indian people. It will serve no purpose to cite from each one of them, but one or two quotations may be given as specimens to convey the general trend of their impressions. Pelsaert, a Dutch visitor during Jahangir's reign, observes: 'The common people (live in) poverty so great and miserable that the life of the people can be depicted or accurately described only as the home of stark want and the dwelling place of bitter woe' their houses are built of mud with thatched roofs. Furniture there is little or none, except some earthenware pots to hold water and for cooking'. Salbank, writing of people between Agra and Lahore of about the same period, says that the 'plebian sort is so poor that the greatest part of them go naked.' These two quotations would suffice to show how miserable the common people in the middle of the seventeenth century were. These and many others that follow lead one to the inescapable conclusion that the condition of the peasantry in India during the sixteenth and seventeenth centuries had considerably deteriorated.

It is pertinent to ask how the peasant during this period was reduced to such straits. India of the medieval times was mainly agricultural, and histories and legends of the times do not tire of singing in praise of the wealth and glory of the Great Mughals. Then how did the peasant become so miserably poor' Were there any ideas and actions of rulers which led to the impoverishment of the agriculturists? Also, were there any ideas of the peasants themselves which taught them to reconcile themselves to their lot and did not prompt them to fight against their economic disablement? Contemporary chronicles do betray the existence of such ideas. That these have not yet been analysed by historians, does not mean that these ideas were not there. An attempt is being made here to discover such ideas and assess their effects.

To find the roots of the miserable condition of the agriculturists in the seventeenth century, one has naturally to look back to earlier times and, indeed, at the very nature of the Muslim conquest of India beginning with the thirteenth century. In the history of Muslim conquest, a unique phenomenon was witnessed in India. Contrary to what happened in Central Asia, Persia or Afghanistan, India could not be completely conquered, nor could its people be converted to the Islamic faith. On the other hand, a ceaseless resistance to the Muslim rule in the thirteenth, fourteenth and fifteenth centuries is clearly borne out by the records of the times. If Muslim chroniclers gloat over unqualified victories for their Turkish kings, there are a large number of inscriptions of Hindu kings who too lay exaggerated claim to military successes. One thing which is clear beyond doubt is that throughout the Sultanate period (and also the Mughal period), there was stiff resistance to Muslim rule, and in one region or the other of the country, the authority of the Sultanate was being openly challenged.

Naturally, the Muslim kings gave much thought to finding some means to suppress the recalcitrant elements. Besides other things, one idea that struck Alauddin Khalji (1296-1316) was that it was 'wealth' which was the 'source of rebellion and disaffection.' It encouraged defiance and provided means of 'revolt'. He and his counsellors deliberated that if somehow people could be impoverished, 'no one would even have time to pronounce the word 'rebellion'. How was this to be done'? The Ulama would not have found it difficult to suggest a remedy. It is laid down in the *Hidaya* that when an 'infidel country' is conquered, the Imam can divide it among the Muslims. He can also leave it in the hands of the original inhabitants, 'exacting from them a capitation tax, and imposing a tribute on their lands.' If the infidels are to lose their lands, their entire moveable property should also be taken away from them. In case they are to continue with cultivating the land, they should be allowed to retain 'such a portion of their moveable property as may enable them to perform their business.' In India the conquered land was divided among Muslim officers, soldiers and Ulama in lieu of pay or as reward. Some land was kept under *Khalisa* or directly under the control of the regime. But in all cases the tiller of the soil remained the original Hindu cultivator. As an infidel he was to be taxed heavily, although a minimum of his moveable property like oxen, cows and buffaloes (*nisab*) was to be left with him. The principle of the *Shariah* was to leave with him only as much as would have helped him carry on with his cultivation, but at the same time to keep him poor and subservient.

Bare Subsistence

According to W.H. Moreland 'the question really at issue was how to break the power of the rural leaders, the chiefs and the headmen of *parganas* and villages'? Sultan Alauddin therefore undertook a series of measures to crush them by striking at their major source of power-wealth. But in the process, leaders and followers, rich and poor, all were affected. The king started by raising the land tax (*Kharaj*) to fifty percent. Under rulers like Iltutmish and Balban, it does not seem to have been above one-third of the produce. Furthermore, under Alauddin's system all the land occupied by the rich and the poor 'was brought under assessment at the uniform rate of fifty per cent'. This measure automatically reduced the chiefs practically to the position of peasants. The king also levied house-tax and grazing tax. According to the contemporary chronicler Ziyauddin Barani, all milk-producing animals like cows and goats were taxed. According to Farishtah, animals up to two pairs of oxen, a pair of buffaloes and some cows and goats were exempted. This concession was based on the principle of *nisab*, namely, of leaving some minimum capital to enable one to carry on with one's work. But it was hardly any relief, for there were taxes like *kari*, (derived from Hindi word Kar), *charai* and *Jiziyah*. The sultans of Delhi collected *Jiziyah* at the rate of forty, twenty and ten *tankahs* from the rich, the middleclass and the poor respectively.

In short, a substantial portion of the produce was taken away by the government as taxes and the people were left with the bare minimum for sustenance. For the Sultan had 'directed that only so much should be left to his subjects (*raiyyat*) as would maintain them from year to year' without admitting of their storing up or having articles in excess.' Sultan Alauddin's rigorous measures were taken note of by contemporary writers both in India and abroad. In India contemporary writers like Barani, Isami and Amir Khusrau were inclined to believe him to be a persecutor of the Hindus. Foreigners also gathered the same impression. Maulana Shamsuddin Turk, a divine from Egypt, was happy to learn that Alauddin had made the wretchedness and misery of the Hindus so great and had reduced them to such a despicable condition 'that the Hindu women and children went out begging at the doors of the Musalmans.' The same impression is conveyed in the writings of Isami and Wassaf. While summing up the achievements of Alauddin Khalji, the contemporary chronicler Barani mentions, with due emphasis, that by the last decade of his reign the submission and obedience of the Hindus had become an established fact. Such a submission on the part of the Hindus 'has neither been seen before nor will be witnessed hereafter.' In brief, not only the Hindu Zamindars, who had been accustomed to a life of comfort and dignity, were reduced to a deplorable position, but the Hindus in general were impoverished to such an extent that there was no sign of gold or silver left in their houses, and the wives of *Khuts* and *Muqaddams* used to seek sundry jobs in the houses of the Musalmans, work there and receive wages. The poor peasants (*balahars*) suffered the most. The fundamentalist Maulana Ziyauddin Barani feels jubilant at the suppression of the Hindus, and writes at length about the utter helplessness to which the peasantry had been reduced because the Sultan had left to them bare sustenance and had taken away everything else in *kharaj* (land revenue) and other taxes.

But there was much greater oppression implicit in this measure. It was difficult to collect in full so many and such heavy taxes. 'One of the standing evils in the revenue collection consisted in defective realization which usually left large balances,' and unrealised balances used to become inevitable. Besides, lower revenue officials were corrupt and extortionate. To overcome these problems, Sultan Alauddin created a new ministry called the *Diwan-i-Mustakhraj*. The *Mustakhraj* was entrusted with the work of inquiring into the revenue arrears, and realizing them. We shall discuss about the tyranny of this department a little later; suffice it here to say that in Alauddin's time, besides being oppressed by such a grinding tax-structure, the peasant was compelled to sell every maund of his surplus grain at government controlled rates for replenishing royal grain stores which the Sultan had ordered to be built in order to sustain his Market Control.

After Alauddin's death (C.E. 1316) most of his measures seem to have fallen into disuse, but the peasants got no relief, because Ghiyasuddin Tughlaq who came to the throne four years later (C.E. 1320) continued the atrocious practice of Alauddin. He also ordered that 'there should be left only so much to the Hindus that neither, on the one hand, they should become arrogant on account of their wealth, nor, on the other, desert their lands in despair.' In the time of Muhammad bin Tughlaq even this latter fear turned out to be true. The Sultan's enhancement of taxation went even beyond the lower limits of 'bare subsistence.' For the people left their fields and fled. This enraged the Sultan and he hunted them down like wild beasts. Still conditions did not become unbearable all at once. Nature's bounty to some extent compensated for the cruelty of the king. If the regime was extortionist, heavy rains sometimes helped in bumper production.

Babur noted that 'India's crops are all rain grown'. Farming in north India depended upon the monsoon rains coming from the Bay of Bengal. Artificial irrigation was there on a very limited scale, for irrigation 'is not at all a necessity in cultivating crops and orchards. Autumn crops (*Kharif* season) grow by the downpour of the rains themselves; and strange it is that spring crops (*Rabi* season) grow even when no rain falls.' Young trees are watered during two or three years 'after which they need no more (watering)' as the ground gets soaked with rain in the monsoon season. Ibn Battutah gives a detailed description of the crops grown in India and adds: 'The grains that have been described are *Kharif* grains. They are harvested 60 days after sowing. Thereafter *Rabi* grains like wheat, barley and massoor are sown. These are sown in the very same field in which *Rabi* grains (are harvested). The soil of this country is very fertile and is of excellent quality. Rice is sown three times in the year. Production of rice is the largest in the country. Sesame and sugar-cane are also sown with *Kharif*.' Shams Siraj Afif writes that when, during the monsoon season, 'there were spells of heavy rains, Sultan Firoz Tughlaq appointed officers to examine the banks of all the water courses and report how far the inundations had extended. If he was informed that large tracts had been made fertile by the spread of waters, he was overwhelmed with joy. But if any village went to ruin (on account of floods), he treated its officials with great severity.'

But the basic policy of impoverishing the people, resulted in crippling of agricultural economy. By the Mughal period the condition of the peasantry became miserable; if there was any progress it was in the enhancement of taxation. According to W.H. Moreland, who has made a special study of the agrarian system of Mughal India, the basic object of the Mughal administration was to obtain the revenue on an ever-ascending scale. The share that could be taken out of the peasant's produce without destroying his chances of survival was probably a matter of common knowledge in each locality. In Akbar's time, in Kashmir, the state demand was one-third, but in reality it came to two-thirds. The Jagirdars in Thatta (Sindh) did not take more than half. In Gujarat, according to Geleynsen who wrote in 1629, the peasant was made to part with three-quarters of his harvest. Similar is the testimony of De Laet, Fryer and Van Twist. During Akbar's reign, says Abul Fazl, evil hearted officers because of sheer greed, used to proceed to villages and *mahals* and sack them. Conditions became intolerable by the time of Shahjahan when, according to Manucci, peasants were compelled to sell their women and children to meet the revenue demand. Manrique writes that the peasants were 'carried off' to various markets and fairs, (to be sold) with their poor unhappy wives behind them carrying their small children all crying and lamenting'. Bernier too affirms that the unfortunate peasants who were incapable of discharging the demands of their rapacious lords, were bereft of their children, who were carried away as slaves. Here was also confirmation, if not actually the beginning, of the practice of bonded labour in India.

In these circumstances the peasant had little interest in cultivating the land. Bernier observes that 'as the ground is seldom tilled otherwise than by compulsion' the whole country is badly cultivated, and a great part rendered unproductive? The peasant cannot avoid asking himself this question: 'Why should I toil for a tyrant who may come tomorrow and lay his rapacious hands upon all I possess and value' without leaving me the means (even) to drag my own miserable existence'. The Timariots (Timurids), Governors and Revenue contractors, on their part reason in this manner: Why should the neglected state of this land create uneasiness in our minds, and why should we expend our own money and time to render it fruitful' We may be deprived of it in a single moment? Let us draw from the soil all the money we can, though the peasant should starve or abscond'?

The situation made the tax-gatherer callous and exploitative on the one hand and the peasant fatalistic and disinterested on the other. The result, in Bernier's own words, was 'that most towns in Hindustan are made up of earth, mud, and other wretched material; that there is no city or town (that) does not bear evident marks of approaching decay.' Wherever Muslim despots ruled, ruin followed, so that, writes he, similar is the 'present condition of *Mesopotamia, Anatolia, Palestine*, the once wonderful plain of Antioch, and so many other regions anciently well cultivated, fertile and populous, but now desolate' Egypt also exhibits a sad picture' '

To revert to the Mughal empire. An important order in the reign of Aurangzeb describes the Jagirdars as demanding in theory only half but in practice actually more than the total yield. Describing the conditions of the latter part of the seventeenth century Mughal empire, Dr. Tara Chand writes: 'The desire of the State was to extract the economic rent, so that nothing but bare subsistence remained for the peasant.' Aurangzeb's instructions were that 'there shall be left for everyone who cultivates his land as much as he requires for his own support till the next crop be reaped and that of his family and for seed. This much shall be left to him, what remains is land tax, and shall go to the public treasury.'

Conditions could not always have been that bad. There were steps taken from time to time to help cultivation and ameliorate the condition of the agriculturists. Shamsuddin Iltutmish constructed a large tank called *Hauz-i-Shamsi*. Traces of Alauddin Khalji's *Hauz-i-Khas* and Firoz Tughlaq's irrigation canals still exist. Similar steps taken in Mughal times are also known. But such steps in aid of the development were taken because these could offer better means of increasing the revenue. Some steps which looked like helping the agriculturists, sometimes resulted in their perpetual penury. For example, a very common administrative measure of the medieval times was to advance loans to peasants to help them tide over their difficulties. But the important ideal entertained by rulers can be best summarized in the words of Sher Shah's instructions to his *Amils*: 'Be lenient at the time of assessment, but show no mercy at the time of collection.' This was, on the face of it, a good principle. But even Sher Shah Suri, renowned for his concern for the well being of cultivators, was much more keen about the benefits to be drawn by his Afghan clansmen from the lands they administered. He sent his 'good old loyal experienced servants' to districts which yielded good 'profits' and 'advantages' and after two years or so transferred them and sent 'other servants like them that they may also prosper.' It was of course the peasant who paid for this prosperity.

Collection of Arrears

We have earlier referred to the problem of collection of arrears. When agriculture was almost entirely dependent on rainfall and land tax was uniformally high, it was not possible for the peasants to pay their revenue regularly and keep their accounts ever straight with the government. The revenue used to fall into arrears. From the study of contemporary sources it is almost certain that there were hardly any remissions-even against conversion to Islam. Muslim rulers were very keen on proselytization. Sultan Firoz Tughlaq rescinded *Jiziyah* for those who became Muhammadan. Sometimes he also instructed his revenue collectors to accept conversions in lieu of *Kharaj*. Rajas and Zamindars who could not deposit land revenue or tribute in time had to convert to Islam. Bengal and Gujarat provide specific instances which go to show that such rules prevailed throughout the Muslim-ruled regions. But remissions of *Kharaj* were not allowed. On the other hand arrears went on accumulating and the kings tried to collect them with the utmost rigour.

In the Sultanate period there was a full-fledged department by the name of the *Diwan-i-Mustakharaj*. The work of this department was to inquire into the arrears lying in the names of collectors (*Amils* and *Karkuns*) and force them to realize the balances in full. Such was the strictness in the Sultanate period. Under the Mughals arrears were collected with equal harshness.

The system then existing shows that the peasants were probably never relieved of the 'burden' of arrears. In practice it could hardly have been possible always to collect the entire amounts and the balance was generally put forward to be collected along with the demand of the next year. A bad year, therefore, might leave an intolerable burden for the peasants in the shape of such arrears. These had a natural tendency to grow It also seems to have been a common practice to demand the arrears, owed by peasants who had fled or died, from their neighbour. And peasants who could not pay revenue or arrears frequently became predial slaves.

In short, between the thirteenth century when armies had to march to collect the revenue, and the seventeenth century when peasants were running away from the land because of the extortions of the state, no satisfactory principle of assessment or collection except extortion could be discovered. The situation became definitely worse in the eighteenth and nineteenth centuries as attested to by contemporary historians Jean Law and Ghulam Hussain. It is this general and continued stringency that was the legacy of the Mughal empire and the Indian Muslim states which continued under the British Raj.

Another idea of the rulers of medieval India was to keep the prices of commodities of everyday necessity low. This idea too emanated in the time of Alauddin Khalji. It was either his own brain-child or that of his courtiers and Ulama. His passion for incessant conquests and constant invasions of Mongols had rendered maintenance of a large army unavoidable. Even if he had recruited the large number of soldiers on a moderate salary, the entire treasure of the state would have been exhausted in five or six years. Alauddin, therefore, decided to cut down the salary of soldiers; but to prevent their falling victim to economic distress, he also decided to reduce the prices of commodities of daily use.

To the contemporary chronicler these prices were quite low and fluctuation, not even of a *dang* (small copper coin), was ever allowed whether in seasons of drought or of plenty. Indeed the 'low' and 'fixed' prices in the market were 'considered to be one of the wonders of the age.' But 'when a husbandman paid half of his hard earned produce in land tax, some portion of the remaining half in other sundry duties, and then was compelled to sell his grain at cheap rates' to the governments, it does not speak well of the general condition of the peasantry in those days.' They could never have been happy in selling their grain cheap in the open market nor to the government itself at fixed rates without making profit. Profit is the greatest incentive to production, but it was completely checked by Alauddin's market regulations and the peasants seem to have lived a life of monotony and low standard.

Without caring to understand that low prices cripple production and impoverish the producer, many sultans after Alauddin Khalji took pride in competing with him in keeping prices low. But their actions led not only to the impoverishment of the peasantry but also of shopkeepers and businessmen. Shams Siraj Afif feels jubilant at describing and listing the low prices during the reign of Firoz Tughlaq, claiming that while Alauddin had to make strenuous efforts to bring down the prices, in the time of Firoz Tughlaq they remained low without resorting to any coercion. 'Like Alauddin, Sikandar Lodi also used to keep a constant watch on the price-level' in the market. Abdullah, the author of *Tarikh-i-Daudi*, says that 'during the reign of Ibrahim Lodi the prices of commodities were cheaper than in the reign of any other Sultan except in Alauddin's last days', and adds that whereas in Alauddin's time the cheapness of prices was maintained through compulsion, force and dire punishments, in Ibrahim's reign prices remained low 'naturally.'

So Alauddin Khalji had pioneered the idea of maintaining prices of necessaries at cheap rates. It was followed by his successors up to the beginning of the sixteenth century, without perhaps caring for its implications on the condition of the peasantry. Historians of Sher Shah affirm that he was indebted to Alauddin in laying down his agrarian policy and Akbar adopted many measures of Sher Shah. During the Mughal period prices by and large went up, although as late as in the reign of Aurangzeb, sometimes the prices reported were regarded as exceptionally cheap. But since the land revenue accounted for by far the larger portion of the peasant's surplus produce, it is obvious that this increase must have wiped out any possible advantage that the peasantry might have obtained through a rise in the prices.

Besides these handicaps, the peasant suffered because there were no clear ideas about a regular commissariat service to maintain supply-line for the army during a campaign. There is evidence that camp-markets were sometimes established for the convenience of soldiers. There are also situations on record when the soldiers were encouraged to loot the peasants to obtain grain. Sher Shah took appropriate measures to see that agriculturists were not harassed by an army on march, but Babur noted that on the news of the arrival of an army the peasants used to leave their land, flee for life and establish themselves elsewhere. Encouragement to soldiers to loot was inherent in *khums* tax, through which the state obtained as its share one-fifth of the booty collected by the troops, while four-fifth was left with the soldiers.

And above all, one fact is clear in the chronicles of medieval India-any measures against the higher classes ultimately affected the peasants, because any loss to the former was surreptitiously transferred to the peasants. For, as Sir Thomas Roe (1615-19) wrote, the people of Hindustan lived 'as fishes do in the sea-the great ones eat up the little. For first the farmer robs the peasant, the gentlemen robs the farmer, the greater robs the lesser and the King robs all.' Bernier corroborates the conclusion when he writes: 'In eastern countries, the weak and the injured are without any refuge whatever; and the only law that decides all controversies is the cane and the caprice of a governor.'

Of all the ideas, motivations and actions mentioned above leading to the impoverishment of the peasantry, the one of leaving 'nothing but bare subsistence', was the most atrocious. Writing about the times of Aurangzeb, Dr. Tara Chand rightly observes that 'the policy (of leaving) bare subsistence was suicidal for it killed the goose that laid the golden eggs. It left no incentive for increasing the production or improving the methods of cultivation.' Consequently, there was a progressive deterioration in the living standards of the peasantry as decades and centuries passed. As said earlier, Alberuni, Barani, Ibn Battutah and Shams Siraj Afif talk about the prosperity of the people right up to the fourteenth century. R.H. Major in his translation of the works of Nicolo Conti, Athnasius Nikitin, Santo Stefano etc., only refers to the poverty of the Indian peasant in the fifteenth century. But Babur in the sixteenth century witnessed extreme poverty; he repeatedly talks about *langoti* as the only apparel and *khichri* as the only food. Witnesses for the seventeenth century are unanimous in observing extreme poverty of the peasantry.

Resistance of the Peasantry

The idea of leaving only the bare minimum to the peasant and collecting the rest of his hard-earned produce in land revenue and other taxes, remained the basic policy of the rulers during the medieval times. Some chroniclers were aware of its evil effects. Shams Siraj Afif, writing in the days of Firoz Shah Tughlaq (1351-88) says that 'Unwise regulations had been made in former reigns, and the *raiyyats* and subjects were oppressed in the payment of revenue. Several writers told the author of this work that it was the practice to leave the *raiyyat* one cow and take away all the rest.' Such a policy proved counter-productive. It not only harmed the agriculturists but also the Muslim regime, for, in place of minimising opposition, it actually encouraged resistance. In the unequal struggle between the poor peasantry and the mighty government carried on over a long period of time the tillers of the soil ultimately lost. But not without stiff resistance. Hindu Zamindars as the leaders and the peasants as their followers, both fought against the unjust demands of the king. Under Alauddin himself the Khuts and *Muqaddams* (Zamindars) avoided to pay taxes, did not care for the summons of the *Diwan-i-Wazarat* or Revenue Department, ignored to call at his office and paid no heed to the revenue officials. And the peasants, finding continuance of cultivation uneconomic and the treatment of the regime unbearable, left the fields and fled into the jungle from where they organized resistances. In this confrontation Zamindars played the role of leaders and the peasants joined under their banner.

Ibn Battutah describes this scenario. 'The Muslims dominate the infidels,' writes he, 'but the later fortify themselves in mountains, in rocky, uneven and rugged places as well as in bamboo groves (or jungles)' which serve them as ramparts. Hence they cannot be subdued except by powerful armies.' The story of the resistance of the Hindus to Muslim dominance and injustice is repeated by many contemporary writers. Ziyauddin Barani says that if the Hindus ' do not find a mighty sovereign at their head nor behold crowds of horse and foot with drawn swords and arrows threatening their lives, they fail in their allegiance, refuse payment of revenue and incite a hundred tumults and revolts.' Similar is the testimony of Amir Khusrau, Ibn Battutah, Vidyapati and the Muslim chroniclers of the fifteenth century. In the fifteenth century, when the Sultanate of Delhi had grown weak, the tillers of the soil evaded, more than ever, payment of land tax, and revenue could be collected only through army sorties in regular yearly or half-yearly expeditions. Such resistance continued throughout, for the Indian peasant had his own survival strategies. These comprised mainly of two options-to fight with determination as far as possible, but, if resistance proved of no avail, to flee and settle down elsewhere. Medieval Indian society, both urban and agrarian, was to some extent an armed society. In cities and towns the elite carried swords like walking sticks. In villages few men were without at least a spear or bow and arrows, and they were skilled in the use of these arms. In 1632, Peter Mundy actually saw in the present day Kanpur district, 'labourers with their guns, swords and bucklers lying by them while they ploughed the ground'. Similarly, Manucci described how in Akbar's days the villagers of the Mathura region defended themselves against Mughal revenue-collecting officers: 'The women stood behind their husbands with spears and arrows, when the husband had shot off his matchlock, his wife handed him the lance, while she reloaded the matchlock.' The countryside was studded with little forts, some surrounded by nothing more than mud walls, but which nevertheless provided centres of the general tradition of rebellion and agrarian unrest. Armed peasants provided contingents to Baheliyas, Bhadauriyas, Bachgotis, Mandahars and Tomars in the earlier period, to Jats, Marathas and Sikhs in the later.

But as the people put up a continual resistance, the Muslim government suppressed them ruthlessly. In this exercise the Mughal emperors were no better than the pre-Mughal sultans. We have often referred to the atrocities of the Delhi sultans and their provincial governors. Abul Fazl, Bernier and Manucci provide detailed accounts of the exertion of the Mughals. Its summing up by Jahangir is the most telling. In his *Tarikh-i-Salim* Shahi he writes:

'I am compelled to observe, with whatever regret, that notwithstanding the frequent and sanguinary executions which have been dealt among the people of Hindustan, the number of the turbulent and disaffected never seems to diminish; for what with the examples made during the reign of my father, and subsequently of my own, there is scarcely a province in the empire in which, either in battle or by the sword of the executioner, *five or six hundred thousand human beings* have not, at various periods, fallen victims to this fatal disposition to discontent and turbulence. Ever and anon, in one quarter or another, will some accursed miscreant spring up to unfurl the standard of rebellion; so that in Hindustan never has there existed a period of complete repose.'

'In such a society,' observes Kolf, 'the millions of armed men, cultivators and otherwise, were its (government's) rivals rather than its subjects.' This attitude was the consequence of the Mughal government's policy of repression. As an example, the exploits of one of Jahangir's commanders, Abdullah Khan Uzbeg Firoz Jung, can provide an idea of the excessive cruelty perpetrated by the government. Peter Mundy, who travelled from Agra to Patna in 1632 saw, during his four days' journey, 200 minars (pillars) on which a total of about 7000 heads were fixed with mortar. On his way back four months later, he noticed that meanwhile another 60 *minars* with between 2000 and 2400 heads had been added and that the erection of new ones had not yet stopped. Abdullah Khan's force of 12,000 horse and 20,000 foot destroyed, in the Kalpi-Kannauj area, all towns, took all their goods, their wives and children as slaves and beheaded and 'immortered' the chiefest of their men. Why, even Akbar's name stands besmeared with wanton killings. In his siege of Chittor (October 1567) the regular garrison of 8000 Rajputs was vigorously helped by 40,000 armed peasants who had shown 'great zeal and activity'. This infuriated the emperor to massacre 30,000 of them.

In short, the Indian peasant was clear in his mind about meeting the onslaughts of nature and man. Attached to his land as he was, he resisted the oppression of the rulers as far as his resources, strength and stamina permitted. If conditions went beyond his control, he left his land and established himself in some other place. Indeed, migration or flight 'was the peasant's first answer to famine or man's oppression.' Babur's description of this process may be quoted in his own words: 'In Hindustan,' says he, 'hamlets and villages, towns indeed, are depopulated and set up in a moment. If the people of a large town, one inhabited for years even, flee from it, they do it in such a way that not a sign or trace of them remains in a day or a day and a half. On the other hand, if they fix their eyes on a place in which to settle,' they make a tank or dig a well; they need not build houses or set up walls, *khas*-grass abounds, wood is unlimited, huts are made and straightaway there is a village or a town.'

Similar is the testimony of Col. Wilks about South India. 'On the approach of a hostile army, the' inhabitants of India bury underground their most cumbrous effects, and' issue from their beloved homes and take the direction' sometimes of a strong fortress, but more generally of the most unfrequented hills and woods.' According to Amir Khusrau, 'wherever the army marched, every inhabited spot was desolated' When the army arrived there (Warangal, Deccan), the Hindu inhabitants concealed themselves in hills and jungles.' This process of flight seems to have continued throughout the Mughal period, both in the North and the South. Writing of the days of Shahjahan, Bernier says that 'many of the peasantry, driven to despair by so execrable a tyranny, abandon the country and sometimes fly to the territories of a Raja because they find less oppression and are allowed a greater degree of comfort.'

To flee was a good idea, when it is realised that this was perhaps the only way to escape from the cruel revenue demand and rapacious officials. Some angry rulers like Balban and Muhammad bin Tughlaq hunted down these escapists in the jungles, others clamped them in jails, but, by and large, the peasants did survive in the process. For, it was not only cultivators alone who fled into the forests, but often even vanquished Rajas and zealous Zamindars. There they and people at large organized themselves to defend against the onslaughts of the regime. For it was not only because cultivation was uneconomic and peasants left the fields; it was also a question of saving Hindu religion and Hindu culture. Under Muslim rule the two principal Muslim practices of iconoclasm and proselytization were carried on unabated. During the Arab invasion of Sind and the expeditions of Mahmud of Ghazni, defeated rulers, garrisons of captured forts, and civilian population were often forced to accept Islam. The terror-tactics of such invaders was the same everywhere and their atrocities are understandable. But even when Muslim rule had been established in India, it was a matter of policy with Muslim rulers to capture and convert or disperse and destroy the male population and carry into slavery their women and children. Minhaj Siraj writes that Sultan Balban's taking of captives, and his capture of the dependents of the great Ranas cannot be recounted. In Katehar he ordered a general massacre of the male population above eight years of age and carried away women and children. Muhammad Tughlaq, Firoz Tughlaq, Sikandar Lodi, Sikandar Butshikan of Kashmir, Mahmud Beghara of Gujarat and emperor Aurangzeb were more enthusiastic, some others were lukewarm, but it was the religious duty of a Muslim monarch to capture people and convert them to Islam.

In these circumstances the defeated Rajas and helpless agriculturists all sought refuge in the forests. Forests in medieval India abounded. Ibn Battutah says that very thick forests existed right from Bengal to Allahabad. In his time rhinoceroses (*gender*) were to be found in the very centre of the Sultanate, in the jungles near Allahabad. There were jungles throughout the country. Even the environs of Delhi abounded in forests so that during the time of Balban, harassed Mewatis retaliated by issuing forth from the jungles in the immediate vicinity of the southwest of Delhi, attack the city and keep the king on tenter-hooks. When Timur invaded Hindustan at the end of the fourteenth century, he had learnt about this resistance and was quite scared of it. In his *Malfuzat* he notes that there were many strong defences in India like the large rivers, the elephants etc. 'The second defence,' writes he, 'consists of woods and forests and trees, which interweaving stem with stem and branch with branch, render it very difficult to penetrate the country. The third defence is the soldiery, and landlords and princes, and Rajas of that country, who inhabit fastnesses in those forests, and live there like wild beasts.'

Growth of dense forests was a cause and effect of heavy rains. Forests precipitated rainfall and rains helped in the growth of forests. Therefore, like forests, rains also helped the freedom loving 'wild-beasts' living in the jungles in maintains their independence and culture. It is truly said that in India it does not rain, it pours. The rainfall in the north and the northeastern India-Uttar Pradesh, Bihar and Bengal, including eastern Bengal (now Bangla Desh) and parts of Assam (the Hindustan of medieval times)-is in the following order: The average annual rainfall in U.P., Bihar and Bengal is 100 to 200 cms. (40 to 80 inches), in eastern Bengal and Assam it is 200 to 400 cms. and in some parts above 400 cms. (80 to 160 and above 160 inches). In all probability a similar average obtained in the medieval period also. Medieval chroniclers do not speak in quantitative terms: in their language 'rivulets used to turn into rivers and rivers into seas during the rainy season.' The situation is best depicted by the sixteenth century conqueror Zahiruddin Muhammad Babur himself in his memoirs *Tuzuk-i-Baburi* or *Babur Nama*. He writes about Hindustan: 'Sometimes it rains 10, 15, or 20 times a day, torrents pour down all at once and rivers flow where no water had been.' Such intensity of rainfall had rendered precarious the grip of Turkish rulers in many parts. For example, the government at Delhi could not always maintain its hold on Bengal effectively. There were very few roads and hardly any bridges over rivers in those days, and the almost primitive medieval communication system used to break down during the rainy season. Local governors of the eastern region-Bihar and Bengal-did not fail to take advantage of this situation and used to declare independence. Governor Tughril Beg of Bengal 'depended on the climate and waterlogged soil of the province to wear out the Delhi forces,' for three years (1278-81). Bengal almost remained independent till the middle of the sixteenth century.

In short, heavy rains and thick forests affected the mobility of the government's army, leaving the refugees safe in their jungle hide-outs and repulse any intrusion. Ibn Battutah describes how people used to fight behind barricades of bushes and bamboo trees. 'They collect rain water' and tend their animals and fields, and remain so strongly entrenched that but for a strong army they cannot be suppressed. Babur confirms this: 'Under the monsoon rains the banks of some of its rivers and torrents are worn into deep channels, difficult and troublesome to pass through anywhere. In many parts of the plains (because of rains) thorny jungle grows, behind the good defence of which the people' become stubbornly rebellious and pay no taxes.' It was because of this that Muslim conquest could not penetrate the Indian countryside nor Muslim rule affect it. If there was any fear of attack, the villagers just fled and re-established themselves elsewhere, or returned after the storm was over.

SC, ST and OBC

Those who took to the jungle, stayed there, eating wild fruits, tree-roots, and the coarsest grain if and when available, but surely preserving their freedom. But with the passing of time, a peasant became a tribal and from tribal a beast. William Finch, writing at Agra about 1610 C.E., describes how Jahangir and his nobles treated them-during *Shikar*. A favourite form of sport in Mughal India was the *Kamargha,* which consisted in enclosing a tract of country by a line of guards, and then gradually contracting the enclosure until a large quantity of game was encircled in a space of convenient size. 'Whatever is taken in this enclosure' (*Kamargha* or human circle), writes Finch, 'is called the king's *shikar* or game, whether men or beasts? The beasts taken, if man's meat, are sold' if men they remain the King's slaves, which he sends yearly to Kabul to barter for horses and dogs: these being poor, miserabie, thievish people, that live in woods and deserts, little differing from beasts.' W.H. Moreland adds: 'Other writer (also) tell it besides Finch.' Even Babur, always a keen observer, had not failed to notice that peasants in India were often reduced to the position of tribals. 'In our countries,' writes he in his *Memoirs*, 'dwellers in the wilds (*i.e.* nomads) get tribal names; here (*i.e.* Hindustan) the settled people of the cultivated lands and villages get tribal names.'

In short, the avalanche of Turco-Mughal invaders, and the policy of their Government turned many settled agriculturists into tribals of the jungles. Many defeated Rajas and harassed Zamindars also repaired to forest and remote fortresses for security. They had been defeated in war and due to the policy of making them *nest-o-nabud* (destroy root and branch), had been reduced to the position of Scheduled Castes/Tribes/Backward Classes. For example, many Parihars and Parmars, once upon a time belonging to the proud Rajput castes, are now included in lower castes. So are the 'Rajputs' counted in Backward Classes in South India. Two examples, one from the early years of Muslim rule and the other from its closing years, would suffice to illustrate the point. In the early years of Muslim conquest, Jats had helped Muhammad bin Qasim in Sind; later on they turned against him. Khokhars had helped Muhammad Ghauri but turned hostile to him and ultimately killed him. This made the Turkish Sultanate ill-disposed towards them, and in course of time many of these Jats and Khokhars were pushed into belonging to low castes of to-day. For the later times is the example of the *Satnamis*. This sect was an offshoot of the Raidasis. Their stronghold in the seventeenth century was Narnaul, situated about 100 kms. southwest of Delhi. The contemporary chronicler Khafi Khan credits them with a good character. They followed the professions of agriculture and trade on a small scale. They dressed simply, like *faqirs*. They shaved their heads and so were called *mundiyas* also. They came into conflict with imperial forces. It began as a minor trouble, but developed into a war of Hindu liberation from the persecution of Aurangzeb. Soon some five thousand *Satnamis* were in arms. They routed the *faujdar* of Narnaul, plundered the town, demolished its mosques, and established their own administration. At last Aurangzeb crushed them by sending 10,000 troops (March, 1672) and facing a most obstinate battle in which two thousand *Satnamis* fell on the field and many more were slain during the pursuit. Those who escaped spread out into small units so that today there are about 15 million *Satnami* Harijans found in Madhya Pradesh, Maharashtra, Bihar and Uttar Pradesh.

Thus were swelled the numbers of what are today called Scheduled Castes, Scheduled Tribes and Other Backward Classes (SC/ST/OBC). The eleventh century savant Alberuni who came to India in the train of Mahmud of Ghazni, speaks of eight castes/ sections of *Antajya* (untouchable?), or workers in low professions in Hindustan such as fuller, shoemaker, juggler, fisherman, hunter of wild animals and birds. 'They are occupied with dirty work, like the cleaning of the villages and other services.' In his time their number was obviously not large. Today the SC/ST alone comprise 23 percent of the population or about 156 million, according to 1981 census.

Add to this the Other Backward Classes and they all count to more than fifty percent. This staggeringly high figure has been reached because of historical forces operating in the medieval times primarily. Muslim rule spread all over the country. Resistance to it too remained widespread. Jungles abounded throughout the vast land from Gujarat to Bengal and Kashmir to Kanyakumari, and flight into them was the safest safeguard for the weak and vulnerable. That is how SC/ST people are found in every state in large numbers. During the medieval period, in the years and centuries of oppression, they lived almost like wild beasts in improvised huts in forest villages, segregated and isolated, suffering and struggling. But by settling in forest villages, they were enabled to preserve their freedom, their religion and their culture. Their martial arts, preserved in their *Akharas*, are even now practised in different forms in many states. Such a phenomenon was not witnessed in West Asian countries. There, in the vast open deserts, the people could not save themselves from forced conversions against advancing Muslim armies. There were no forests into which they could flee, hide themselves and organize resistance. Hence they all became Muslim.

In the Indian forest villages these 'primitive' Hindus continued to maintain themselves by engaging in agriculture and simple cottage industries. They also kept contact with the outside world for, since they had remained Hindu, they were freely employed by Rajas and Zamindars. They provided firewood and served as boatmen and watchmen. The Hindu elite engaged them for guard duty in their houses, and as *palki*-bearers when they travelled. Travelling in the hot climate of India was mostly done at night, and these people provided guard to bullock carts and other conveyances carrying passengers and goods. There are descriptions of how these people ran in front and rear of the carts with lighted torches or lanterns in one hand and a *lathi* in the other. They also fought for those Hindu leaders who organized resistance from remote villages and jungle hide-outs. The exaspertated and starving peasantry sometimes took to highway robbery as the only means of living. Raiding bands were also locally formed. Their main occupation, however, remained menial work, including scavenging and leather tanning. But with all that, their spirit of resistance had made them good fighters. Fighting kept their health replenished, compensating for the non-availability of good food in the jungles. Their fighting spirit made the British think of them as *thugs*, robbers and bandits. But the British as well as other Europeans also embarked upon anthropological and sociological study of these poor forest people. In trying to find a name for these groups, the British census officials labelled them, in successive censuses, as Aboriginals (1881), Animists (1891-1911) and as Adherents of Tribal Religions (1921-1931).

These days a lot of noise is being made about helping the SC/ST and OBCs by reserving their quotas in government jobs. It is argued that these people have been oppressed by high caste Hindus in the past and they should now be helped and compensated by them. But that is only an assumption. It is they who have helped save the Hindu religion by shunning all comforts and taking to the life of the jungle. That is why they have remained Hindu. If they had been harassed and oppressed by high-caste Hindus, they could have easily chosen to opt for Muslim creed ever so keen on effecting proselytization. But they preferred to hide in the forests rather than do so. There is another question. Was that the time for the Upper Caste Hindus, fighting tenaciously to save their land, religion and culture, to oppress the lower strata of Hindus whose help they desperately needed in their struggle? The mindset of upper-caste/backward-caste conflict syndrome needs reviewing as it is neither based on historical evidence nor supported by compulsions of the situation. The present day isolated conflicts may be a rural politician/plebian problem of no great antiquity.

Another relic of the remote past is the objection to the entry of men of lower class people into temples. In Islam slaves were not permitted to bestow alms or visit places of pilgrimages. In India, according to Megasthenes, there were no slaves. But slavery (*dasta*) probably did exist in one form or the other. Were the *dasas* also debarred from entering temples and the practice has continued; or, was it that every caste and section had its own shrines and did not enter those of others? The picture is very blurred and origins of this practice are difficult to locate.

Above all, there is the question: Would the SC/ST by themselves accept to change their way of life and accept the assistance? Perhaps yes, perhaps no. An example may help understand the position.

In June 1576 Maharana Pratap of Chittor had to face Akbar's armies in the famous battle of Haldighati. Rana Pratap fought with exemplary courage and of his soldiers only a little more than half could leave the field alive. In the darkness of the evening, the wounded Rana left the field on his favourite horse Chetak. A little later, in October, Akbar himself marched in person in pursuit of the Rana, but the latter remained untraced and unsubdued. Later on he recovered all Mewar except Mandalgarh and Chittor. His nearest associates, the Bhil and Lohia tribals, had taken a vow that until their motherland was not freed, they would not eat in metal plates, but only on leaves; they would not sleep on bedsteads, but only on the ground; and they would renounce all comforts. The bravest among them even left Chittor, to return to it only when Mewar had regained independence. That day was not destined to come in their life-time. It was not to come for decades, for generations, for centuries. During these hundreds of years they lived as tribals and nomads, moving from city to city. On India regaining independence, Prime Minister Jawaharlal Nehru, who knew about these people's poignant history, decided to rehabilitate them in Chittor. In March 1955 an impressive function was arranged there and Pandit Nehru led the descendants of these valiant warriors back to their homes in independent Chittor in independent India. But most of them did not care to return. They live as nomads even today. The SC/ST and OBCs too may find their way of life too dear to relinquish for the modern 'urban' civilised ways. Many welfare officers working in their areas actually find it to be so.

Slaves

The forest-village-dwellers, whether escapees or resisters, suffered untold privations. Still they had the satisfaction of being able to preserve their freedom, their religion and their culture. But all victims of aggression were not so 'lucky'. Many vulnerable groups and individuals could not extricate themselves from the clutches of the invaders and tyranny of the rulers; they used to be captured, enslaved and even sold, not only in India but also outside the country. It was not only Jahangir, a comparatively kind hearted emperor, who used to capture poor people during his hunting expeditions and send them to Kabul in exchange for dogs and horses, all Muslim invaders and rulers collected slaves and exploited them as they pleased.

When Muhammad bin Qasim invaded Sind, he took captives wherever he went and sent many prisoners, especially women prisoners, to his homeland. Parimal Devi and Suraj Devi, the two daughters of Raja Dahir, who were sent to Hajjaj to adorn the harem of the Caliph, were part of a large bunch of maidens remitted as one-fifth share of the state (*Khums*) from the booty of war (*Ghanaim*). The *Chachnama* gives the details. After the capture of the fort of Rawar, Muhammad bin Qasim 'halted there for three day, during which time he masscered 6,000 'men. Their followers and dependents, as well as their women and children were taken prisoner.' When the (total) number of prisoners was calculated, it was found to amount to thirty thousand persons (Kalichbeg has sixty thousand), amongst whom thirty were the daughters of the chiefs. They were sent to Hajjaj. The head of Dahir and the fifth part of prisoners were forwarded in charge of the Black Slave Kaab, son of Mubarak Rasti. In Sind itself female slaves captured after every campaign of the marching army, were married to Arab soldiers who settled down in colonies established in places like Mansura, Kuzdar, Mahfuza and Multan. The standing instructions of Hajjaj to Muhammad bin Qasim were to 'give no quarter to infidels, but to cut their throats', and take the women and children as captives. In the final stages of the conquest of Sind, 'when the plunder and the prisoners of war were brought before Qasim' one-fifth of all the prisoners were chosen and set aside; they were counted as amounting to twenty thousand in number' (they belonged to high families) and veils were put on their faces, and the rest were given to the soldiers'. Obviously, a few lakhs of women were enslaved and distributed among the elite and the soldiers.

In the words of the Andre Wink, 'From the seventh century onwards, and with a peak during Muhammad al-Qasim's campaigns in 712-13, a considerable number of Jats [and also others] was captured as prisoners of war and deported to Iraq and elsewhere as slaves. Some Jat freemen became famous in the Islamic world, as for instance Abu Hanifa (699-767), the founder of the Hanafite school of law.'

So, from the days of Muhammad bin Qasim in the eighth century to those of Ahmad Shah Abdali in the eighteenth, enslavement, distribution and sale of captives was systematically practised by Muslim invaders. A few instances are necessary to have a clear idea of the monstrous practice of taking captives. When Mahmud Ghaznavi attacked Waihind (near Peshawar) in 1001-02, he took 500,000 persons of both sexes as captive. This figure of Abu Nasr Muhammad Utbi, the secretary and chronicler of Mahmud, is so mind-boggling that Elliot reduces it to 5000. The point to note is that taking of slaves was a matter of routine in every expedition. Only when the numbers were exceptionally large did they receive the notice of the chroniclers. So that in Mahmud's attack on Ninduna in the Salt Range (1014), Utbi says that 'slaves were so plentiful that they became very cheap; and men of respectability in their native land (India) were degraded by becoming slaves of common shopkeepers (of Ghazni)'. His statement finds confirmation in Nizamuddin Ahmad's *Tabqat-i-Akbari* which states that Mahmud 'obtained great spoils and a large number of slaves'. Next year from Thanesar, according to Farishtah, 'the Muhammadan army brought to Ghaznin 200,000 captives so that the capital appeared like an Indian city, for every soldier of the army had several slaves and slave girls'. Thereafter slaves were taken in Baran, Mahaban, Mathura, Kannauj, Asni etc. so that when Mahmud returned to Ghazni in 1019, the booty was found to consist (besides huge wealth) of 53,000 captives according to Nizamuddin. But Utbi is more detailed. He says that 'the number of prisoners may be conceived from the fact, that each was sold for from two to ten *dirhams*. These were afterwards taken to Ghazna, and the merchants came from different cities to purchase them, so that the countries of Mawaraun-Nahr, Iraq and Khurasan were filled with them'. The *Tarikh-i-Alfi* adds that the fifth share due to the Saiyyads was 150,000 slaves, therefore the total number of captives comes to 750,000.

This was the practice throughout the medieval period. Furthermore, it was also a matter of policy with the Muslim rulers and their army commanders to capture and convert, destroy or sell the male population, and carry into slavery women and children. Ibn-ul-Asir says that Qutbuddin Aibak made 'war against the provinces of Hind'. He killed many, and returned home with prisoners and booty.' In Banaras, according to the same authority, Muhammad Ghauri's slaughter of the Hindus was immense. 'None was spared except women and children." No wonder that slaves began to fill the households of every Turk from the very beginning of Muslim rule in India. Fakhr-i-Mudabbir informs us that as a result of the Muslim achievements under Muhammad Ghauri and Qutbuddin Aibak, 'even a poor householder (or soldier) who did not possess a single slave before became the owner of numerous slaves of all description (*jauq jauq ghulam har jins*)'.

In 1231 Sultan Iltutmish attacked Gwalior, and 'captured a large number of slave'. Minhaj Siraj Jurjani writes that Sultan Balban's 'taking captives, and his capture of the dependents of the great Ranas cannot be recounted'. Talking of his war in Awadh against Trailokyavarman of the Chandela dynasty (Dalaki wa Malaki of Minhaj), the chronicler says that 'all the infidel wives, sons and dependents' and children' fell into the hands of the victors'.

In 1253, in his campaign against Ranthambhor also Balban appears to have captured many prisoners. In 1259, in an attack on Haryana (the Shiwalik Hills), many women and children were enslaved. Twice Balban led expeditions against Kampil, Patiali, and Bhojpur, and in the process captured a large number of women and children. In Katehar he ordered a general massacre of the male population of above eight years of age and carried away the women and children.

The process of enslavement during war went on under the Khaljis and the Tughlaqs (1290-1414 C.E.). Of Alauddin Khalji's 50,000 slaves some were mere boys, and surely mainly captured during war.

Firoz Tughlaq had issued an order that whichever places were sacked, in them the captives should be sorted out and the best ones should be forwarded to the court. His acquisition of slaves was accomplished through various ways-capture in war, in lieu of revenue and as present from nobles. Soon he was enabled to collect 180,000 slaves.

Ziyauddin Barani's description of the Slave Market in Delhi, (such markets were there in other places also), during the reign of Alauddin Khalji, shows that fresh batches of captives were constantly replenishing them. The practice of selling slaves was well established and widely known. Amir Khusrau in the fourteenth century writes that 'the Turks, whenever they please, can seize, buy, or sell any Hindu'. He is corroborated by Vidyapati in the next century. The latter writes that the Muslim army commanders take into custody all the women of the enemy's city, and 'wherever they happened to pass, in that very place the ladies of the Raja's house began to be sold in the market.'

Alauddin Khalji fixed the prices of such slaves in the market, as he did for all other items of common use like wheat and rice, horse and cattle. The sale price of boys was fixed from 20 to 30 *tankahs*; the ill-favoured could be obtained for 7 or 8. The slave boys were classified according to their looks and working capacity. The standard price of a working girl was fixed from 5 to 12 *tankahs*, that of a good looking girl from 20 to 40, and a beauty of high family even from 1 thousand to 2 thousand *tankahs*. Under Muhammad bin Tughlaq, as per the information of Shihabuddin al Umri, a domestic maid in Delhi could be had for 8 *tankahs* and one deemed fit to be a concubine sold for about 15 *tankahs*.

'In other cities,' says he, 'prices are still lower.' Muhammad bin Tughlaq became notorious for enslaving captives, and his reputation in this regard spread far and wide so that Umri writes about him thus: 'The Sultan never ceases to show the greatest zeal in making war upon the infidels'.

Everyday thousands of slaves are sold at very low price, so great is the number of prisoners.' Ibn Battutah's earwitness account of the Sultan's arranging marriages of enslaved girls with Muslims on a large scale on the two Ids confirms the statement of Al Umri. 'First of all,' writes he, 'daughters of *Kafir* (Hindu) Rajas captured during the course of the year, come, sing and dance.

Thereafter they are bestowed upon Amirs and important foreigners. After this the daughters of other *Kafirs* dance and sing' the Sultan gives them to his brothers, relatives sons of Maliks etc. On the sixth day male and female slaves are married.' It was a general practice for Hindu girls of good families to learn the art of dancing. It was a sort of religious rite. They used to dance during weddings, festivals and *Pujas* at home and in temples. This art was turned ravenous under their Muslim captors or buyers.

In short, female slaves were captured or obtained in droves throughout the year. Such was their influx that Ibn Battutah appears having got bored of them when he wrote: 'At (one) time there arrived in Delhi some female infidel captives, ten of whom the *Wazir* sent to me. I gave one of them to the man who had brought them to me, but he was not satisfied. My companion took three young girls, and I do not know what happened to the rest.' 'Thousands (*chandin hazar*) of non-Muslim women (*aurat va masturat*) were captured during the yearly campaigns of Firoz Tughlaq' and under him the Id celebrations were held on lines similar to those of his predecessor.

Their sale outside, especially during the Hajj season, brought profits to the state and Muslim merchants. Their possession within, inflated the harems of Muslim kings and nobles beyond belief. Some feeble attempts were sometimes made by some kings to put a stop to this inhuman practice.

The Mughal emperor Akbar, for example, abolished the custom of enslaving helpless women and children in times of war. *Jahangir* ordered that 'a government collector or Jagirdar should not without permission intermarry with the people of the *pargana* in which he might be' for abduction and forced marriages were common enough.

But there was never an abjuration of the policy of enslavement as mainly it was not the Mughal emperors but the Mughal nobility who must have taken the lion's share of the state's enslavement, deportation and sale. To make the long and painful story short, it may just be mentioned that after the Third Battle of Panipat (1761), 'the plunder of the (Maratha) camp was prodigious, and women and children who survived were driven off as slaves-twenty-two thousand (women), of the highest rank in the land, says the *Siyar-ul-Mutakhkhirin*.'

The above study points to some hard facts about enslavement of Hindus under Muslim rule. It is not pertinent here to make a detailed study of the Muslim slave system which was an institution as peculiar as it was unique. Examples of men like Iltutmish and Balban are cited to show how well the slaves fared in the Islamic state and society, how well they were brought up and how easily they could rise to the highest positions in life.

'Iltutmish received nourishment like a son' in the house of his master. Firoz Tughlaq and his nobles too treated their slaves in a similar fashion. But it is the captured and enslaved victims who felt the pinch of slavery. Here only their sufferings may be briefly recapitulated under three separate sections-the fate of men, of women and of children. Of the men captives, the Muslim regime did not have much use. Male prisoners were usually put to the sword, especially the old, the overbearing and those bearing arms, as had happened during Muhammad bin Qasim's invasion, Ghauri's attack on Banaras, Balban's expedition to Katehar, Timur's campaign in Hindustan or Akbar's massacre at Chittor.

Of the captured men, those who could fetch good price were sold in India and outside. A lucrative trade in Indian slaves flourished in the West Asian countries.

Many chroniclers aver that an important export item of commerce abroad comprised of Indian slaves who were exchanged for horses. If the trade in slaves was as brisk as the horse-trade, then many thousands of people must have been deported from India each year. For example, over the years from the eleventh to the early years of the nineteenth century, three quarters of the population of Bukhara was of mainly Indian slave extraction. The Hindu-Kush (Hindu-killer) mountain ranges are so called because thousands of Indian captives 'yoked together' used to die while negotiating them. Ibn Battutah himself saw Indian slaves being taken out of the country.

Many of the slaves who were not sold by their captors, served as domestic servants, as artisans in the royal *Karkhanas* and as Paiks in the army. The Paiks cleared the jungles and prepared roads for the army on march.

They were also sometimes used as human 'shields' in battle. But others, especially professional soldiers captured in war and willing to serve the Muslim army, joined the permanent cadre of the infantry, and were known for their loyalty. Alauddin Khalji, Mubarak Khalji, and Firoz Tughlaq were saved by Paiks when attempts were made on their lives.

Child captives were preferred to grown up men. It may be recollected that in his campaigns in Katehar, Balban massacred mercilessly, sparing only boys of eight or nine. The age factor is material. As these boys grew in years, they gradually forgot their parents and even their native places and developed loyalty only to the king. They could thus be reared as Janessaries were brought up in the Ottoman Empire. The price-schedule of Sultan Alauddin Khalji is evidence of the importance attached to boy-slaves. In his time, while the price of a handsome slave was twenty to 30 *tankahs* and that of a slave-servant ten to 15 *tankahs*, the price of a child slave (*ghulam bachchgan naukari*) was fixed at 70 to 80 *tankahs*. Therefore during a campaign it was aimed at capturing lots of children. But no Hindus wished their children to become slaves, and in the face of an impending defeat Hindu mothers used to burn their little children in the fire of *Jauhar* rather than let them fall into the hands of the enemy to lead the life of perpetual bondage and sometimes meet a most detestable death.

The women captives in Muslim hands were treated as objects of sex or for making money through sale. Al'Umri writes that 'in spite of low prices of slaves, 200,000 *tankahs* and even more, are paid for young Indian girls. I inquired the reason' and was told that these young girls are remarkable for their beauty, and the grace of their manners.' This was the position from the very beginning. It has been mentioned before that Muhammad bin Qasim sent to Hajjaj some thirty thousand captives many among whom were daughters of chiefs of Sind. Hajjaj forwarded the prisoners to Caliph Walid I (C.E. 705-15).

The latter 'sold some of those daughters of the chiefs, and some he granted as rewards. When he saw the daughter of Rai Dahir's sister, he was much struck with her beauty and charms' and wished to keep her for himself'. But as his nephew Abdullah bin Abbas desired to take her, Walid bestowed her on him saying that 'it is better that you should take her to be the mother of your children'. Centuries later, in the time of Jahangir, Abdullah Khan Firoz Jung expressed similar views when he declared that 'I made prisoners of five lacs of men and women and sold them. They all became Muhammadans. From their progeny there will be crores by the day of judgment'. The motive of having progeny from captured women and thereby increasing Muslim population was at the back of all marriages, abductions and enslavements throughout the medieval period.

One recognised way of escape from sex exploitation in the medieval period was *Jauhar* or group-self-immolation. *Jauhar* also was naturally resorted to because the motives and actions of the victors were never in doubt. For example, before Qasim could attack the Fort of Rawar many of the royal ladies themselves voluntarily immolated themselves. The description of the holocaust in the Chachnama is like this: 'Bai, the sister of Dahir, assembled all her women and said' 'God forbid that we should own our liberty to these outcast cow-eaters. Our honour would be lost' there is nowhere any hope of escape; let us collect wood, cotton and oil' and burn ourselves.

'If any wish to save herself she may.' So they went into a house, set it on fire and burnt themselves.' It is those of the lesser mettle who used to save themselves and used to be captured. The repeated *Jauhars* at one place, Chittor, during the attacks of Alauddin Khalji, Bahadur Shah of Gujarat and Emperor Akbar have become memorable for the spirit shown by the Rajputnis. Captured and enslaved women often had to lead a life of misery and dishonour as happened with Deval Devi, daughter of Raja Karan Baghela of Gujarat.

As the legacy of this scenario, Indian girls are still being sold to West Asian nationals as wives, concubines and slave girls. For example, all the leading Indian newspapers like *The Indian Express, The Hindustan Times* and *The Times of India* of 4 August 1991, flashed the news of a sixty year old 'toothless? Arab national Yahiya H.M. Al Sagish 'marrying' a 10-11 year old Ameena of Hyderabad after paying her father Rs. 6000, and attempting to take her out of the country.

Al Sagish has been taken into police custody and the case is in the law-court now. Mr. I.U. Khan has 'pointed out that no offence could be made out against his client as he had acted in accordance with the Shariat laws. He said that since this case related to the Muslim personal law which permitted marriage with girls who had attained Puberty (described as over 9 years of age), Al Sagish could not be tried under the Indian Penal Code (IPC). Besides Ameena's parents had not complained.' (*Times of India*, 14 August 1991).

But this is not an isolated case. I was in Hyderabad for about four years, 1979-1983. There I learnt that such 'marriages' are common. There are regular agents and touts who arrange them. Poor parents of girls are handsomely paid by foreign Muslims for such arrangements. Every time that I happened to go to the Hyderabad Airlines office or the Airport (which was about at least once a month), I found bunches of old bridegrooms in Arab attire accompanied by young girls, often little girl brides. 'A rough estimate indicated that as many as 8000 such marriages were solemnised during the past one decade in Hyderabad alone.' (*Indian Express Magazine*, 18 August 1991). In short, the sex slave-trade is still flourishing not only in Hyderabad but in many other cities of India after the medieval tradition.

Artisans and Labourers

After a brief survey of the misery and exploitation of the peasants, backward classes and slaves, let us look at the condition of artisans and labourers. In the medieval period, as sometimes even now, the work and vocation of agriculturists approximated, bordered, converged and telescoped into many other subsidiary professions. A peasant, when he was free from his field, in terms of time and seasons, or was compelled to leave his village, generally worked as basket-maker, weaver or water-carrier in his village or in the town nearby temporarily or after migrating to it. With the passage of time some of these agriculturalists became efficient and skilled craftsmen while the majority remained engaged in unskilled jobs. In urban setting their life-style may have improved a little-only a little in the medieval age-but they all remained an exploited lot. There was hardly any contemporary foreign visitor to India who was not struck by the extremely miserable existence of the lower class people. Such a situation obtained in all parts of the country, north and south, east and west.

Athnasius Nikitin, who travelled in the Deccan between 1470 and 1474 says that 'the land is overstocked with people: but those in the country are very miserable'. Durate Barbosa (1600-1615) was horrified by the poverty existing on the Malabar coast and says that some of the lower classes in the region were so poor that they lived on roots and wild fruits and covered themselves with leaves. His near contemporary Varthema (1504-06) and the later visitor Linschoten wrote in a similar strain. Writing around the year 1624, Della Valle gives glimpses of life in Surat by pointing out that the people were numerous, wages were low, and slaves cost practically nothing to keep. Similar is the testimony of Pyrard. The Portuguese writer Paes (wrote in 1520) and Nuniz (1536-37), confirm the assertion that the mass of the people were living in the greatest poverty and distress. In the seventeenth century John

De Laet (1631) summarised the information he had collected from English, Dutch and Portuguese sources regarding the Mughal empire as a whole. 'The condition of the common people in these regions (south and west) is,' says he, 'exceedingly miserable'; wages are low; workmen get only one regular meal a day, the houses are wretched and practically unfurnished, and people have not got sufficient covering to keep warm in winter.

This about the south and west. About the east and north, Bengal and the region between Agra and Lahore, Joseph Salbank (1609-10) writing of the thickly populated country between Agra and Lahore observes that while the nobles 'are said to be very wealthy' the plebian sort, is so poor that the greatest part of them go naked.' In this regard, and for the urban scene in particular the testimony of Pelsaert (1620-27) and Bernier (1656-68) is of immense value. They lived and wrote mainly about Agra and Delhi respectively. Pelsaert laments 'the utter subjection and poverty of the common people-poverty so great and miserable that the life of the people can be depicted or accurately described only as the home of stark want and the dwelling place of bitter woe.'

He continues: 'There are three classes of people who are indeed nominally free, but whose status differs very little from voluntary slavery-workmen, peons or servants and shopkeepers. For the workmen there are two scourges, the first of which is low wages. Goldsmiths, painters (of cloth or chintz), embroiderers, carpet makers, cotton or silk weavers, black-smiths, copper-smiths, tailors, masons, builders, stone-cutters, a hundred crafts in all-any of these working from morning to night can earn only 5 or 6 *tackas (tankahs)*, that is 4 or 5 strivers in wages. The second (scourge) is (the oppression of) the Governor, the nobles, the *Diwan*, the *Kotwal*, the *Bakshi*, and other royal officers.

If any of these wants a workman, the man is not asked if he is willing to come, but is seized in the house or in the street, well beaten if he should dare to raise any objection, and in the evening paid half his wages, or nothing at all. From these facts the nature of their food can be easily inferred' For their monotonous daily food they have nothing but a little *khichri'* in the day time, they munch a little parched pulse or other grain, which they say suffices for their lean stomachs? Their houses are built of mud with thatched roofs. Furniture there is little or none, except some earthenware pots to hold water and for cooking? Their bedclothes are scanty, merely a sheet or perhaps two' this is sufficient in the hot weather, but the bitter cold nights are miserable indeed, and they try to keep warm over little cowdung fires' the smoke from these fires all over the city is so great that the eyes run, and the throat seems to be choked.'

In 1648 the capital shifted from Agra to Delhi, but the story of exploitation remained the same. Bernier writes that' 'grandees pay for a work of art considerably under its value, and according to their own caprice.' 'When an *Omrah* or *Mansabdar* requires the services of an artisan, he sends to the *bazar* for him, employing force, if necessary, to make the poor man work; and after the task is finished, the unfeeling lord pays, not according to the value- of the labour, but agreeably to his own standard of fair remuneration; the artisan having reason to congratulate himself if the *Korrah* has not been given in part payment.'

The artisans and craftsmen in the permanent service of the monarch and the principal *Omarahs* were a little better off than the casual wage earners. They tended to preserve the arts for they were paid more and regularly. Akbar sanctioned the following daily wages for workers and artisans-2 *dams* (copper coins, 1/40 of *Rupia*) for ordinary labourers, 3 to 4 *dams* for superior labourers, 3 to 7 *dams* for carpenters and 5 to 7 *dams* for builders. According to Moreland carpenters and builders got, in Akbar's days, equivalent to about one rupee per day on the average, and they were rather better off than the modern workmen of the United Provinces, if not Punjab in the early years of the twentieth century. But there are many buts.

It is not certain if the workmen got full sanctioned rates. Then for the slightest mistake they were heavily fined. 'If a horse lost condition, the fines came down to the water carriers and sweepers employed in the stable. When an elephant died through neglect, the attendants (some of whom drew less than three rupees a month) had to pay the price of the animal.' During the process of investigation and imposition of punishment some money had to be paid to middlemen and Mughal officers.

Naturally, such artisans and workers 'can never become rich, and he feels it no trifling matter if he have the means of satisfying the cravings of hunger and of covering his body with the coarsest raiment'.

'Peons or servants are exceedingly numerous in this country,' writes Pelsaert, 'for every one-be he mounted soldier, merchant or king's official-keeps as many as his position and circumstances permit. Outside the house, they serve for display, running continually before their master's horse; inside, they do the work of the house, each knowing his duty,' like the *bailwan*, the *farrash*, the *masalchi*, the *mahawat* etc. Edward Terry (1616-19), Pelsaert and many others note that men stood in the market places to be hired and many of them were paid very low wages or even paid in kind, 'for most of the great lords reckon 40 days to the month, and pay from 3 to 4 rupees for that period: while wages are often left several months in arrears, and then paid in worn-out clothes or other things.'

Such fleecing was naturally responded to by cunning and 'very few of them serve their master honestly; they steal whatever they can; if they buy only a piece-worth of food, they will take their share or *dasturi* (commission).'

Transporters and coolies were no better off. On land, elephants, camels, horse, bullocks and donkeys were the main means of conveyance of kings, nobles, landlords and big merchants.

Agricultural products were transported from fields to the markets in the cities in bullock carts. Grain was also carried and sold by roving merchants (*banjaras*) on mules in places which were not easily accessible. Big merchants with their merchandise generally moved only in large convoys using chariots, horses, bullock carts, mules, camels, and even buffaloes, depending on the terrain. The government officials with treasures also travelled in convoys and under proper escorts.

Transport between rural and urban areas, between cities and within the city was provided by coolies, horses, bullock carts and *dola* or *doli*. In the days of Firoz Tughlaq, hire for a bullock cart was 4 to 6 *jitals*, and 12 *jitals* for a horse. A *dola* which was carried by *kahars* cost half a *tankah*. The *dola* or palanquin was the common conveyance of ladies of high rank. But this sophisticated means of transport was also being brought into more and more use by the old and infirm and the ease loving elite.

When Qutbuddin Mubarak Khalji (1316-20) felt miserable without the company of his favourite Khusrau Khan, he sent orders to the latter to return from the Deccan as quickly as possible (about C.E. 1320), and Khusrau Khan was taken in a palanquin post haste from Devagiri to Delhi. And Sikandar Lodi's boast, 'if I order one of my slaves to be seated in a palanquin, the entire body of nobility would carry him on their shoulders at my bidding', clearly indicates that besides ladies, the use of palanquin had also become a fashion with men of means. In the fifteenth century *Ekka* and *Tonga* had also come into vogue, but for long journeys the horse was the common conveyance.

A footman's services could be requisitioned for 5 *tankahs* a month, and a man could travel from Delhi to Agra spending only one *Bahloli,* which sufficed for him, his horse and his small escort/ retinue during the journey. A large number of people were engaged on this work, and they plied a brisk trade. In the Mughal times comparatively better roads added some sort of sophistication to land travel. Those employed by the Government on the work of transport and communication were not ill paid. Ibn Battutah's description of the same pertains to government's communication system which facilitated smooth running of administration.

According to Barani and Ibn Battua there were two types of news-carriers: the mounted runners (*Aulaq*) and the foot runners (*Dhava*). The administration of the Sultanate, Sur and Mughal governments 'was greatly facilitated by an efficient postal service which connected different parts of the empire.' According to Pelsaert, postmen carrying their master's letters could cover 25 to 30 Kos a day, but that was also because they ate opium regularly.

To sum up, Professor Mohammad Habib in his review of G.N. Sharma's *Social Life in Medieval Rajasthan* (1500-1800) has this to say about artisans and workers and their wages in northern India of the Mughal times: 'The industries of Rajasthan were well-developed, (but) further progress was made impossible owing to the low social position assigned to the worker, forced labour or *begar* and administrative oppression of all types.

'The cultivator had to be satisfied with a meagre reward for the hard work of himself and his family'. The inventories of thefts committed show that a well-to-do peasant had two dhotis and two turbans for himself, four saris costing about Rs. 2-4 for his wife and some ten utensils costing Rs.25.' The wages recorded tell the same sad tale. 'The account papers (1693-1791 A.D.) of the construction of the palaces of Jaipur and Kotah show that skilled labourers got annas 6 to 8 and a supervising architect Rs.1/2 per day.' The wages of un-skilled labourers as mentioned in the Kotah records of 1689 A.D. vary from one anna to two annas. Payment was sometimes made in grain-14 *Chataks* daily for skilled workers and 2 to 4 *Chataks* for women workers.

The Bikaner *Bahis* throw some light on wages-a *chaukidar* Rs.2 per month, grooms, sweepers and gardeners Rs.1 to Rs.3 per month. 'From the point of view of wages the prospects of government officials were not very encouraging.' The pay of officers of position, according to the Bikaner *Bahi* (V.S.1764) varied from Rs.21 to Rs.28 per month. An accountant's pay according to the Kotah records was Rs. 135 per year. An ordinary clerk could be engaged for Rs. 60 per year, while a senior clerk's pay was about Rs. 235 a year. A *Kotwal* was generally paid Rs. 15 to 20 a month. Such low wages would only be possible with the low price of grain. According to Dr. Sharma 10 maunds of wheat could be purchased for Rs. 14 to 16; the same quantity of millet for Rs. 11 to 12 and of barley for Rs. 9 to 10.

The low scale of both grain prices and wages proves only one thing, the thorough exploitation of the peasants and the workers. But this was an Indian and not a Rajasthani-misfortune. Tavernier, for example, could on his journey from Surat to Agra get 50 guards at Rs.4 per month each. The states and the governing classes tried to appropriate the whole surplus value of labour. Still the condition of the workers and peasants was probably better in Rajasthan than in, the Mughal empire. The situation in the Mughal empire is summed up by W.H. Moreland like this: 'In several instances the lowest grades of servants were entitled to less than two rupees monthly (65 dams for a sweeper, 60 for a camel-driver, 70 for a wrestler, and so on), while the bulk of the menials and of the ordinary foot-soldiers began at less than three rupees.

The minimum for subsistence at the court is probably marked by the lowest grade of slaves, who were allowed one *dam* daily, equivalent to three-quarters of a rupee monthly in the currency of the time' artisans were, as a rule badly off, and they can scarcely have been able to pay high wages to their journeymen' The facts available regarding the wages paid by travellers and merchants come almost entirely from the south and west of India. Terry insists on the excellence of the servants obtained for five shillings, or say two rupees a month, and he adds that they would send half this sum home; probably this statement relates to servants hired in Surat, but in any case it refers to this part of the country, as Terry went no farther north than Mandu.

Valle, writing of Surat about ten years later put the rate at not more than three rupees, while De Laet's informants gave him from three to four rupees, which could be supplemented in some cases by commission charged on purchases. A messenger between Surat and Masulipatam was in 1641 allowed seven or eight *mahmudies* (say something between three and four rupees) for the journey. These instances appear to justify the conclusion that early in the seventeenth century foreigners could secure capable servants for somewhere about three rupees a month. What this represents in real wages is uncertain. (But) The rates struck Europeans as extraordinarily low, and taken with those which prevailed in the northern capital they enable us to understand the great development of domestic employment which' characterised the life of India at this period.

The important point to note is that servants, messengers and escorts were in great demand. Any journey seems to have been inconceivable without a certain number of them. William Hawkins, who was in India in Jahangir's reign, found that 'almost a man cannot stir out of doors throughout all his dominions without great forces, for they are all become rebels'. Tavemier said that, in about 1660, 'to travel with honour in India, one hired 20 to 30 armed men, some with bows and arrows and others with muskets. They cost Rs.4 a month'. The profession must have been well organised and yet the wages were miserably low.

The economic position of artisans was no better. Bernier writing to Colbert, said: 'No artisan can be expected to give his mind to his calling in the midst of a people who are either wretchedly poor, or who, if rich, assume an appearance of poverty, and who regard not the beauty and excellence but the cheapness of an article; a people whose grandeess pay for a work of art considerably under its value and according to their own caprice? For it should not be inferred that the workman is held in esteem, or arrives at a stage of independence. Nothing but sheer necessity or blows from a cudgel keeps him employed; he never can become rich, and he feels it no trifling matter if he have the means of satisfying the cravings of hunger and of covering his body with the coarsest garment. If money be gained it does not in any measure go into his pocket, but only serves to increase the wealth of the merchant.' Bernier's description is corroborated by what Thevenot was told about the same period of the state of the arts in Delhi.

The story of the exploitation of the poor, both rural and urban, is unending. And the guiding principle of this pernicious practice was to leave the people with bare subsistence. No foreign traveller fails to notice it with disapproval if not actual disgust.

It would appear that the lords and the upper classes in Turco-Mughal India derived a cynical pleasure in oppressing the poor. The result was as expected. Artisans, workers and labourers became lazy. Scarcely any one made an effort to climb the ladder to better prospects, so that 'for a job which one man would do in Holland, here passes through four men's hands before it is finished.' Such exploitation in the Mughal period provided droves of *khidmatgars* to British officers and men when they established and ran their Raj in this country.

11

European Domination of the Indian Ocean Trade

Prior to the arrival of the Portuguese in the in the Indian Ocean in 1498, no single power had attempted to monopolize the sea lanes that connected the ports of the Indian sub-continent with the Middle East and East Africa on the West, and the ports of South East Asia and China to the East. Unlike in the Mediterranean where during Roman (and earlier) times, rival powers attempted to control the oceanic trade through military means, peaceful trade had remained the norm in the Indian Ocean. Although there were periods when coastal rulers of the Malabar coast and Southern India were powerful enough to demand toll taxes from passing ships, (and Arab rulers had attempted to control the shipping lanes through the Red Sea) there had not been any systematic attempt by any single political power to eliminate all others from the oceanic trade that touched the Indian subcontinent.

Indian ports that demanded high taxes from docking ships invariably lost out to "free ports"-i.e. ports that demanded very low tariffs from docking ships. In fact, several of the Indian ocean ports were politically neutral entities-giving free and equitable access to shippers of varied nationalities and religious affiliations.

Whereas pre-15th century Arab and Chinese geographical texts spoke of various natural hazards involved in long-distance shipping, they did not cite any significant political or military impediments to undertaking long-distance voyages other than the risk from pirates. Thus, evidence left behind by chroniclers such as Marco Polo, Ibn Batuta, Persian ambassador Abdur Razzaq, the Venetian Nicolo Conti, and Genoan Santo Stefano-all indicate that the Indian Ocean was the scene of thriving trade in the 14th and 15th centuries.

But once the Portuguese had discovered their new route to India, they displayed considerable zeal in seizing the most profitable ports of East Africa, the Persian Gulf, and the Saurashtran, Konkan and Malabar regions in India. A chain of fortified coastal settlements backed by regular naval patrols allowed the Portuguese to gradually eliminate many rivals, and enforce a semi-monopoly in the spice trade by the middle of the 16th C. Local traders were coerced into buying safe passes and paying customs duties to the Portuguese. However, this attempt at a monopoly was challenged by the maritime powers of North Sumatra based in Aceh, as well as by the Omanis, and by Gujarati traders. And as the Portuguese expanded with settlements in South East Asia, China and Japan-the Western monopoly became harder to maintain.

Initial success came to the Portuguese because they had been shrewd enough to develop a strategy of divide and conquer-first concentrating on isolating Muslim traders from the Hindu monarch of Calicut and demonstrating their fire power by launching a two-day bombardment of the vital port city (which was then the largest spice market of the Indian Ocean). These intimidating tactics worked in the favour of the Portuguese who repeated this strategy at other key trading destinations. In 1510, Bijapur's Adil Shahi ruler ceded the control of Goa to the Portuguese. Having realized that the bulk of trade moving out of India landed at one of three ports in the Indian Ocean-i.e. Hormuz in the Persian Gulf, Aden on the Red Sea, and Malacca in the Malay Peninsula-Goa's Indian Governor, Alfonso Albuquerque then shifted his attention to capturing each of these crucial ports. Malacca fell in 1511 and Hormuz in 1515. Only Aden proved elusive.

In 1505, the spice trade from Asia to Europe was declared a 'royal monopoly' by the Portuguese, who saw in this the possibility of extorting tribute through military means. Once Hormuz and Malacca came under the military and political control of the Portuguese, the Portuguese then attempted to expand their monopoly to the inter-Asian trade. For this they needed to seal off independent access to the Gujarati traders who although cut off from Malacca could continue to trade through the Red Sea. For twenty years, the Portuguese kept attacking the ports of Gujarat, even gaining a military victory in 1509 (after an earlier defeat against the combined defences of Diu and an Egyptian naval fleet that had been sent to aid the defences of Diu's Amir Hussain). But nevertheless, Diu did not fall; and attempts to defeat Malik Ayaz, (the next governor of Diu) also failed in 1520-1. In 1530, the Portuguese colonists looted and burned the ports of Cambay, Surat and Rander, but it was only in 1534, when in a moment of weakness, Sultan Bahadur of Gujarat relinquished control of the small port of Bassein. Diu-which had held out for two decades, suddenly became vulnerable when Mughal emperor Humayun cut a deal with the Portuguese to defeat Sultan Bahadur. The Portuguese were given permission to build a fort on the island, which allowed the Portuguese to garner complete political control over the territory by 1555. Portuguese naval control over the Gulf of Cambay became complete when they also captured the port of Daman in 1559. Thus the merchants of Gujarat were brought under control by the Portuguese, and Gujarat-(which on account of its thriving industry and trade may have been one of the richest of India's provinces) saw its fortunes steadily decline.

Following their conquests in Gujarat, the Portuguese then proceeded to augment their control in Sri Lanka by taking over Colombo, and founding a settlement in Meliapur (Sao Tome) on the Coromandel coast. Realizing that the trade from Goa to Bengal was even more lucrative than the Coromandel trade, they then turned their aggressive energies on Bengal. After initial resistance, they were allowed to settle in Chittagaon and Satgaon (near Kolkata), and later moved up-river to Hooghly. This enabled them to establish a virtual monopoly on the trade out of West Bengal by the end of the 16th C, until they were expelled by the Mughal armies in 1632. The Livra das cidades, e fortalezas documented in detail Portuguese control over numerous Indian ocean ports (in addition to those previously mentioned), such as Sofala in Mozambique-a major supplier of African gold, Mangalore, Cannanore, Cranganore, Cochin and Quilon-all important sources for spices and other tropical produce.

This success had come about mainly because unlike the trading ships of their Asian predecessors, the Portuguese ships were extremely well-armed for their times. Moreover, they were fortunate to arrive in the Indian sub-continent at a time when many of the ports were outside the political control of any powerful local ruler who could mount any effective resistance against their superior fire-power and their willingness to use it without hesitation. This was also due to the fact that the great Asian economies of the time were essentially land-based self-reliant economies. External trade did not comprise a significant portion of the economy, and the rulers had little stake in defending the interests of the sea-faring merchant classes. Where the merchant class was of some local significance-such as in Gujarat, the Portuguese did meet with considerable resistance (as also in Sumatra). But when squeezed between two enemies (the Mughals to the North and the Portuguese to the South), Gujarat had little choice but to give in.

Smaller and less-established traders from the Southern and Eastern Indian coast were completely eliminated from the inter-Asian trade, and were never able to recover. Others survived by accepting Portuguese conditions and demands of tribute for safe passage. However, some Gujarati and other Indian traders (along with their counterparts from East Africa, the Middle East and Indonesia) tried hard to bypass the Portuguese monopoly by using smaller ports that were relatively free from Portuguese domination. In addition, Gujarati traders began to emulate the Portuguese practice of arming their fleets, so as to resist the attacks from their Portuguese rivals.

However, the bulk of the profits went to the Portuguese who shipped highly-prized Indian textiles to Indonesia-picking up valuable spices in return for shipment to Europe. But the very profitability of this trade brought competitors. First the Dutch, and soon after the English and the French. In 1656, Colombo fell to the Dutch, and in 1663, the Portuguese lost Cochin to the Dutch. Competition with the British East India Company had led to the loss of Hormuz earlier.

Very quickly, the Dutch and then the English attempted to replace the monopoly of the Portuguese with a monopoly of their own. This led each of them to form their own fortified settlements along the chief trading routes as alternatives to the former Portuguese trading bastions. At first, the Dutch appeared to be more successful than their British and French rivals, and succeeded in establishing their pre-eminence in Indonesia, and once they had outmaneuvered the Portuguese, also came to dominated the shipping out of Gujarat and Sind. It was now the Dutch that imposed their will on most Indian shippers, exacting the taxes that were earlier levied by the Portuguese. At the same time, each of Portugal's European rivals began setting up local factories and trade outlets that matched or exceeded Goa.

Surat (1612), Madras (1639), Bombay (1668), Pondicherry (1674) and Calcutta (1698) thus gradually overshadowed Goa, and took over as the main centres of Indo-European trade. Nevertheless, the Indian (and other Asian) ship-building industry continued to thrive, as ships built in the ports of the Indian Ocean often matched (or even exceeded) the European-built ships in finish and craftsmanship.

Impressed by the range of Indian manufactures (especially textiles), and to supplement their trade, Dutch and British merchants established factories not only in their new port settlements, but also inland. Factories in the centres of textile weaving-such as Bahruch and Ahmedabad in Gujarat, and further inland in Burhanpur, Agra and Lahore were set up. Masulipatam, Pipli, Balasore and Dhaka also drew their attention as did Patna later. In this way, the Dutch and British merchants could keep a much more significant share of the profits that would have otherwise gone to local Indian middlemen. Manufacturing and trading emporiums were also set up in Indonesia by the Dutch.

But even as European-initiated manufacturing grew quite dramatically in the period leading up to direct colonial rule, a successively smaller proportion of the revenues that were generated in Europe reached the highly skilled and industrious Indian or Indonesian workers.

However, with only limited political control in India, British and Dutch traders could not entirely control the price of skilled labour, and had to deal somewhat respectfully with local factory owners, traders and tax officials. India continued to maintain a positive trade balance with respect to its European trade, and European traders were compelled to cover this trade deficit with a steady supply of precious metals. And as long as the European traders furnished the Indian subcontinent with gold and silver, Indian monarchs had some incentive to tolerate the European traders even as they continued to expand their presence, and artfully resisted political control over their Indian activities.

For a while, an equilibrium was maintained; but the European trading companies were always trying to increase their bargaining power by exhibitions of their steadily improving military might. They were constantly testing their powers-probing any weakness on the part of the Indian rulers. In 1691, the East India Company even attempted to challenge Mughal authority, but lost to Aurangzeb's armies, who was determined not to allow the European traders any more concessions than what they had already won.

But once the Mughal empire began to disintegrate, it was only a matter of time before one or the other of the European powers that dominated the Indian Ocean trade would find a way to extend its domination on the Indian heartland as well. In the end, it was the British who won the battle to rule over India, edging out their European rivals who found other territories to colonize in Asia and Africa.

The colonization of India was followed up by the colonization of Burma, Indo-China, the Middle East and virtually all of Africa. China's coastal areas also come under European domination. By the dawn of the 20th century, the US had also emerged as a colonial power, as it took over Spanish colonies in the Caribbean and in the Philippines.

Thus what began as a war against the unarmed free-trading merchants of the high seas, ultimately led to the almost complete subjugation of much of the planet by the Western European (and American) powers, and an enormous and unprecedented flow of wealth from the colonies to Europe and North America. For a century, the Portuguese managed to exact tribute from most of the regional traders who were active in the Indian Ocean. This was followed by a period of Dutch domination, although there were also pockets (and periods) of competitive trade as other European rivals attempted to outflank the Portuguese (and later the Dutch). But in the end, it was the British who won the largest prize-direct colonial rule over two-thirds of mainland India (and indirect rule of the rest)-allowing for the extraction of tributes far greater in magnitude than what had accrued to the Portuguese and the Dutch before them.

But even as much of Asia and Africa were forced into a state of unprecedented poverty and misery, Europe and North America witnessed astonishing developments in science, technology and culture. What was for the West, a triumph of awesome proportions, became an unmitigated tragedy for those that had to suffer the tortuous ordeal of colonization. It is important not to ignore this tragic dialectic of history-that the wealth (that in large part) funded the foundation and sustenance of "Western Civilization" came from the South and the East.

Western champions of "free trade" might also note that it was the armed and willing European monopoly traders who destroyed the free trade of the Indian Ocean. Not the other way around. Protected trade, at the barrel of the gun, not "free" or "fair" trade was at the very heart of the West's early contacts with the South and the East, and to this date, it is the West that appears most unwilling to bring down its own trade barriers even as it attempts to preach "free trade" to the rest of the world.

Bibliography

Adikaram, E. W.: *Early History of Buddhism in Ceylon,* D. S. Puswella, Migoda, 1946.

Agrawala, V. S.: *Shiva Mahadeva: The Great God,* Veda Academy, Varanasi, 1966.

Ahmad, Imtiaz: *State and Foreign Policy: India's Role in South Asia,* Vikas, New Delhi, 1993.

Ahmad, Jamil-ud-din: *Some Recent Speeches and Writings of Mr. Jinnah,* Lahore, Ashraf, 1952.

Aiyar, R. Krishnaswami: *Outlines of Vedaanta,* Chetana, Bombay, 1978.

Archer, W. G.: *The Kama Sutra,* Unwin Hyman, London, 1990.

Ashton, S.R. : *British Policy Towards the Indian States, 1905-1939,* London, Curzon, 1982.

Aurobindo, Sri: *Vyasa and Valmiki,* Acharya Press, Pondicherry, 1956.

Avalon, Arthur and Ellen: *Hymns to the Goddess,* Ganesh and Co., Madras, 1964.

Aziz, Ashraf: *Light of the Universe: Essays on Hindustani Film Music,* Three Essays Collective, New Delhi, 2003.

Bagchi, P. C.: *Studies in Dharmashastra,* University of Calcutta Press, Calcutta, 1939.

Bahadur, K.P.: *The Wisdom of Vedaanta,* Sterling Publishers Private Limited, New Delhi, 1996.

Banerjea, J. N.: *Pauranic and Vedanta Religion,* University of Calcutta, Calcutta, 1996.

Bankimchandra, C.: *Essentials of Dharma,* Sanskrit Book Depot, Calcutta 1979.

Basu, Manoranjan: *Dharmashastra: A General Study,* Shrimati Mira Basu, Calcutta, 1976.

Beaumont, Roger : *Sword of the Raj: The British Army in India, 1747-1947*, Indianapolis, Bobbs-Merrill, 1977.

Benjamin, Joseph : *Scheduled Castes in Indian Politics and Society*, New Delhi, Ess Ess Publications, 1989.

Bhattacharyya, B.: *Nispannayogavali of Mahapandita Abhyakara Gupta*, Oriental Institute, Baroda, 1949.

Borchert, Bruno: *Mysticism: Its History and Challenge*, Samuel Wiser, York Beach, 1994.

Bose, D. N.: *Dharmashastra: Their Philosophy and Occult Secrets*, Kali Press, Calcutta, 1965.

Bowle, John: *The Imperial Achievement: The Rise and Transformation of the British Empire*, Little, Brown, 1974.

Brockington, J. L.: *Righteous Rama: The Evolution of an Epic*, Oxford, London, 1984.

Bromley, D.: *Krishna Consciousness in the West*, Bucknell University Press, Lewisburg, 1989.

Brooks, E.: *The Original Analects: Sayings of Confucius and His Successors*. Columbia University Press, New York, 1988.

Bruhn, Klaus: *The Jina-Images of Deogarh*, MacMillan, Leiden, 1969.

Burke, Mary Louise: *Swami Vivekananda in America: New Discoveries*, Advaita Ashrama, Calcutta, 1966.

Chaudhary, M.: *Partition and the Curse of Rehabilitation*, Calcutta, Bengal Rehabilitation Organization, 1964.

Chaudhuri, Nirad: *Thy Hand, Great Anarch! India: 1921-1952*, London, Chatto & Windus, 1987.

Coomeraswamy, Ananda K.: *Buddha and the Gospel of Buddhism*, MacMillan, London, 1928.

Crawford, Cromwell S.: *Ram Mohan Roy: His Era and Ethics*, Acharya Press, New Delhi, 1984.

Dalton, Dennis : *Gandhi's Power : Nonviolence in Action*, New Delhi, OUP, 2001.

Danielou, Alain: *The Complete Kama Sutra*, Park Street Press, Rochester, 2000.

Dasgupta, Shahana: *Rani Lakshmibai: The Indian Heroine*, Rupa & Company, Calcutta, 2002.

Datta, V.N.: *Sati: Widow Burning in India*, Manohar, New Delhi, 1990.

David, M. D.: *John Wilson and his Institutions*, Mumbai, 1957.

De Bary: *Self and Society in Ming Thought*, Columbia University Press, New York, 1970.

De, Sushil Kumar: *Ancient Indian Erotics and Erotic Literature*, Firma K. L. Mukhopadhyay, Calcutta, 1959.

Deak, Istvan: *The Lawful Revolution: Louis Kossuth and the Hungarians 1848-1849*, Columbia University Press, 1979.

Dhar, Niranjan: *Vedanta and Bengal Renaissance*, Minerva Associates, Calcutta, 1977.

Dikshit, D.P. *Political History of the Chalukyas of Badami*. New Delhi: Abhinav, 1980.

Donat, K.: *Meditate the Tantric Yoga Way*, George Allen and Unwin, London, 1973.

Doniger, W.: *The Rig Veda: An Anthology*, Penguin, New York, 1981.

Duboi, Abbe: *Hindu Manners, Customs and Ceremonies*, Fifth Indian Impression, CUP, 1985.

Dwivedi, M.: *The Principal Upanishads*, Adyar Library, Madras, 1931.

Eaton, Richard M.: *Sufis of Bijapur, 1300-1700: Social Roles of Sufis in Medieval India*, Princeton University Press, Princeton, 1978.

Edwardes, Michael: *Battles of the Indian Mutiny*, London; B. T. Batsford Ltd., 1963.

Erickson, Erik H.: *Gandhi's Truth: On the Origins of Militant Nonviolence*, Norton, New York, 1970.

Farquhar, J.N.: *Modern Religious Movements in India*, Munshiram, New Delhi, 1967.

Fay, Peter Ward: *The Opium War, 1840-42*, University of North Carolina Press, 1975.

Fisher, Michael H.: *The Politics of British Annexation of India - 1757-1857*, Oxford, 1996.

Frauwallner, E..: *History of Indian Philosophy*, Motilal, Delhi, 1973.

Gambhirananda, S.: *Brahma Sutra Shamkar Bhasya*, Adavita Ashrama, Calcutta, 1977.

Gambhirananda, Swami: *Brahma Sutra Shamkar Bhasya*, Adavita Ashrama, Calcutta, 1977.

Gandhi, M. K.: *The Story of My Experiment With Trust*, Washington, Public Affairs Press, 1948.

Garbe, R.: *The Philosophy of Ancient India*, Chicago University Press, Chicago, 1899.

Goradia, Nayana: *Lord Curzon: The Last of the British Moghuls*, New Delhi, Oxford University Press, 1993.

Goudriaan, T.: *Ritual and Speculation in Early Tantrism*, State University of New York Press, New York, 1992.

Gough, A.E.: *The Philosophy of the Upanisads and Ancient Indian Metaphysics*, MacMillan, London, 1882.

Grant, G. P.: *Philosophy in the Mass Age*, Copp Clark, Toronto, 1959.

Grisenold, H.D.: *Insights into Modern Hinduism*, Oxford, New York, 1934.

Growse, F. S.: *The Ramayana of Tulasidasa*, Motilal Banarsidass, Delhi, 1995.

Gurumurthy, S. : *Hindu Heritage, Assimilative, Not Divisive*, Vigil, Madras 1993.

Haich, E.: *Sexual Energy and Yoga*, Aurora Press, New York, 1982.

Hasan, Murhirul: *Legacy of a Divided Nation: India's Muslims Since Independence*, New Delhi, Oxford, 1997.

Hasan, Mushirul: *India's Partition: Process, Strategy and Mobilization*, New Delhi, Oxford UP, 1993.

Heifetz, Hank: *The Origin of the Young God: Kalidasa's Kumara-sambhava*, University of California Press, Berkeley, 1985.

Heimann, Betty: *Facets of Indian Thought*, Geroge Allen & Unwin, London, 1964.

Heinsath, Charles: *Indian Nationalism and Hindu Social Reform*, Princeton University Press, Princeton, 1964.

Heschel, J.: *God in Search of Man: A Philosophy of Judaism*, Noonday Press, New York, 1997.

Hirschman, Edwin: *White Mutiny: The Ilbert Bill Crisis in India and the Genesis of the Indian National Congress*, New Delhi, Heritage, 1980.

Hixon, L.: *Mother of the Universe: Visions of the Goddess, Tantric Hymns of Enlightenment*, Quest Books, Wheaton, 1994.

Hopkins, J.: *Kalachakra Tantra Rite of Initiation*, Wisdom Publications, Boston, 1982.

Hopkirk, Peter: *The Great Game: The Struggle for Empire in Central Asia*, Kodansha, 1992.

Hume, R.E.: *The Thirteen Principle Upanishads*, Oxford University Press, London, 1971.

Hutchins, Francis: *Spontaneous Revolution: The Quit India Movement*, New Delhi, Manohar, 1971.

Irene, S.: *Vedic Heritage Teaching Program*. Arsha Vidya Gurukulam, Coimbatore, 1994.

Iyar, K.: *Vedanta: The Science of Reality*, Ganesh and Co., Mardas, 1930.

Iyengar, B.K.S.: *Light on the Yoga Sutras of Patanjali*, Aquarian Press, London 1993.

Jacob, K.: *Religion and Ethics in Advaita*, C.M.S. Press, Kottayam, 1982.

Jafar, Malik Muhammad: *Jinnah as a Parliamentarian*, Lahore, Afzar Publications, 1977.

Jain, Kailash Chand, *Lord Mahavira and His Times*, Saraswati Press, Delhi, 1974.

James, Lawrence: *The Rise and Fall of the British Empire*, St. Martin's, 1997.

James, Robert Rhodes: *The British Revolution, 1880-1939*, New York, Knopf, 1976.

Jean, M.: *Tantrik Yoga*, The Aquarian Press, Wellingborough, 1970.

John, B.: *Mantras: Sacred Words of Power*, George Allen and Unwin, London, 1977.

John, Elsner: *Pilgrimage: Past and Present in the World Religions*, Harvard University Press, Cambridge, 1995.

John, K.: *The Origin and Development of the State Cult of Confucius*, Paragon Book, New York, 1966.

Karmarkar, D.: *Sankara's Advaita*, Karnatak University, Dharwar, 1976.

Kaushik, Asha : *Globalization, Democracy and Culture : Situating Gandhian Alternatives*, Jaipur, Pointer, 2002.

Kaviraj, G.: *Aspects of Indian Thought*, University of Burdwan, Calcutta, 1966.

Kavlekar, K.K. : *Non-Brahmin Movement in Southern India, 1873-1949*, Kolhapur, Shivaji University, 19790

Keith, A.B. : *Rigveda Brahmanas*, Harvard University Press, Cambridge, 1920.

Keith, Arthur Berriedale: *The Religion and Philosophy of the Veda and Upanishads*, MacMillan, Delhi, 1925.

Kishwar, Madhu : *Religion at the Service of Nationalism, and Other Essays*, OUP, Delhi, 1998.

Klaus, K.: *A Survey of Hinduism*, State University of New York Press, Albany, 1989.

Knipe, M.: *Hinduism: Experiments in the Sacred*, Harper, San Francisco, 1991.

Knott, K.: *Hinduism, A Very Short Introduction*, Oxford University Press, New York, 1998.

Kosambi, D. D. : *The Culture and Civilisation of Ancient India in Historical Outline*, London, Routledge and Kegan Paul, 1956.

Kottackal, Jacob: *Religion and Ethics in Advaita*, C.M.S. Press, Kottayam, 1982.

Kuiper, F.B.J. : *Aryans in the Rigveda*, Rodopi, Amsterdam, 1991.

Kuppuswamy, Sastri S.: *Compromises in the History of Advaitic Thought*, Kalyani Press, Madras, 1940.

Louis, Fischer: *Essential Gandhi: An Anthology of His Writings*, Vintage, New York, 1983.

Low, D. A. and Brasted, Howard: *Freedom, Trauma, Continuities: Northern India and Independence*, New Delhi, Sage Publications, 1998.

Maheshwari, Shriram: *Rural Development in India: A Public Policy Approach*, New Delhi, Sage, 1995.

Makhan, L.: *The Ramayana of Valmiki*, Munshiram Manoharlal, New Delhi, 1978.

Mathew, Arnold: *Culture and Anarchy*, The University Press, Cambridge, 1935.

Mayer, A. : *Caste in an Indian Village: Change and Continuity 1954-1992*, Delhi, OUP, 1996.

Mazumder, Sukhendu : *Politico-Economic Ideas of Mahatma Gandhi: Their Relevance in the Present Day*, New Delhi, Concept Pub., 2004.

Mearns, David J.: *Shiva's Other Children: Religion and Social Identity amongst Overseas Indians*, Sage, Walnut Creek, 1995.

Mearns, J.: *Shiva's Other Children: Religion and Social Identity amongst Overseas Indians*, Sage, Walnut Creek, 1995.

Mehra, Parshotam: *A Dictionary of Modern Indian History, 1707-1947*, New Delhi, Oxford University Press, 1985.

Metcalf, Thomas R.: *The Aftermath of the Revolt: India, 1857-1870*, Princeton, Princeton University, 1964.

Mohan, K.: *The Mahabharata*, Munshiram Manoharlal, Delhi 1997.

Mookerjee, Ajit: *Kali The Feminine Force*, Thames and Hudson, London, 1988.

Mookerji, Satkari: *Modern Polity and Vedanta*, Sanskrit College, Calcutta, 1972.

Moon, Penderel: *The British Conquest and Dominion of India*, London, Duckworth, 1989.

Morris-Jones, W.H.: *The Government and Politics of India*, London, Hutchinson, 1971.

Nanda, B. R. : *Gandhi and His Critics*, Oxford University Press, Delhi, 1993.

Neale, Walter C.: *Economic Change in Rural India: Land Tenure and Reform in the United Provinces, 1800-1955*, New Haven, 1962.

Nevile, P.: *Lahore: A Sentimental Journey*, New Delhi, Penguin, 1993.

Oddie, G.A. : *Hindu and Christian in South-East India*, London, Curzon Press, 1991.

Pathak, Dr S.P.: *Jhansi during the British Rule*, Ramanand Vidya Bhawan, Delhi, 1987.

Preston, Diana: *The Boxer Rebellion*, Berkley Books, 2000.

Raimundo Panikkar: *The Vedic Experience: Mantramanjari*, Longman Todd, London, 1977.

Raja, C. Kunhan : *The Taittiriya Sarvanukramani of Yaska*, Madras, 1931.

Ramamurti, A.: *Advaitic Mysticism of Sankara*, Visvabharati, Santiniketan, 1974.

Ranajit Guha: *A Construction of Humanism in Colonial India*, CASA, Amsterdam, 1993.

Renou, Louis: *The Nature of Dharmashastra*, Walker and Co., New York, 1997.

Robson, Brian: *Sir Hugh Rose and the Central India Campaign*, Sutton Publishing Ltd for the Army Records Society, UK, 2000.

Satyapal Verma: *Role of Reason in Sankara Vedanta*, Parimal Publication, Delhi, 1992.

Savarkar, Vinayak Damodar : *The Indian War of Independence* 1857 Rajdhani Granthagar, Delhi, 1988.

Scheftelowitz, Isidor : *Die Kasmirische Rezension von Katyayanas Sarvanukramani,* Zeitschrift fur Indologie und Iranistik, 1922.

Shukla, D. N.: *Vastu-Shastra,* Motilal Banarsidass, Delhi, 1966.

Singh, Birendra Kumar: *Early Chalukyas of Vatapi, circa A.D. 500 to 757*, Delhi, Eastern Book Linkers, 1991.

Smith, Col. J. T. : *Silver and the India Exchanges,* Effingham Wilson, London, 1876.

Strauss, L.: *Political Philosophy*, The Bobbs Merrill Co., New York, 1975.

Swami Vishnu Tirtha: *Devatma Shakti,* Swami Shivom Tirth, Rishikesh, 1962.

Talageri, Shrikant : *Aryan Invasion Theory and Indian Nationalism,* Voice of India, Delhi, 1993.

Tejomayananda, Swami: *Hindu Culture: An Introduction,* Chinmaya Publications, Piercy, 1993.

Thapar, Romila : *Ashoka and the Decline of the Mauryas,* London, Oxford University Press, 1961.

Thompson, Edward: *The Making of the Indian Princes,* Oxford University Press, London, 1943.

Trautmann, Thomas R.: *Kautilya and the Arthasastra: A Statistical Study,* Leiden, Brill, 1971.

Trimingham, J.: *Sufi Orders in Islam,* Oxford University Press, New York, 1998.

Utpat, V.N.: *Riddles of Buddha and Ambedkar,* Itihas Patrika Prakashan, Thane 1988.

Vable, D.: *The Arya Samaj. Hindu without Hinduism.* Vikas Publ., Delhi, 1983.

Vedalankar, Pandit Nardev : *Basic Teachings of Hinduism,* Veda Niketan, Durban, 1978.

Visvantha, K.: *Essentials of Hinduism,* Narosa Pub. House, New Delhi, 1989.

Wendy Doniger: *Siva: The Erotic Ascetic,* Oxford University Press, Delhi, 1998.

Zaidi, A. Moin: *Evolution of Muslim Political Thought in India,* New Delhi: S. Chand, 1975.

Index

K

L

M

O

P

□□□